AN   ON

ORGANISATION FOR ECONOMIC CO-OPERATION AND DEVELOPMENT

307.76
ORG

ORGANISATION FOR ECONOMIC CO-OPERATION AND DEVELOPMENT auth e pub.

Pursuant to Article 1 of the Convention signed in Paris on 14th December 1960, and which came into force on 30th September 1961, the Organisation for Economic Co-operation and Development (OECD) shall promote policies designed:

– to achieve the highest sustainable economic growth and employment and a rising standard of living in Member countries, while maintaining financial stability, and thus to contribute to the development of the world economy;
– to contribute to sound economic expansion in Member as well as non-member countries in the process of economic development; and
– to contribute to the expansion of world trade on a multilateral, non-discriminatory basis in accordance with international obligations.

The original Member countries of the OECD are Austria, Belgium, Canada, Denmark, France, Germany, Greece, Iceland, Ireland, Italy, Luxembourg, the Netherlands, Norway, Portugal, Spain, Sweden, Switzerland, Turkey, the United Kingdom and the United States. The following countries became Members subsequently through accession at the dates indicated hereafter: Japan (28th April 1964), Finland (28th January 1969), Australia (7th June 1971), New Zealand (29th May 1973), Mexico (18th May 1994) and the Czech Republic (21st December 1995). The Commission of the European Communities takes part in the work of the OECD (Article 13 of the OECD Convention).

Publié en français sous le titre :
STRATÉGIES POUR LE LOGEMENT ET L'INTÉGRATION SOCIALE DANS LES VILLES

Preface

The OECD Project on Housing, Social Integration and Livable Environments in Cities, was launched in 1991 to study the current critical factors of change in cities. Its primary objective was to examine policy and programme strategies involving all levels of government, the private sector and community groups that are being applied in OECD Member countries to provide more affordable housing and improving social integration and residential environments. Seventeen countries (Australia, Austria, Belgium, Canada, Finland, France, Germany, Ireland, Japan, Netherlands, Norway, Spain, Sweden, Switzerland, United Kingdom, United States and Turkey) participated in the Project Group which was chaired by Mr. Jan O. Karlsson (Sweden). The work was supported by two major international Conferences. The first **"Integrated Housing Strategies: Creating Opportunities for People and their Community"** was hosted by the Scottish Office in Edinburgh, United Kingdom, on 6-8 October 1992. The second **"Partnerships for People in Cities"** was co-sponsored by the OECD and the European Foundation for the Improvement of Living and Working Conditions. The Conference was held in Dublin, Ireland on 19-21 October 1993.

The report was prepared by Dr. Richard Kirwan in collaboration with Mrs. Lindsay MacFarlane of the Urban Affairs Division of the OECD Territorial Development Service.

The summary and policy conclusions were approved by the Group on Urban Affairs. This report is published on the responsibility of the Secretary-General.

Contents

7

Introduction

Background to the project

The Project on Housing, Social Integration and Livable Environments was initiated under the aegis of the Group of Urban Affairs in April 1991. The declared aim of the activity was to develop goal-oriented, sustainable and holistic strategies to address the current dynamic problems faced by OECD Member countries in the economic, environmental and social development of their cities. The Group expressed a general concern for ensuring viable urban structures and promoting national economic competitiveness through well-functioning cities, as well as a desire to achieve social justice and equity of access to facilities, services and opportunities for all urban residents, especially those currently most disadvantaged.

The specific objectives of the project were:

-- to examine the main factors of change in cities through the collection of social, economic and environmental data and case study examples and to develop valid and inter-related strategies for the achievement of multiple societal goals such as economic growth, affordable housing, social integration and environmental quality in cities;
-- to examine holistic and horizontal frameworks of alternative policy and programme mixes involving all levels of government, the private sector and community groups that are in use for the provision of affordable housing and the successful achievement of social integration and economic performance in the context of long-term sustainable development;
-- to consider and make recommendations on how, in conjunction with other social, economic and environmental policies, housing policy within Member states can contribute to housing affordability and social integration within cities, in particular through multi-sectoral and strategic policies.

Seventeen countries participated in the Project Group (Australia, Austria, Belgium, Canada, Finland, France, Germany, Ireland, Japan, Netherlands, Norway, Spain, Sweden, Switzerland, United Kingdom, United States and Turkey).

The countries provided information and were represented at working sessions from which the conclusions of the project have been derived. The main sources of information[1] for the project were:

-- Country reports, submitted by Member countries, which described the main urban issues confronting each country and the policies and programmes currently in place.
-- Papers prepared by experts on single issues such as crime prevention and housing affordability. These papers identified key elements, inter-relationships with other problems in the urban system and promising policy strategies to address the issue. Comparative information from Member countries was used, whenever possible, and country experiences with innovative policies were reported.
-- Case studies, presented by Member countries, which described successful strategies that had been undertaken. Information was shared on modifications or abandonment of traditional strategies and experiments with new policies. Lessons learned and transferable information were emphasised.
-- Two international conferences were held in support of the project: the first hosted by the Scottish Office of the United Kingdom in Edinburgh on "Integrated Housing Strategies: Creating Opportunities for People and their Community" (October 1992); and the second "Partnerships for People in Cities" (October 1993) co-hosted in Dublin, Ireland, by the European Foundation for the Improvement of Living and Working Conditions and supported by the governments of Canada and Japan and by the United States Federal National Mortgage Association (Fannie Mae). These conferences brought together government officials, representatives of Member countries and researchers. Theoretical and research information was enriched by practical policy experience during discussions.

---

[1]Persons requiring specific information on Country reports, Issue papers and case studies should contact the OECD Secretariat, Urban Affairs Division, Territorial Development Service in writing. Chapter References do not include these OECD documents.

--   Several interim reports produced as the project advanced, forming the basis for the development of the final report.

The project culminated in this final report, which consolidates the work of the Project Group.

Structure of the report

The report comprises eight chapters.

The first chapter, "The Urban Policy Context", describes the development of urban regeneration policy and outlines the changes that have taken place in the urban environment such as globalisation, fiscal restraint and so on. It explains the limitations of current single-sector urban policies and introduces the need for a new, integrated approach to policy-making.

The second chapter "Different Approaches to Urban Policy among OECD Members" discusses the process of urban change, both growth and decline, and the impact of this process on the components of the urban system. The major part of the chapter is devoted to a synthesis of policies and programmes that are currently being utilised in Member countries of the OECD.

Chapter 3 defines the rationale and a conceptual framework for a strategic multi-sectoral approach to urban policy. Member countries accept the need for holistic policy making, but the transformation is difficult and complex. This chapter introduces a clear framework around which national policy programmes can be redesigned.

The next three chapters form a useful link between past policy experience and promising future approaches to solving urban problems. The policies identified are designed to address clusters of problems, which are divided into three groups. Chapter 4 "Social Renewal and Livable Environments" concentrates on policies for social integration, employment, homelessness and improving the quality of housing and residential environments. Chapter 5 "Housing Affordability: Key Issues and Policies" addresses ways of making housing more affordable; while Chapter 6 "The Collection and Use of Data" examines the role of data in the formulation, implementation and evaluation of policies.

To assist the understanding of the policy strategies, the key elements of each issue are presented in a subsection, followed by a discussion of the policies in force. Specific examples from Member countries are described in the text and in Insets. Problems of policy design or implementation are highlighted in the discussion. Links between the problem areas, that call for careful design of a multi-sectoral approaches, are also identified. An overview of the collection and use of data for the formulation, implementation and evaluation of multi-sectoral urban strategies highlights key issues in this important policy area.

In the seventh chapter "Examples of the Multi-sectoral Approach: National Strategies and Local Initiatives" successful multi-sectoral approaches, illustrated with case studies from Member countries, are documented. The range of institutional arrangements and policy characteristics used is specified and the advantages and disadvantages associated with them are noted. Particular attention is paid to the role of partnerships.

In the final chapter "The Challenge of the Multi-sectoral Approach" the conclusions suggested by the project are drawn together and an attempt is made to highlight: the characteristics of current urban problems; the opportunities for innovative policy experimentation; the potential role of multi-sectoral policy in tackling urban problems, as well as some of the possible pitfalls; and the elements that would benefit from further examination.

Chapter 1

The Urban Policy Context

As can be seen from the objectives noted above, the project and the present report focus on the severe concentrations of disadvantage, unemployment, poverty and alienation that have emerged in recent years throughout OECD Member countries. Although most countries have suffered to some degree the effects of the recent economic recession, with widespread increases in unemployment and a straitened fiscal climate, it was not the aim of the project to address broad macroeconomic issues. Nonetheless these issues provide the context within which the processes of urban change under review have evolved. The subject matter of this report is both more limited and more problematic than this. It is the emergence and persistence within cities of areas of severe deprivation and exclusion in which the disadvantages of individuals and families are compounded by the poor quality of the environment and housing and by the lack of adequate and appropriate community facilities.

This is not the first time that the problems of urban deprivation or the need for urban regeneration have become matters of major concern for governments. The 1960s, for example, also witnessed an upsurge of concern about the specifically urban manifestations of discrimination and neglect. The difference on this occasion is that the problems in large numbers of OECD Member countries are seen to stem from mainstream, structural changes in social and economic development: from new attitudes to household formation, from the ageing of the population, from the much higher levels of labour force participation, from the globalisation of national economic processes and from the unwillingness of governments to expand public spending and borrowing. The centrality of these causes represents a new challenge for policy makers. Successful adaptation to new global economic and social trends must involve a solution of the urban problems that are their direct outcome: urban regeneration and social inclusion, as much as environmental and ecological sustainability, are therefore essential components of the process of adaptation.

Past experience of urban regeneration

Since the beginnings of the modern industrial and commercial city in the nineteenth century, areas of acute social and economic deprivation have co-existed side by side with areas of affluence and settled prosperity. In each generation social reformers and activists have looked to reduce these disparities and improve the welfare of the most disadvantaged. In the nineteenth century, the emphasis was on measures to improve public health and prevent epidemics through better sanitation and building design, as well as through improvements in medical services and research. Education was seen as the key to the advancement of individuals in the labour market, leading to universal, compulsory public education. Towards the turn of the century the emphasis shifted to the scope for the resettlement of the most disadvantaged populations through planned housing developments, low cost transportation and urban expansion. During the inter-war period, localised social and economic disparities were to some extent concealed by the wider impacts of the Great Depression. And in the immediate post-war period they tended to take second place in the policy agenda to the rapid expansion of suburban, middle-class housing development, especially in the "new worlds" of North America and Australasia, and to the large-scale programmes of post-war reconstruction and universal social housing in Europe. The defence-led full employment policies of the 1950s also helped to disguise the disparities.

It took the racial conflicts and the civil rights movement of the 1960s in the United States, crowning decades of periodic social unrest and racial tension in America's largest cities, to focus attention once again on the acute differences between areas of urban prosperity and areas of neglect and on the up-hill struggle faced by those least favoured by the processes of urban change.

The explosion of analysis that accompanied the attempt to respond to the emerging urban crisis in the United States highlighted the significant role of a conjunction of factors. Localised urban deprivation at its most acute arises from the coincidence of three sets of causal influences: first, the mix of personal characteristics or endowments and labour market conditions (including racial, ethnic, gender or religious discrimination), that determines the ability of the individual to find and retain a secure source of income; second, the workings of the housing market, or its administered social housing equivalent, in rationing access to the available housing stock in favoured, easily accessible locations and in creating the incentives, and the means, for housing maintenance, improvement and disinvestment; and finally, the fiscal and administrative mechanisms which determine the availability of community facilities and services (including such things as education, health services, public transport, policing, etc.) and which control the allocation of resources to programmes of social and individual welfare and rehabilitation. In the United States of the 1960s the dominant influences included racial antipathies and discrimination, rent control and the incentives to housing disinvestment and the effects of local fiscal autonomy on the distribution of resources and on the locational preferences of businesses and households. In contemporary OECD cities, the mix of factors is different; but they stem from the same three main sources.

The United States experience at that time also focused attention on the role of area-based policies. The Model Cities programme, established as part of the Johnson administration's Great Society initiative, reflected a serious attempt to devise area-based, multi-sectoral programmes for urban social and economic regeneration. The failure of this initiative due to a combination of factors, including administrative complexity, local political controversy and corruption and fiscal constraints, tended to divert attention away from the scope for integrated, holistic area-based regeneration programmes. The subsequent attempt towards the end of the 1970s, under the Carter administration, to refocus United States urban policy around area-based initiatives has even stronger echoes in the current debate about methods of tackling urban and social regeneration. For it was explicitly based on three concepts which remain high on the contemporary policy agenda: the neighbourhood focus; partnership; and the role of voluntary or community agencies. Moreover, a great deal of attention was also paid in this programme to the role of Urban Impact Analysis (*Cf.* Glickman, 1980). In this case the failure of the specifically area-based policy was due, on the one hand, to the much more widespread impact of generalised, counter-cyclical fiscal and employment programmes, and, on the other hand, to the equally cataclysmic effect of subsequent attempts to rein in Federal government spending in the fight against inflation (*Cf.* R. Kirwan, 1981).

Echoes of the United States experience of urban policy formulation in the 1960s and 1970s were felt in most OECD Member countries, especially those like the Netherlands and the United Kingdom which recognised the close affinity with their own emerging problems. But in reality none faced problems of the same magnitude as the United States, nor did many share the peculiar mix of circumstances which underlay the worst manifestations of urban deprivation in United States cities at that time.

Nonetheless the lessons of the United States experience in attempting to apply a nationally co-ordinated set of area-based strategies for urban social and economic regeneration remain worthy of note, not just for the causes of their failure but also for the profound disagreement it engendered between those who advocated different policy approaches, notably those for and against an explicit area focus.

New influences

In the period since 1980, the situation has changed significantly, so that the present-day concern with localised areas of acute deprivation in cities, and with persistently disadvantaged groups of individuals, displays many different characteristics to that of earlier decades. Above all, the experience is far more widespread. It affects almost all OECD Member countries to some degree, many acutely. Moreover, it seems to arise in most cases from similar causes. The specificity that characterised United States experience in the 1960s is less evident today, though significant local differences inevitably persist. The current problems follow, and in many cases seem to have flowed from, a period of profound economic and political change. Economic growth, it is true, has reduced the magnitude of some problems: for example, housing standards have risen universally and there are few examples of outright housing shortage (apart from the special case of Germany) or of severely deficient housing stock. Education, health and welfare services have generally improved, even where their targeting has been criticised. But the form that economic growth and social change have taken has been critical to the emergence of new problems in cities.

Four main processes account for the persistence of low quality neighbourhoods and persistently disadvantaged groups in cities: socio-demographic trends; labour market changes; the globalisation of economic processes; and fiscal restraint.

Socio-demographic trends: Since the 1960s almost all OECD Member countries have experienced profound socio-demographic changes, the origins of which can be traced to earlier decades but which have become quantitatively much more significant in the recent past. Overall, populations have been ageing, with increased longevity and advances in medical science. At the same time, the labour market has had to absorb the children of the post-World War II "baby boom", most of whom have been educated to much higher levels of skill and competency than previous generations. Economic growth and changing social attitudes have encouraged a significant increase in the propensity of all age groups to form separate, smaller households, with increasing rates of divorce and household fission, the postponement of marriage and child-rearing and the survival of elderly, single people to an advanced age.

These developments are closely tied up with the changes that have been occurring in the labour market. But they also reflect changing social attitudes, such as the increasing tendency for women to accept sole parenthood from the outset. The implications for the structure of households have been particularly important, since the household remains the unit which determines the incidence of poverty and affluence and largely influences the access of children and others to favourable life chances. This is reflected in the high incidence of poverty among single parent families and the single elderly, together with families with large numbers of children.

Labour market changes: The thirty years between 1960 and 1990 saw massive changes in the structure and availability of jobs throughout OECD Member countries. But there have been some important differences. Whereas in some countries, notably the United States, Sweden and to a lesser extent the United Kingdom and Australia, there was a substantial increase in the number of available jobs per person of working age (16 to 65 years) (and the ratio remained high in Japan), in many European countries, notably France and Italy, there was little effective increase. As a consequence, participation in the labour force increased to a high level in the United States, Sweden, Japan, and the United Kingdom, while it remained significantly lower in France, Italy and Spain.

In North America, where the rate of job creation was most rapid, the rate of increase of labour productivity was lowest; the opposite was true of Europe. Women have accounted for a major share of the increase in labour force participation and employment, but many jobs for women, as also increasingly for men, have been part-time or temporary. In almost all countries there has been a widening of wage differentials, most notably in Australia, Canada, Japan, Sweden and the United Kingdom. However, where in Europe the rate of new job creation has been lowest, wage differentials have increased much less. On the other hand, the unemployment rate has been much lower in the United States and Japan, while in Europe it has risen markedly since the 1960s, with a much more significant component of long-term unemployed. Many European countries have in fact succeeded in maintaining greater job stability and narrower wage differentials at the expense of the number of available jobs and hence labour force participation.

Significant differences also show up when these labour market experiences are converted into patterns of household formation. For example, in many European countries, notably Denmark, Sweden and Germany, the incidence of single-parent families is large but relatively few are wholly dependent on

17

welfare, a high proportion deriving the major share of their income from employment. On the other hand, in countries like Ireland, the United States and the United Kingdom, single parent families are much more likely to be dependent on transfer payments and a high proportion of this group are as a consequence classified as poor. In general, however, the "new poor" have come to be defined as much by their household status as by their success in finding a secure and stable source of income from employment or from their provision for old age: the single elderly and those of an advanced age, single parent families, families with large numbers of children and, to some extent, older people of working age, living alone, without secure employment.

Globalisation of economic processes: Associated with these broad changes in the labour market has been a significant change in the economic structure of cities and in the composition of the labour force. This reflects the progressive globalisation of national and local economies. Since the 1970s the dismantling of barriers to international trade and the deregulation of the foreign exchange markets have encouraged the restructuring of industry and employment and have led to the loss of large numbers of previously stable jobs in vulnerable branches of activity. Throughout OECD Member countries the occupational structure has become increasingly tertiarised, in response partly to the consequent movement of manufacturing employment to locations outside the OECD and partly to the effects of technological change and capital investment designed to increase labour productivity in goods production. At the same time the demand for more skilled employees has grown, reducing the opportunities for the older, less skilled workers and those unable to adjust to the emerging conditions or accept retraining.

There is of course nothing essentially new about the impact of international trade and foreign competition on the economic performance of cities. Many OECD cities, like Kobe, Genoa, Boston, Marseille or Liverpool, have been profoundly affected in the past by changes in trading conditions and the international competitiveness of particular industries. But the emerging situation differs from the conditions experienced in previous eras in the breadth and generality of its impact. No longer is the impact of competition confined to single industries, or even to manufacturing. Almost all branches of activity, including a significant share of services are now exposed to the effects of global exchange.

This has had two main effects: to require continuous attention to the need to improve productivity; and to increase uncertainty about the future. What is clear, however, is that this is not a once-for-all process, following which stability will be re-established. It is a continuing state in which businesses in all countries will face increasingly fierce international competition and will as a consequence have to ensure that their investment in technology and labour productivity are adequate for the task.

The changing skill mix of those in employment, the emphasis on training, the loss of unskilled job opportunities and the increasing reliance of firms on part-time or casual employment are thus not merely a reflection of the substantial changes in the supply of labour over the last thirty years but also a recognition of the changing context for the demand for labour which the progressive globalisation of economic activity has created. The employment situation of many marginal groups is, as a consequence, increasingly precarious. On the positive side, however, this process has involved the creation of large numbers of new and varied jobs in the service industries, many requiring new and rewarding skills, and has resulted in a much more diversified array of jobs, matched to the capabilities and preferences of employees, providing more jobs for women and special needs groups (such as the disabled) and much more flexible arrangements for employment than in the past.

Fiscal restraint: Allied to this process of opening up national economies has been the much greater attention paid by governments to the control of inflation, the imposition of limits on public spending and borrowing and the efficiency of the public sector. This has had two direct consequences for cities. Firstly, it has seen the loss of large numbers of often unskilled but secure jobs in public sector agencies, in particular public utilities and traded services. In return many new, more skilled jobs have been created; but the overall numerical shift has been negative and the opportunities for unskilled employment have decreased. And secondly, it has set new limits to the volume of resources available to assist disadvantaged areas and groups and to create programmes for urban regeneration. This has encouraged policy makers to look elsewhere, to the private sector and to local communities, for additional resources to fund their efforts.

In many countries fiscal restraint has also been accompanied by a reduction in the volume of resources available for subsidised social housing. Where the private rental market is not sufficiently buoyant to provide an alternative, this has left a gap in the supply of affordable rental housing.

Social security and welfare payments have tended to become more selective, with means testing and other forms of rationing more likely to be imposed. In many ways this should help the most disadvantaged, since improved targeting of programmes and benefits has become a significant goal of most governments. In practice, however, it appears that, to date, the long-standing tension between universalism and selectivity in social welfare policy has prevented a major diversion of resources in favour of the most needy in a great many countries.

Old approaches to new problems

As a result of these processes and their largely adverse impact, there is a growing image of a dystopian future for cities. In the 1970s, the impact of urban decentralisation and incipient deindustrialization on inner cities was widely recognised and reacted to. By 1980 almost every OECD country with older industrial cities had inner city problems and policies. As these policies were introduced, policy-makers began to realise that the problem points within the urban mosaic were not only related to the inner city; nor were they always due to easily separable or identifiable causes. In the Mediterranean countries, and parts of North America, Australasia and Japan, for example, the declining quality of life, manifest in many older core cities, was induced by growth-related congestion rather than economic decline. Congestion and environmental damage were also seen to characterise numerous suburban office and retailing centres, set in a sea of mono-functional residential development. Decay and decline, exacerbated by the changing demographics of the 1980s, also became evident in numerous social housing systems (generally in North and Western Europe) and affected both inner and outer areas of cities. Thus, the pattern of urban problems, whether defined in relation to location or socio-economic well-being or environmental quality, became more complex in its geography and its form during the period 1970-90: the mosaic of difficulties had moved beyond the inner city and was driven by many, complex factors.

These changes, bearing in mind the endemic tendency of cities to unbalanced and separating growth, are hardly surprising. Increased global economic competition has been manifested in the pressure for greater efficiency and flexibility in urban production. All too often, neither the labour force nor management has reacted quickly to the new "footlooseness" of production. In consequence, in almost all OECD Member countries, long term unemployment (adjusted for stage in the business cycle) has increased. This has tended to reinforce the income gaps between those in and out of work. At the same time social trends have resulted in more disrupted housing and family life cycles (for example, the early departure of children from home, increased divorce and separation rates, larger numbers of poor, elderly widows, etc.). This has created

20

a "new poor" in cities throughout the OECD, whose numbers are often swollen by the growing number of ethnic minority and migrant households now living in advanced economy cities.

Furthermore, in policy terms, where the larger concentrations of the "new" and "old" poor are now to be found, there is a concern that persistent, long term unemployment and benefit-dependency will create or sustain new cultures of poverty. Secondly, there is also a worry that central to this "culture" is a dependence on benefits and a focus on the "here and now" rather than the "future". Arguably such an orientation de-emphasises such things as educational attainment, saving and individual health awareness, boosts alcohol and drug dependency and encourages increased criminality (*Cf.* OECD, R. Kirwan, 1993).

All these negative reinforcements, if and where they exist, have led to a growing recognition that urban regeneration policy is not just about bricks and mortar but about reconnecting the links between such areas or groups and the rising economic mainstream. In short, the "urban" dimension of policies must now be regarded as a key integrative concern and not a minor addendum to national sectoral policies. Single sector policies have major limitations where re-integration is the focus of regeneration.

However, at the close of the 1970s urban policies in many countries remained highly sectoral. Mainstream policies often had divergent spatial foci. There was little policy integration. From an urban perspective there were serious deficiencies in each of the main policy areas.

Economic policy

Prior to the mid-1970s urban analysis and policy had tended to make a sharp distinction between the economic and social dimensions of urban problems. In Europe, inter-urban differences in economic well-being were largely addressed as regional problems: indeed the spatial economic problem was thought to comprise "depressed" regions (with above average unemployment rates and under-utilisation of infrastructure), on the one hand, and "congested" or "pressure-cooker" regions (where in-migration, labour shortages and over-utilisation of the social infrastructure caused unacceptable inflationary pressure), on the other hand. Intra-urban disparities in unemployment within the more prosperous conurbations were regarded as a local policy concern of little relevance to national economic policy formulation. Little regard was paid moreover to the tendency for diversionary, and expensive, regional policies to shift manufacturing firms or offices from their original core city locations to the more peripheral parts of the depressed metropolitan regions. For regional policies to have benefited those living in the worst areas of the declining conurbations, further transport, training and related measures would have been required to ensure the required urban impact.

In North America, and to a lesser extent Australia, urban policy had a much higher profile in the national policy agenda, stemming largely from the civil rights movement of the 1960s and the Johnson administration's Great Society initiatives. But the urban focus floundered in the course of the 1970s, partly due to the perceived inadequacies of the preceding initiatives and partly under the weight of the economic recession caused by the two "oil shocks" and of the accompanying tendency to hyper-inflation. Urban policy became increasingly synonymous with counter-cyclical measures, whose public finance implications were unsustainable.

In Japan, while there was a growing awareness of the need for improvements to the social infrastructure of urban areas, economic policy was directed almost exclusively towards economic growth, export competitiveness and the need to secure adequate supplies of energy and raw materials from overseas. From an economic perspective, urban policy was low on the agenda.

Social policy

In Europe, the traditional concern of welfare state policy since the 1950s has been the establishment of an adequate "safety net" for individuals and families in employment and retirement. While this has played a vital role in sustaining those most in need, many of whom were to be found in the most run-down neighbourhoods within the major cities, it was not until the 1980s that serious attention began to be paid to the longer run incentive effects or to the fiscal cost. Social justice and equality were, and remain, predominant concerns; but the spatial and longitudinal impact of welfare spending in the cities received little attention.

In the United States, greater attention was paid to the relationship between social welfare programmes and urban problems, not least because a much higher proportion of welfare expenditure is financed locally. The main criticism was that the resulting system was a variegated patchwork, without any comprehensive basis for addressing social needs. For one reason or another -- geographical, ethnic or political -- large numbers of people in need fell into the interstices between the programmes. The growing criticism of many of these programmes at the beginning of the 1980s has been reinforced by the recognition that poverty in the United States cities increased most rapidly while these initiatives were in place and has declined since many were abandoned.

Housing policy

Housing policies have largely been pursued in a vacuum from other social and economic policies, with disastrous consequences in some cities. In Europe, much of housing policy was seen as an extension of the welfare state. Rent controls, for periods exceeding half a century in much of Western Europe, contributed to older neighbourhood decay, whilst tax expenditure policies encouraged middle income groups to become home-owners and suburbanise. Major social housing schemes often cleared city centres in the 1950s and 1960s (with some of the land still lying derelict three decades later), disrupted communities and placed low-income, low-skill and low-mobility households on the edge of cities.

Regional policy, social policy and housing policies, which were key central government policy thrusts in many OECD countries in the 1950-75 period, were usually pursued by different government ministries with different intellectual motivations and objectives. There was minimal local co-ordination and the existence of these policy thrusts frustrated the development of truly urban policies.

In the United States, the period of large-scale urban renewal came to an end in the early 1960s; but the long-standing incentives to middle-class suburbanisation -- reinforced by racial prejudice and local fiscal autonomy -- continued to encourage new housing development at increasing distances from core cities. In Australia, the same effect was induced by governments' willingness to release serviced land at the urban periphery at significantly below its true economic cost.

When the economic conditions in Europe and North America did eventually begin to favour private re-investment in inner city neighbourhoods, the effects of "gentrification" brought additional hardship to the more disadvantaged households living in previously neglected areas.

Meanwhile, national housing finance systems tended to protect home purchasers by allowing housing funds to enjoy a privileged status within the

23

overall financial system. As a result, the cost of capital for house construction and purchase was kept artificially low, encouraging investment in new housing stock. In Japan, the same phenomenon was due to the government's broader macroeconomic approach to maintaining a high savings ratio and to keeping down the cost of capital for business.

Planning policy

The task of local co-ordination could, arguably, have fallen to the town planning system (at least where it was well developed). However, the theoretical objectives of positive town planning were focused on a balanced, integrated vision of cities, the instruments and processes of planning tended to emphasise the bureaucratic control of growth. Town planning had primarily physical concerns, was more comfortable allocating state investment than dealing with market processes, was often non-participatory in nature and was in essence more concerned with regulation than the creation of alternative futures. It was also strongly sectoral in focus. The urban elements of planning policy in many countries were disparate in focus, objectives and technical expertise. Despite the concern generated during the 1960s -- notably in the United States -- environmental policies were often limited in scale and diffuse in nature, with integrated control of atmospheric pollution the exception rather than the rule, and were unlinked to social and economic policies at the urban scale.

References

BARCELONA DECLARATION on the Revitalisation of Neighbourhoods in Crisis, signed in Barcelona, October 1992.

EUROPEAN FOUNDATION FOR THE IMPROVEMENT OF LIVING AND WORKING CONDITIONS (1992), *Out of the Shadows -- Local Community Action and the European Community*, Loughlinstown House, Dublin.

GHEKIERE, L. (1991), *Marché et politiques du logement dans la CEE*, Union nationale des fédérations d'organismes d'HLM, La documentation française, Paris.

GLICKMAN, N. (ed.) (1980), *The Urban Impacts of Federal Policies*, Johns Hopkins University Press, Baltimore.

JENCKS, C. and PETERSON, P. (eds.) (1991), *The Urban Underclass*, Brookings Institution, Washington D.C.

JENCKS, C. "Is the American underclass growing?" in Jencks, C. and Peterson, P. (eds.) *op. cit.*, 28-100.

KIRWAN, R. (1981), "The American experience" in Hall, P. (ed.), *The Inner City in Context*, Heinemann, 71-87, London.

NETHERLANDS MINISTRY OF HOUSING, PHYSICAL PLANNING AND ENVIRONMENT (1991), *Statistics on Housing in the European Community*, The Hague.

OECD/EUROPEAN FOUNDATION FOR THE IMPROVEMENT OF LIVING AND WORKING CONDITIONS (1993), Keynote Presentation: *Strategic Alliances for Social Regeneration and Prosperity* by Dr. Satya Brink, Conference on Partnerships for People in Cities, Dublin, Ireland, 18-21 October 1993.

OECD (1992), Background Document: *Cities and the Environment*, International Conference on the Economic, Social and Environmental Problems of Cities, 18-20 November, Paris.

OECD (1992), Background Document: *Policies for the Future of Cities*, International Conference on the Economic, Social and Environmental Problems of Cities, 18-20 November, Paris.

OECD/SCOTTISH OFFICE (1992), Issue Paper: *Strategic, Multi-sector Approaches to Urban Regeneration: City Policy for the Future* by Professor Duncan MacLennan, Conference on Integrated Housing Strategies: Creating Opportunities for People and their Community, Edinburgh, Scotland, 6-8 October 1992.

VAN VLIET, W. (ed.) (1990), *International Handbook of Housing Policies and Practices*. Green Press, New York.

WILSON, W. (1991), "Public policy research and The Truly Disadvantaged" in Jencks, C. and Peterson, P. (eds.) *op. cit.*, 460-481.

WORLD BANK (1992), *World Development Report, 1992: Development and the Environment*. Oxford University Press, New York.

Chapter 2

Different Approaches to Urban Policy among OECD Member Countries

The emerging policy context

The single-sector emphasis of traditional urban policies began to change in the 1980s, not because national governments put in place a clearly thought through strategic or integrated urban policy, but because city and provincial governments had to face new economic challenges as well as a major shift in the tenor of national government policies. Heightened economic competition and increased international exchange, leading to significant economic restructuring, on the one hand, and public expenditure cutbacks, deregulation and, to a lesser extent, privatisation, on the other hand, have created a new backcloth to city policies and led to new urban policies with both strengths and weaknesses.

Older forms of policy were quickly de-emphasised or changed. In many European countries, diversionary regional policies were largely curtailed and governments dropped any real attempt to shape the spatial pattern of economic development. The regulatory impact of town planning became subject to critical scrutiny by national governments. Markets, and not subsidies and plans, were to dominate the location of industry as inter-urban competition increased. At the same time public capital expenditure, on homes, roads, sewers and so on, became the lead sectors of public spending cutback in many countries. This greatly reduced the power of local planners and politicians to shape urban change unless they made recourse to private sources of support.

In the United States, these tendencies were well established. National government has never had a conscious role in the spatial allocation of economic activity, even though many Federal policies, such as mortgage insurance, defence expenditure, highway construction and the deductibility of State and local taxes, have had a major impact on the location of businesses and households. But the effects of fiscal restraint and international economic competition were nonetheless strongly felt, arising from local responses to the emerging economic conditions.

The new economic conditions of the decade placed fresh strains on cities: for example, long term unemployment and homelessness rates have increased in most OECD cities in the 1980s. But, at the same time, it created new opportunities for change. The more restrictive climate for national government spending in Europe and Australasia and the newly-imposed local fiscal constraints in the United States left urban governments to find new ways of coping with competition and change. In some countries, such as France, Canada and Spain, the 1980s saw a deliberate strengthening of the governance roles and competence of local and provincial authorities. In others, most notably the United Kingdom, the national government increased its control over the volume and mix of urban municipal expenditure. Indeed in the fields of housing and urban policy, new specialised government agencies were formed in the United Kingdom to provide localised alternatives to municipal government in providing homes, local economic development, training and so on. In both these contexts the imperative for local cross-sectoral co-ordination increased.

In Europe, the structure and role of participatory government also changed sharply in the 1980s. Citizens groups and individual citizens have played a growing role in shaping public planning, investment and public service delivery. Governments have encouraged these changes which are gradually modifying the character and quality of public services for the better, though the process has not been without controversy or difficulty. One notable outcome has been the greatly increased time now required in most countries to obtain agreement to any form of development or investment.

In the United States, cities and counties have for long recognised that the responsibility for their economic success rests largely in their own hands. Enjoying a large measure of fiscal autonomy, with or without the support of State legislatures, cities have played a significant role in attracting additional funds and economic activity to their area. In many parts of Europe, for example Germany and Italy, cities have enjoyed a similar degree of autonomy, in the one case supported by the federal constitution (in former West Germany) and in the other by the patronage system of distributing central funds. In Japan too, city mayors have enjoyed considerable powers to pursue independent initiatives.

But in much of Europe, the emerging conditions have come as something of a shock. Local governments, now more than ever responsible for the destiny of their own cities, have come to form purposive relationships not only with local citizens but also with the voluntary and private sectors. The effect has been a broadening of the local community and local economy role in shaping change. Municipal governments, now less reliant on national governments, have become more dependent on the active involvement of local citizens, communities and the corporate sector. In this context a local, inter-sectoral view of cities and neighbourhoods is more likely to prevail than when local bureaucrats see their main support coming from remote, sectorally divided branches of higher levels of government.

The 1980s also saw, within cities, a growing emphasis on area-based policy initiatives, not least because of the emerging concentrations of dysfunctional problems. Increasingly communities recognised the linkages between housing rehabilitation and environmental, social and economic policies. Local economic development policies, replacing regional policies, in many cases had direct neighbourhood dimensions and community connections. The locus of policy moved to "areas", forcing a gradual holistic perspective, and moving decisions downwards within the urban context. The "bottom-up" process and the infrastructure for devising new urban policies were thus greatly strengthened.

Urban deprivation and exclusion thus stems from the changing socio-demographic structure of urban populations and the increased competition for employment, with higher skill requirements and greater likelihood of irregular or unstable income, that affects all OECD countries to one extent or another.

If a difference does exist between Member countries, it relates primarily to the role and relevance of housing and the physical environment. In North America and Australasia, the housing situation is considered less important than the socio-economic determinants of persistent disadvantage in the urban context, while in Japan the emphasis is almost wholly on housing market failures. In Europe, by way of contrast, both dimensions have played a part.

In Australia, for example, problems in the housing market are minor by the standards of many other countries and are mainly that affordable housing of relatively good quality has been made available only at the cost of increasing inaccessibility to employment and community services (as well as at considerable environmental cost). In the United States, the housing market is generally a much less important element than it was in the 1960s: the pressure on inner city housing markets has generally diminished and housing costs in low income areas have fallen relatively. Where racial and ethnic minorities were once thought to suffer a cost penalty, their housing costs are now lower in many cases than the average. (The concentration of poverty in the small public housing sector in the United States, however, remains a serious problem.) In Japan, in contrast, the pressure of rising land and housing costs in the major metropolitan areas is the most significant component of localised urban disadvantage. In Europe, the physical, housing problem still looms large, in part because the localisation of disadvantage is in many cases directly related to the existence of badly planned and badly maintained social housing complexes and partly because housing market responses, such as discrimination in access or rents against foreign migrants or the lack of appropriate small units of accommodation for single migrant workers persist.

The differences, however, remain ones of emphasis, with the specific causes of localised disadvantage varying as much from city to city as between countries.

The current concern with disadvantage in cities, and in particular to its spatial distribution, has revived the earlier debate about the relative merits and roles of "people-oriented" versus "place-oriented" policies. The respective arguments are well known though their validity remains a matter of controversy.

The argument in favour of "people-oriented" policies rests in part on grounds of efficiency: the most effective way of building bridges between the disadvantaged and the mainstream is to ensure that individuals have the training, the skills, the income support and the services they need; and in part on grounds of equity: in the great majority of cases, the most disadvantaged and those in greatest need of assistance, identified in terms of separate criteria, are not clustered residentially into small areas. Indeed they tend to be widely dispersed. Only a very small proportion of the severely poor, for example, live in the areas that are themselves the poorest; only a minority of the long-term unemployed or school-leavers unable to find suitable employment reside in the areas of concentrated neglect; single parent families and poor elderly couples and single people are found throughout most urban areas.

The argument in favour of area-based programmes depends more on the scope for efficiency gains. Appropriately co-ordinated multi-sectoral policy initiatives are likely to yield a better return on the resources devoted to them, because the value of the individual component measures will not be dissipated by the failure to back them up with action targeted to related needs: employment initiatives are more likely to be successful if the shortage of public transport is tackled at the same time; inducements for single mothers to re-enter the labour market are more likely to be successful if child care facilities are provided and affordable housing is available; and so on. Moreover, it is the consequences of the failure to adopt a "place-oriented" approach which command attention. For, if it is correct to say that the problems of disadvantage are compounded by their spatial concentration, the costs to society of the failure to devise strategies adequate to address the problems of the worst concentrations of neglect will be that much greater.

The simple solution is of course to meet the arguments of social justice by providing adequate and appropriate universal programmes, at the same time as targeting customised, multi-sectoral initiatives at the worst concentrations of urban deprivation and neglect. Unfortunately few governments are in a position to be able to meet both agendas simultaneously to a level which their advocates would regard as ideal. Some choice is unavoidable.

The difference in the weight attached to the physical and housing dimensions of the problem in different Member countries is reflected in the emphasis given to area-based strategies. While in the United States, for example, there are strong advocates of a "place-orientation", it is accepted that the rationale for area-based initiatives rests on the claim that -- to quote one leading analyst -- "what distinguishes members of the underclass from those of other economically disadvantaged groups is that their marginal economic position or weak attachment to the labour force is uniquely reinforced by the neighbourhood or social milieu" (*Cf.* Wilson, 1991, p. 474). Clearly the implications for policy are different if the source of the problem is thought to be spatial concentration *per se* rather than a contingent association with pockets of poor quality housing or deficiencies in the housing allocation process.

In Europe, by contrast, there is also increasing concern about the cumulative effects of the spatial concentration of disadvantage. This view is especially acute when the spatial concentrations can at the same time be correlated clearly with ethnic minorities or groups of recent migrants. But the prominence given to housing and physical environment-led policies in many European countries, as the key to successful urban regeneration and socio-economic inclusion -- albeit in concert with a broad array of social and economic initiatives -- arises exactly because it is the deficiencies in the systems for planning, providing, allocating and maintaining the housing stock, and the related community facilities, that are thought to have been primarily responsible for the emergence of significant concentrations of acute disadvantage.

Once again it is a difference of emphasis but it underlies the differences of approach found in different Member countries. In the United States many commentators would echo Jencks' conclusion that "looking for metasolutions is almost certainly time wasted...[To] reduce...poverty, joblessness, illiteracy, violence or despair, we will surely need to change our institutions and attitudes in hundreds of small ways, not one big way" (*Cf.* Jencks, 1991, p. 98). In Europe the concern is not so much with metasolutions as with the conscious integration of initiatives to comprise a measured, holistic response to the problems of particular areas and particular groups.

Key policy issues in OECD countries

In order to identify the main issues of concern, Member countries were asked to submit short reports on what they saw as their major urban-housing policy problems, setting out the objectives of the policy programmes, both national and local, which they have introduced to tackle the twin concerns about social integration and housing affordability. This section brings together the experiences of the participating countries and describes how they approached these questions. Although there are always problems of comparability, given the differences in economic, social and institutional arrangements throughout the OECD, it is evident from this exercise that there are striking parallels in terms of the problems faced in OECD cities, the ways in which they are being tackled and the extent to which policy objectives are being successfully achieved.

Shared problems

There is a strong connecting thread among the problems faced by mature OECD cities and metropolitan regions.

Firstly, *severely disadvantaged neighbourhoods* co-exist with areas of affluence and economic success. These are often in the inner city, but are also to be found on the periphery, especially where large areas of low-cost or social housing have been built at the outer edge of the metropolitan area. Typically these areas lack access to basic amenities and community facilities; employment opportunities are limited; and housing tenure and social mix are uniform. Social deprivation tends to be concentrated in these areas.

Secondly, there are also clear and sometimes related problems of *housing affordability*. A shortage of cheap rental housing or difficulties of access to finance for first time buyers, combined with high land and housing prices, have made it increasingly difficult for low-to-middle income families to find affordable housing in suitable locations.

Thirdly, there are problems relating to *social and demographic change*. The growing number of elderly households in OECD countries, the numbers of young households moving into property for the first time, and, arguably most pressing in much of Europe at least, the upsurge in immigration into the cities of Member nations are each having a major impact on the volume and structure of urban housing demand.

Finally, despite major improvements in recent decades, there remains a problem of overall *physical housing quality* in many of these neighbourhoods. These will now be examined in greater detail.

Severely disadvantaged neighbourhoods

In Sweden, most rental housing has been built since the 1950s. It is mainly situated in large scale urban housing projects, and much of the stock is in severe need of major renovation. Social housing estates built in the 1960s and 1970s have alleviated sectoral shortages; but they too have become characterised by unsatisfactory services and a visually unattractive and run-down outdoor environment.

In Western Germany, large housing estates were built in the 1960s and 1970s, characterised by high density and multi-storey built form. Most of these were rented social housing units. These estates were developed in response to continuous demographic and economic growth. Insufficient attention was paid to environmental quality or to the various needs of a highly differentiated social structure among the tenants. Until the mid-1980s, there was little tenant participation. Surprisingly, studies indicate that despite the generally low social status of the tenants, rents in these estates are often set above comparable commercial residential rents. This is all the more significant because of the socio-demographic structure of the households: comprising low-to-moderate income households; a disproportionate number of families with young children; and migrants. As in many other OECD countries, the peripheral location and absence of transport facilities among the large German housing estates has severely impaired the economic potential of residents. By the mid-1980s, housing shortages were reversed and large numbers of vacancies began to appear on these estates, reflecting the low demand for this type of housing arrangement. However, while this was a true reflection of the intrinsic demand for this type of housing, this quickly became of second order importance, once the large scale immigration of the late 1980s began, accompanied by a growing shortage of housing in the unified Germany.

In the Netherlands, there is considerable evidence of neighbourhoods with a high incidence of unemployment, criminality, bad housing, low incomes and poor levels of training and education.

In the United Kingdom, a significant part of public sector housing was built at high densities, in unpopular housing forms, often in peripheral locations. About 10 per cent of these dwellings face severe management problems. Recent experience highlights the downward spiral into decay and deprivation which can affect this type of housing, to the point where areas become stigmatised. As in the German case noted above, in these cases much of the stock is left empty with the remainder frequently housing only "problem" tenants. High levels of unemployment, crime and poverty characterise these areas.

In Switzerland, France and Belgium, the deteriorating position of what may be called the "marginal" households -- the elderly, the handicapped, single parents, immigrants, ex-criminal offenders, drug addicts and others who together make up the "new poor" -- has also been especially highlighted. Undoubtedly this is a widespread problem that has to be tackled systematically if social renewal is to make progress in OECD countries.

The Swiss report provides a breakdown of the types of housing problems faced by underprivileged groups (see Table 2.1). This matrix would almost certainly be applicable to many other OECD countries. In particular, it emphasises the affordability problem of excessive housing cost-to-income burdens and the probability of discrimination faced by these types of households. Within individual categories of the underprivileged, it is evident that immigrants, the young and others subject to discrimination (e.g. drug addicts, ex-criminal offenders and AIDS or HIV carriers) are all likely to be poorly treated by current urban housing systems.

Table 2.1 **Overview of under-privileged groups and their housing problems**

Problem group	Over-crowding	Substandard equipment, noise, other disturbances	Excessive rents in relation to income	Discrimination by landlords and other residents
Elderly	seldom	seldom	sometimes	seldom
Handicapped and ill	seldom	seldom	sometimes	sometimes
Single parents	seldom	seldom	sometimes	sometimes
Young families	seldom	sometimes	very often	seldom
Large indigenous families	sometimes	seldom	sometimes	sometimes
Large immigrant families	very often	often	often	very often
Other immigrants	often	very often	sometimes	very often
Unemployed	seldom	often	often	often
Students	sometimes	sometimes	sometimes	seldom
Other youth	sometimes	often	often	very often
Released prisoners	seldom	very often	often	very often
Drug addicts	seldom	very often	often	very often
AIDS	seldom	sometimes	sometimes	very often

Source: Switzerland Country Report.

Housing affordability

Affordability problems arise in a number of guises but generally refer to situations where housing cost-to-income ratios are unacceptably high for certain groups or where a shortage of available housing puts pressure on land and housing costs. In Finland the average housing cost-to-income ratio is 16 per cent of income, whereas in Spain the comparable figure is 31 per cent. In Italy, on the other hand, rents tend to be held down to a fixed percentage of income, and similar systems are found in many OECD Member countries, even where there has been resistance to the specification of precise affordability ratios.

But averages can be deceiving. A high ratio is less of a problem to a high income household than it is to a low-to-medium income household. The most severe affordability problems occur when low or variable income households face higher than OECD average ratios of housing costs to income. At the same time high house price-to-income ratios often co-exist with low rent-to-income ratios, where supply shortages push up land and housing asset prices at the same time as rent controls and subsidy measures act to keep rents and rental returns low. This type of housing market failure has adverse distributional effects for many of the underprivileged groups described above, as well as for those first time buyers who could easily afford the purchase of housing if it was provided in a more efficient housing market context.

In Table 2.2, evidence from three major capital cities illustrates the extent of the pressure on housing affordability faced in many places during the late 1980s. The figures indicate the year-on-year rate of house price inflation for Greater London, Paris and the Tokyo metropolitan region. In Greater London, average house prices rose from £55 000 in 1986 to over £82 000 by the end of 1989. In Paris, over a roughly equivalent period, house prices increased from an average of FF 1.472 million to FF 2.258 million. In Japan, again in the same period, Tokyo house values increased from Y 31 million to Y 57 million on average. In every case, these increases were far higher than income growth, putting severe pressure on moderate income and first time house purchasers, and fuelling speculative housing demand on the part of established home owners. It should be noted, however, that these very rapid rates of increase in house prices during the boom period were followed by significant falls during the ensuing economic recession. In many instances the effect has been to leave those who purchased housing at inflated values with substantial negative equity in their property.

Table 2.2 **Annual house price increases, selected cities**
1987-89 percentage change

Year	London	Paris	Tokyo
1987	20	7	39
1988	18	30	31
1989	5	11	12

Source: OECD Issue Paper: Economic Growth, Concentration of Service Industries and Provision of Affordable Housing in Big Cities.

The recent Swiss experience has been of high urban land prices and high construction standards, making new "brownfield"-sited housing completely unaffordable to target social groups. This affordability gap has coexisted with large numbers of empty properties in less attractive areas. In Finland, the average housing cost-to-income ratio is low by international standards; but it is much higher for young households and for the poor, who face ratios of as high as 37 per cent (for the lowest quintile). In Finland also, as in many other countries, there have been state-led efforts to increase the production of rented housing through subsidies; but there has still been insufficient new housing to cope with the increase in demand brought on by income growth and financial deregulation.

The affordability problem has also been keenly felt in urban Japan where land prices and long term locational decisions by business and government have created unsustainable housing cost-to-income ratios for most ordinary families. This situation has encouraged speculation and hoarding on the land market. Similar problems have also been experienced in Belgium and in the United Kingdom, a country which has a very highly regulated planning and land release system. Italy has faced serious housing shortages for low-to-medium income tenants, under-investment in real property generally and a lack of affordable housing for students, young families and temporary workers. The absence of new supply reflects the longer term consequences of rent control, although there are major regional differences: in North and Central Italy there are large numbers of under-used, seasonal second homes.

Table 2.3 **Saving ratios and mortgage debt to GDP ratios**

Country	Saving ratios		Mortgage debt: GDP	
	1982	1989	1983	1989
Japan	13.7	14.4	18.7	25.1
Germany	13.8	13.6	22.2	21.9
France	19.5	11.4	19.2	21.0
United States	9.3	7.4	33.5	45.2
United Kingdom	11.6	5.0	32.1	58.3

Source: OECD Issue Paper: Recent Developments in Financing Home Ownership in OECD Countries.

Table 2.3 gives details of the savings ratio and proportion of GDP taken up by mortgage debt in a number of OECD Member countries. This illustrates some of the macroeconomic consequences of the liberalisation of housing finance. Across the OECD savings ratios have fallen in order to allow mortgage indebtedness to rise (for the financing both housing and non-housing spending). In other words, the increase in people's capacity to borrow has increased housing market pressure, on the one hand, and may in turn have reduced individual countries' ability to save and invest, on the other hand. The United Kingdom in particular experienced a considerable reduction in the personal sector savings ratio during the second half of the 1980s, a period during which its mortgage debt grew to more than half of GDP.

Social and demographic change

Housing needs, housing demand, the use which is made of the housing stock and the composition of neighbourhoods all depend fundamentally on demographic dynamics. There have been at least three main sources of change in recent years. First, household formation is increasingly starting at an early age, related to which is the growing proportion of new types of household in urban areas, for instance, single parent families. Second, there is the cumulative structural change brought on by increasing numbers of elderly citizens, particularly in the over 75 age group. These households have specialised housing requirements, often in the form of sheltered housing, with concomitant additional resource requirements. This trend needs to be seen in the context of the wider long term, structural pressure placed on welfare states and social security systems by the increasing ratio of dependent to economically-active households in OECD cities, regions and nations. Third, there is the issue of immigration. In the case of Europe, migration from Africa and from Eastern Europe, has had an especially serious impact, as has the rural-urban migration in Turkey, with the consequent issues of squatter housing, inadequate infrastructure provision, etc. This is perhaps most visible in the housing pressures faced in the newly-unified Germany; but it is also having a major impact on countries like France and Italy.

In Italy, the main difficulties in relation to the creation of livable urban environments stem from increasing environmental deterioration and the lack of well co-ordinated financial support for urban public services. But undoubtedly the main housing problem has been how to cope with immigration. In the last five years of the 1980s between 1.5 and 2 million immigrants arrived in Italy, mainly from the developing countries, and since then there has been additional pressure from Eastern Europe, notably Albania and former Yugoslavia. In France the core urban areas house about 45 per cent of the population but more than two thirds of the immigrant population. The elderly and other atypical household types are most likely to be found in these areas, whereas families tend to be located in suburban areas. In Norway and Germany, immigrant households are more likely to live in over-crowded housing.

The situation of other countries is much more diverse. While a number of countries, including Australia and Canada, maintain active migration policies reflecting the contribution migration makes to their national and local economic and social outcomes, migration can also accentuate problems particularly at the urban level. In Canada, for example, the three major cities, Vancouver, Toronto and Montreal, face immigration of more than 250 000 persons each year. This scale of immigration has created demands and tensions which have led to problems. Undoubtedly, devising strategies for an integrated, non-segregated urban future in the face of these dynamics represents a major, visible, political challenge to forward-looking governments in the OECD.

Physical housing quality

The fourth dimension of the problem faced by urban areas in OECD Member countries relates to the question of housing quality. The United Kingdom provides one among many examples of a pattern of spiralling decay, as entire streets, usually in areas of social housing, become difficult to let, common areas are allowed to deteriorate and residents lose interest in their neighbourhoods. Average housing quality indicators relating to floor space, overcrowding, standard amenities and the like show that in general the quality of housing is improving throughout the OECD. But they ignore the very real problems that exist for these marginal groups and in marginal areas. In Scotland, the problems of decay and the need for major repairs in peripheral public housing neighbourhoods are well beyond the financial capacity of the relevant municipal governments to tackle within a reasonable time-scale without assistance from higher levels of government. In Japan and Europe, the problems are exacerbated by the relatively high population density in most cities, (see Table 2.4), though it must be remembered that the much lower densities found in the United States and Australasia, for example, are there often seen to be the cause of other very serious environmental problems -- the problems of urban sprawl.

Policy responses

Faced with these major problems, OECD governments have developed policies and programmes aimed at the social and economic integration and the physical rehabilitation and revitalisation of their worst urban neighbourhoods. The following sections highlight some of the main approaches adopted by Member countries. Detailed analysis follows in Chapters 4, 5 and 6.

Table 2.4 **Population density in selected OECD cities**

City	Population density persons/ha
Tokyo	105
London	56
Frankfurt	54
Zurich	54
Stockholm	51
Amsterdam	51
Paris	48
Copenhagen	30
New York	20
Washington D.C.	12
Perth	11

Source: Newman P., 1991, "Greenhouse, Oil and Cities", Futures Magazine, May 1991.

Policy objectives

National approaches can be grouped into two types: those fundamentally concerned with what the Netherlands calls social renewal, that is the redevelopment of the socio-economic as well as the physical fabric of deprived neighbourhoods; and those found in countries such as Japan, Australia, Spain and Canada which are directed in the main at achieving affordability objectives. The two are, of course, interdependent; but an emphasis on affordability tends to spotlight questions of market efficiency; targeting subsidies and improving housing finance; land release and planning; and the supply of low cost housing. Arguably, this should be an integral part of all social renewal initiatives. However it tends in practice to play only a small part in the much broader array of social renewal policies, which include community participation, horizontal co-operation (between public and private sectors) and vertical co-operation (between different tiers of government) and the concept of the multi-sectoral approach to social integration and renewal, for example, as seen in France in the last ten years.

In Spain, the government set out a number of plans to tackle the question of housing affordability, for the periods 1981-83, then 1984-87 and the period post-1988. In the first of these, the Government attempted to stabilise the protected part of the housing market and slow down the reduction in the level of new construction. The second plan had the concrete objectives of switching housing aid from a supply-side orientation to personal subsidies, in the pursuit of renovation and housing market deregulation. In the most recent period, the Spanish authorities have sought to modernise and improve the housing finance system and thereby provide wider opportunities for households to enter into mortgage commitments. The Spanish case is characteristic of the trend in urban and housing policy evident in many OECD Member countries towards personal subsidies, deregulation and more of an enabling role for the state than that of regulator and provider. In Spain's forward-looking housing plan, the key aims are to provide easy access to housing for those facing access difficulties, by reducing building costs through freeing the release of building land. The complementary objective is to diversify the supply of housing by development of the rented housing market.

A different story emerges in the Netherlands where several cities, such as Rotterdam, had been pursuing policies of social renewal prior to the adoption of the policy in a national context. An important objective in the Netherlands has been the full participation of all the relevant parties in a multi-sectoral approach to social renewal. In order to monitor the degree of participation and to help evaluate individual renewal projects, a key component of the programme became the design of monitoring and evaluation models which could play a part in the local and national political debate. The Netherlands, along with Japan and France, has been in the forefront of data-led and data supported policies, a critical first step in pursuing relevant policies in urban areas.

In France, the position of disadvantaged groups in run-down neighbourhoods has been accorded top priority. Here, the multi-sectoral approach was pursued most vigorously, using extensive data collection to target the most deprived neighbourhoods and then focus a whole range of initiatives on the target neighbourhood. More recently attention has shifted to city-wide regeneration.

The need for a holistic approach is also recognised in the United Kingdom's policies which emphasise the connection between housing and local economic development and therefore the need to combine agencies and different parts of the private and voluntary sectors in order to achieve the desired objectives.

In tackling the problems faced on Germany's social housing estates, the policy-makers began by recognising the multi-faceted nature of the problem. The response, it was realised, would therefore need to be multi-sectoral. This has been reflected in the measures taken by the planning authorities in relation to building control, participation by tenants in the ownership, management, design and control of their estates, and new ways of tackling the problems of affordability through improvements to subsidy design. Policies have also been co-ordinated to develop employment schemes and to modernise and target community-oriented social work.

The Finnish government policies directed at specific population groups have been explicitly housing-orientated and have become increasingly targeted and means-tested (for example, through housing allowances). A second set of policies has had the objective of "asserting the responsibility of citizens for their housing and environment", in other words, enabling households, including tenants, to participate in the control of their housing affairs. A third policy objective has been the design of explicit measures to prevent housing segregation. This policy uses a strongly interventionist collection of planning, provision and tenant allocation instruments within the social housing sector to achieve an acceptable social mix.

Canadian housing policy, which is administered by Canada Mortgage and Housing Corporation includes three broad strategies. This first relies on providing support for the private sector in the task of providing adequate, suitable and affordable housing, through finance and affordability initiatives. The second targets federal aid to those in need; while the third fosters research and development and the gathering of information to promote market efficiency.

The Norwegian government has, through the State Housing Bank, explicitly pursued a policy of linking housing standards to certain livability-qualities of the dwelling and neighbourhood. The Housing Bank has a dominant position in pursuing the goals of stable and sufficient new construction and renewal. It also provides grants and additional loans for young people, the elderly and disabled in close co-operation with local authorities. The challenge of social regeneration should be met at the local level in joint efforts between the municipal and the voluntary (*i.e.* co-operative) sector, supported by funds, research and development assistance from the national level.

Policy instruments and strategies

When one considers the many and varied types of subsidy, regulation, initiative and partnership that have been, and are being, used across the OECD to tackle the unintended impacts of previous housing and related policies, it is easy to miss the strategic level of thinking that must underpin the regeneration and rehabilitation of depressed neighbourhoods. The approach adopted by France demonstrates most clearly the value of combining a strategic vision of what is needed with an acknowledgment that housing policies alone will not revitalise neighbourhoods. The French authorities have recognised that what is required is more flexible and more wide-ranging multi-sectoral approaches to the problem that extend into the fields of local employment and education as well as to the physical improvement of the housing stock. This lesson was also learnt in Scotland after the failure of the Glasgow Eastern Area Renewal Programme -- a predominantly "physical" renewal programme -- to stimulate permanent jobs for East Glasgow residents. This led to the adoption of a multi-pronged, multi-sectoral approach in the subsequent initiatives established to revitalise four pilot peripheral social housing estates.

The Social Development of Neighbourhoods Programme in France took as its starting point the need to target resources to those areas most requiring regeneration. The need to select, monitor and evaluate urban projects is a critical requirement of housing-led holistic strategies. In the French case,

43

neighbourhood policy was intended to focus on areas of public housing where alienation was at its worst. Thus national-led policy selected 12 high-priority neighbourhoods and subsequently another 136 neighbourhoods signed neighbourhood development contracts for renewal as part of a partnership between national and regional government. A fundamental principle in this selection exercise was the collection of extensive data with which to identify accurately and consistently the worst spatial pockets of disadvantage.

In the Netherlands, the national government, in employing what is also a multi-sectoral approach to social renewal, has sought to evaluate progress in their projects through a four-pronged exercise. First, there is a requirement for a financial report, in which the relevant local authority presents an annual financial account of the use of funds. This feeds back into the calculation of future funding. Second, there is a requirement for a report on the results of social renewal. This is a quantitative exercise which describes the process of renewal, including measures which improve its effectiveness and efficiency. It details the nature of the organisational partnerships within a project and the individual effectiveness of components of the project (for example, housing, education, labour market, child care, crime prevention). Third, the Social and Cultural Planning Bureau conducts a research programme to provide a global inventory of the experience of social renewal at the local level. Finally, and related to this, the research bureau of the Dutch Municipalities Association (DMA) is developing a database on local experiences of social renewal using quantitative data, a systematic dossier library and local level project data.

Efforts to stabilise urban land markets in Japan, as a springboard to the rapid development of new affordable housing, hinge on four factors; the interaction between land policy and data, policy to restrict the growth of real estate lending, the revision of land taxation and particularly the restriction of land trading. These policies require high degrees of monitoring and good information flows. Similarly, the large scale plans to rapidly increase the supply of urban housing through national-local government co-ordination -- a recognition of the fact, common to many countries, that individual local governments do not have the resources on their own for projects of such a scale -- which involve setting concrete targets and using the specific mechanisms of land release, land use conversion and the targeting of under-utilised land, all require a high level of information and communication between the different agencies involved.

The Japanese experience underlines the fact that, in order for social renewal programmes to be undertaken successfully, policy makers must have access to appropriate and comprehensive data or indicators. Most countries have information available from periodic censuses; but some OECD Member countries have moved much further. Belgium, for example, collects substantial and innovative qualitative data on dwelling quality in terms of technical, functional, dimensional and locational criteria. The integration of data of this type with the more traditional measures of housing needs, income and related-household information is a necessary first step in making useful prioritised decisions concerning the targeting of social renewal programmes and policies.

Another vital element in the continuance of policies to rejuvenate neighbourhoods is the design of subsidy mechanisms. While there is a great diversity of approaches within OECD Member countries, most use supply-side subsidies to encourage the development of new affordable housing or the rehabilitation of existing stock, often through grants offered by increasingly local tiers of government. However, there are other trends emerging. Italy, for example, spent US$20 000 million on residential building, administered by 20 regional governments to develop over 300 000 units to a variety of landlord types and housing tenures for social housing in the decade to 1987. This is close to an eighth of the entire housing stock.

In the United Kingdom, policy has explicitly sought to change the role of the dominant social housing landlords, the local and municipal authorities, from that of provider to one of overall housing enabler. Social housing will in future be developed by smaller often community-based housing associations. These receive large capital grants for approved developments, but will in future draw a significant and growing proportion of their finances from the private sector. In Sweden, by contrast, large scale renovation has been subsidised by low interest government loans and other subsidies, improving about 200 000 units in the period after 1983. There is some evidence that, with the intention of "turning around" problem estates, in order to attract middle class households, rents have risen substantially.

Canadian housing project expenditure targets a wide range of activities. Approximately 30 per cent of housing units benefiting from programmes were new while the remainder included rent supplements for low income persons in existing rental units and loans or grants to low income homeowners for home repairs and rehabilitation. Some 22 per cent of the 1990 housing programme was focused on the "not for profit" sector contributing to over 9 000 units. In Spain, where policy aims to increase supply access and affordability, supply measures include a preferential credit line to finance land purchase and building, the creation of rented housing investment funds, and subsidised loans for social housing production.

A key element of Canada's housing strategy refers to social housing partnerships. Social housing agreements are made between the federal, provincial and territorial governments to establish a process and protocol for the delivery and evaluation of social housing programmes. Typically, this also involves non-profit housing organisations, municipalities and local housing authorities. In order to make management of these units more effective, a process of national public consultation on social housing and related issues is used. The prepared consultation paper is an invitation to participate, and the responses are used to build consensus about the future direction of social housing programmes. The Canadian Mortgage and Housing Corporation is presently involved in consultations on the way public housing can be of most use to society, and to focus on ways in which the complex needs of poorer residents in public housing can be better addressed by providing opportunities to access services, training and employment. Another aspect of this consultation is to improve life in public housing by addressing concerns such as security and by providing more channels for tenant participation in the management of their communities.

Another clear-cut example of the multi-sectoral, partnership approach is provided by the "New Life in Urban Scotland" initiative set up in 1988. This recognised that the real future challenge lay not in inner city regeneration but in improving and revitalising the peripheral housing estates in urban Scotland. It was also recognised that renewal had to embrace more than physical housing improvements and that all the relevant agencies and actors had to be fully involved. In other words, each contributor had to feel that they "owned" the project. The problems faced were many and varied and the response had to be targeted, comprehensive and consensual. In each of the four partnership areas, the following three principles have been employed. First, an integrated approach to economic, social and physical regeneration, firmly grounded in analysis and long term strategy (requiring the co-operation of a wide range of public bodies), has been adopted. Second, the aim has been to include the private sector as an integral agent in the process, both to advise and provide expertise but also to tackle directly the economic isolation of the housing estates. Third, and most important, the process has been based on the full involvement of the local community in the decision-making process in order to encourage participation, responsibility and a long term commitment to the success of the project.

In relation to the more general objective of neighbourhood renewal and social integration, partnership and multi-sectoral co-operation stand out clearly from the experience of OECD Member countries as key elements in the design of strategies for urban and neighbourhood change. The need to think strategically in terms of pursuing multi-pronged objectives that cover training, employment, crime prevention and the provision of community services, as well as housing, has to be reconciled with the full participation of all relevant groups.

The evidence provided by Member countries highlights both the common trends and the distinctive variety of housing and urban policies in OECD countries. It has focused on two main issues: the problem of housing aff ordability and the task of regenerating neighbourhoods blighted by poverty and social decay.

Most countries are experiencing significant problems, resulting from demographic change, the emergence of the "new poverty", housing and land market failures and the continuing, basic problems of unsatisfactory housing quality. Across the OECD, policy programmes have been developed that seek to co-ordinate physical, social and economic renewal, emphasising co-operation between the public and private sectors, and placing citizen participation in, and control of, housing-led renewal at the forefront of policy objectives, instruments and evaluation. In a context of decentralisation and fiscal prudence, Member countries have reported some measure of success in dealing with issues of social renewal, social housing management and the stabilisation of overheated urban real estate markets using this broader approach. But there is no room for complacency. Key elements in making policy work such as the shared need for improved urban monitoring and information systems remain deficient. Without adequate information and coordination, innovative policy ideas will not be transformed into multisectoral strategies capable of meeting urban challenges.

Chapter 3

The Search for a New Policy Framework

Urban regeneration policy for the 1990s is, in effect, concerned with central societal objectives of growth, equality, and the environment. A strategic, integrated approach to urban regeneration is clearly required in many neighbourhoods and cities. As can be seen from the foregoing summary of the policy approaches currently being undertaken in OECD countries, the move towards strategic policy making is evident; yet it has not been universally adopted, coherently implemented nor even clearly defined. This section describes a new conceptual framework and introduces the key components of an "integrated and multi-sectoral" approach to the tasks facing central and local governments.

Towards a strategic urban policy approach: two helpful conceptions

At the level of the city or the metropolitan area as a whole, it is obvious that cities are complex, open systems. Cities are spatially separated but functionally linked to each other by flows of goods, information, capital and labour. New products and new production processes are increasing the "footlooseness" of location choices -- residential opportunities, environmental quality, cultural and leisure activities associated with places are looming larger in the location decisions of households and firms. Two "policy" consequences flow from these changes:

-- location is no longer driven by narrow production cost factors but by a range of social, environmental and economic aspects of cities which reflect the past as well as the present and which are shaped by state as well as market actions;
-- urban change partly stems from the actions of cities themselves and it is in the power of a city to shape change and innovation.

These observations imply that although cities must react competitively to non-local events they can also do so purposefully and through a range of activities. That is, at the urban level, strategic, integrated policy making will be essential in the face of growing inter-urban competition.

The second concept concerns how the "city" itself is viewed. Many analysts have tended either to talk about the urban economy as an integrated whole, or to make crude core/periphery subdivisions. Much use has been made of the inner city/outer city dichotomy. But this emphasis, which is appropriate in some contexts -- for example, in relation to some United States urban issues -- does not adequately reflect all urban geographies. It tends to have hampered policy development. A more appropriate approach is to conceive of cities, for policy and analysis purposes, as a mosaic of functionally defined neighbourhoods. Urban regeneration policy, whether dealing with a single neighbourhood or a whole city, must be based upon a clear understanding of the neighbourhood structure of cities. And once this approach is adopted a multi-sector/multi-functional approach is almost inevitable, since neighbourhoods are multi-functional phenomena.

A number of observations relevant to policy development emerge:

--   neighbourhoods, though specialised, contain a variety of land uses and socio-economic groups; altering such an environment may require a range of simultaneous actions across a number of sectors;
--   neighbourhoods are defined through patterns of social and economic interaction; social interactions may generate attachment to place and a sense of community; the separation of home and job locations means that neighbourhoods are relatively open economic systems;
--   the openness of neighbourhood economies means that connections, either competitive or complementary, with other neighbourhoods may be strong, and they may be positive or negative; policy must be acutely aware of "displacement" and "shifting" impacts of policies in a specific place;
--   neighbourhoods may generate externalities that impact on the rest of the city, that is, not all inter-neighbourhood flows are "traded";
--   neighbourhoods are often chosen by households or firms because of the people or businesses already resident there; should some decide to leave there are likely to be destabilising effects on the choices of others;

-- as a consequence of the interdependence of locational choices, neighbourhood change trajectories are likely to display cumulative "growth" or "decline" features at key change points; this is important for policy -- it may be about sparking off change as much as lifetime involvement in a place and clearly dynamics of change and the appropriate phasing of change triggers will be important.

Once neighbourhoods, defined in terms of appropriate multi-functional criteria, are recognised as the appropriate building blocks for understanding the dynamics of cities, then it becomes clear that policy design must recognise interactions between areas and functions. Moreover, there is a need to not only examine the articulation of economic and social interconnections but also to recognise that there are changing governance issues and systems at the community level.

It follows that, wherever possible, urban policies should be targeted at neighbourhoods, as the essential building block of urban change, and that they should be linked and multi-sectoral, both at the level of the city and at the level of the neighbourhood.

New connections

It is clear that, in the course of the last decade, national and urban governments have learned much about how to facilitate urban regeneration. But in many cases the experience has been disconnected or un-integrated in two senses. Firstly, in many cities regeneration activities are small in scale and coverage: in Europe, for example, the major developments in places like Glasgow, Berlin and Rotterdam are the exceptions. In most towns and cities in OECD Member countries, integrated area regeneration schemes cover only one or two neighbourhoods. The outstanding questions are: what are the implications of moving beyond demonstration schemes, or restricted areas, to city-wide regeneration strategies; can what works on a restricted scale apply also city-wide? Secondly, in many places projects, even on quite a large scale, have been initiated and driven by a single sector agency or government department. Often the connections to other programmes and market actions, necessary to maximise the benefits of the initiative, have been added in an *ad hoc* fashion as the policies unfolded; frequently they have simply been ignored. Policies need spatial and sectoral integration.

51

The same considerations highlight the need for a strategic approach. Projects should take into account the impacts on connected places and the ways in which project design and phasing change the behaviour of households and firms in ways which support public action and leverage public or private investment. A strategic approach requires a clear forward look, but also a recognition that events will not unfold as predicted and that constant, but consistent, reaction to change will be required.

Strategic, multi-sectoral approaches to urban regeneration must be directed at the urban and neighbourhood scales of action. But they depend ultimately on national or provincial governments having a clear understanding of what urban policy has become and on well articulated national or provincial policies in respect of social, economic and governance affairs, which both recognise and support the urban dimension. Their failure to do this will mean either that urban policy remains an addendum to mainstream policies, rather than a formative influence, and/or that the policies of higher levels of government may actually be inconsistent with and frustrate specific urban actions.

A number of preferred principles for public policy have emerged over the last decade and these are likely to persist into the future. These principles need to be clearly articulated and their urban implications recognised. These key integrating principles are likely to include the following:

-- in general, market solutions or competitive organisation of state provision are likely to be preferred to monopolistic state provision: well organised markets are more likely to emerge if there are underlying formative policies;
-- there is likely to be long-run, downward pressure on public spending; curtailment of services should therefore be based on a coherent understanding of costs and benefits, (cheaper state policies are not always economically more efficient state policies);
-- subsidies, especially in the housing sector, are increasingly related to incomes; but they will need to be well structured to avoid poverty traps and related effects;
-- rising, cyclically adjusted, unemployment rates emphasise the growing attention that needs to be given to education and training policies; but with growing labour demands for urban regeneration projects, the scope for "work-fare" and "green-fare" policies needs to be radically reassessed; and in so doing governments must recognise the potential non-wage benefits to participants in such schemes.

-- the emergence of a "two-thirds favoured/one-third disadvantaged" pattern of prosperity will mean that governments will always be electorally dependent on the middle classes; altruism is not likely to regenerate cities; either spatial or social exclusion must grow to insulate the "haves" from the consequences of the behaviour of the "have-nots", or governments must make clearer the longer term benefits (to society, the economy and the environment) of redistributive policies; if they do not, a dystopian, divided future will unfold;

-- in fostering a broader and longer term view of the costs and benefits of government action, governments must convincingly articulate the interactions between the social and environmental facets of "sustainable development"; at present, international, national and local policy documents are characterised by high expectations, but relatively few real urban programmes actually address such issues; for instance, the underlying connections between the adoption of "user and polluter pay" principles for urban utilities, user-charging for transport, housing investment policies and income-related benefit systems need to be spelled out clearly; inter-sectoral thinking has to apply to the principles that underlie sectoral policies, and their consistency, as well as to spending programmes; if the principles are inconsistent, scarce public resources will be wasted; holistic thinking must precede integrated spending;

-- national governments must set a clear framework for governance; subsidiarity, participation and citizenship are all related issues which have taken root in the 1980s; the geographic structures of government and the balances between participatory and representative democracies are critical to the nature and tone of urban policies; the *ad hoc* growth of urban initiatives and agencies over the last decade now needs rationalisation; and such reconsideration must touch upon the extent and nature of the fiscal resources available for economic development and social renewal; although the process of resource allocation from higher levels of government usually incorporates a "needs" element, there is a growing case for priority distributions to cities which generate creative strategies for change; there may have to be an explicit "triage" process in distributing scarce urban policy resources;

-- any process which reshapes national resource allocation on a competitive or strategic basis will imply, directly or indirectly, the growth of some cities at the expense of others; some countries prefer a "top-down" determination of national spatial priorities; others prefer to leave the outcome to the "bottom up" processes of competition and migration; either way, a clear national planning framework is required; whether based on city competition, needs indicators or centrally determined strategic priorities, governments which tended to de-emphasise national spatial planning in the 1980s will be required to rethink the national framework for urban change.

The evolving administration of policies and programmes

At all levels of government, it is not just urban policies that will require scrutiny but also the structure, tone and style of administration. Public servants may need more urban education. A holistic "urban" view, inter-sectoral policy impact matrices, more extensive value-for-money and cost-benefit evaluations will be required. And responsibility for urban policy should lie with appropriate departments. In many situations the appropriate department might be the first one to admit that its programmes are necessary but not sufficient to achieve urban regeneration. But since the "lead" spending department may vary from city to city (depending on the specific regeneration requirement), a high profile inter-departmental committee might be a better option. Alternatively a multi-purpose urban regeneration agency, with housing, land, environmental and local economic development powers, might be more successful. Such an enabling agency would be more likely to achieve action. In some countries, for example the United Kingdom, multiple regeneration agencies already co-exist; but one might question whether this is sensible. A single regeneration agency might prove more integrated and effective, especially in liaising with local authorities and the private sector.

Although a clear overall approach to urban policy is required, there is little doubt that the main role in implementing effective urban regeneration policies lies at the local level. At this level the key components of an integrated approach to policy formulation and implementation include:

-- the capacity to look across time, to understand past decline trajectories and to aim for better, future patterns;
-- an understanding of the urban mosaic which recognises the connected and competitive nature of neighbourhoods within cities in the selection of regeneration areas and policy instruments;
-- an emphasis on the multi-faceted nature of neighbourhood decline and revitalisation and the consequent requirement for integrated policy action at the very local scale; and

-- the ability to integrate the objectives and actions of potential partners in the process of change, namely citizens, community groups, the private sector and all the relevant public agencies and departments.

Partnerships and individual action at the local level

A vision for change should be based upon the shared aspirations of all the key investors, governors and citizens involved with a place. It is a device for focusing imagination and reducing uncertainty and for articulating the overlaps of partners' strategies and intentions. An effective vision has to be developed in a multi-partner, multi-sector framework, if it is truly to set the tone for coherent change. And a well formed vision must balance creative and imaginative thinking (newly imagined possibilities) with resources and realities (which may narrow probabilities).

If a city does not have the leadership capacity and creative skills to develop a shared, credible vision, then it is unlikely ever to use regeneration resources well. The long term vision, which may be adapted as the uncertain future unfolds, has to be harmonised to present realities by specifying medium term plans, annual programmes and targets, and indeed early action plans for specific projects. As strategies for urban improvement are designed to deal with current problems rather than future objectives their character changes from broadly stated aims about broad outcomes (prosperity, quality, self-sustaining communities, etc.) to increasingly specific statements about programme inputs (housing, job creation, etc.). Of course urban regeneration is about the ends and not the means and local spending agencies, like central government departments, must recognise that the dominant strategy is for "the city" and not "the sector".

In this context it is crucial that multiple agencies and partners (governments, quangos, citizens and the private sector) are involved early in the process and that partners in different sectors are mutually aware of each others' strategies. In many cities, even those well regarded for their urban regeneration programmes, key partners do not share strategy formation and are mutually ignorant of each others' strategies. Such agencies may combine well at the project level but eventual difficulties will occur. Housing spenders in government agencies need to be fully aware of local business development strategies. Housing spenders and local economic development agencies in turn need to be aware of urban environmental strategies, as well as the environmental consequences of their own actions. Recent examples in Europe, including the

Partnerships in Scotland, new planning mechanisms in France and "Social Renewal" in the Netherlands, have all emphasised the importance of multi-sector contributions to regeneration strategy.

Individual private actions, by firms and households, are equally important in moving a city forward. Expectations, shaped by the past, influence present actions: present actions create or foreclose future options. In relation to some of the worst neighbourhoods in North American and European cities, there is a growing concern that the current pattern of social and economic exclusion sustains behaviour and spending patterns which emphasise the present rather than the future. Excluded individuals, with arguably shorter time horizons, are less likely to "invest" in education and are less likely to be health conscious (as reflected in diet, alcohol and drugs dependency and smoking rates). Unless the "telescope" through which individuals and the community view the future in such areas is reconstructed and unless a new appraisal of the future consequences of present actions is made, then city or project "vision" will mean nothing to such groups.

This raises critical issues about education, training and social work as well as the roles of participation and politicians in engaging such communities in purposive change. The approach to such groups is often ambivalent in urban regeneration policies, at least where they are not simply ignored. But rehabilitation strategies must make clear judgements about how to cope with problems of this nature. In all too many cities there are examples of expensive housing, environmental and economic development initiatives which ignored the need to change the expectations of client groups, by education and other programmes, prior to the investment in physical capital. The poorest communities often require the widest multi-sectoral actions.

Institutions, firms and individuals alike need to recognise that regeneration investment or activities create change with new opportunities for action on the part of affected groups: regeneration is a dynamic, changing process. Programmes and strategies for urban regeneration cannot be linear. For instance, the environmental upgrading of sites in Year 1 may induce middle-income home-ownership in Years 3-4 and by Year 5 that growth may make the sites attractive to higher income housing. This may alter the need for subsidy and the scope for leveraging private finance. As neighbourhoods are small, open systems, changes can occur suddenly, quickly revising required policy inputs. This is why a strategic approach is required, if the maximum leverage is to be secured from scarce public funds.

Information for policy action

In many countries, government information systems were designed to address questions about housing need, which was the strategic priority of the 1950s and 1960s. Now, in many run-down cities, housing as shelter is no longer the strategic priority *per se*, but only in relation to broader environmental, neighbourhood and urban economic issues. These new strategic priorities require new spatially referenced multi-functional databases.

When such data is available, a strategic identification of neighbourhoods for action is required which explicitly takes account of shifting, leverage and displacement effects.

But until data collection policies are improved, cities must proceed on the basis of more *ad hoc* approaches to understanding the urban mosaic. For example, when areas are identified for action, baseline survey work on the items noted above is likely to be required, with subsequent monitoring and evaluation. There should then follow a frank assessment of likely impact of regeneration on other areas, some of which may be undergoing similar regeneration in the rest of the city. When the objective is general urban regeneration and not the upgrading of isolated areas, a strategic overview is essential to avoid wasteful inter-area competition or the pre-emption of strategic options. Glasgow, the leading city for urban regeneration in the United Kingdom in the 1970s and 1980s, provides an instructive example of how the failure to adopt a strategic approach may waste resources.

It is important of course to avoid "paralysis by analysis" in the pursuit of urban regeneration. But, equally, failure to consider inter-area and multi-sectoral linkages may jeopardise the success of policy initiatives and on occasion even lead to perverse or unwanted outcomes.

The design of multi-sectoral programmes and policies

Linking sectoral programmes

As rehabilitation policy for housing has evolved into more general urban regeneration initiatives, so single-sector policies have been required to evolve multi-sectoral connections. At one time, housing was the major, though not the only, "single-sector" approach to urban redevelopment and revitalisation in most

OECD Member countries. It is natural therefore that the multi-sectoral approach, developed in countries like France, the Netherlands and Scotland, should have evolved from a housing focus.

The first pre-requisite, as noted above, is that there should be a clearly articulated "city-wide vision". At the same time there needs to be a broad strategic understanding of how housing and other programmes can serve the economic, social and environmental objectives which are components of this "vision". Unfortunately this may prove difficult, since there are few cities in which there is an established matrix of the links between housing and other economic and environmental impacts. In most European countries, the traditional emphasis of housing professionals has been on social effects; only recently have government agencies attempted to establish the role of the housing sector in the local economy.

For the areas or neighbourhoods selected for policy action, there needs to be a clear statement of the aims of each proposal and a more detailed scrutiny of inter-sectoral connections. These can be sub-divided into:

-- *Prerequisites*: definition of the actions which should precede housing change;
-- *Housing action integration*: integration of tenure and management aspects of housing policies and land market issues;
-- *Transport links and circulation*: scrutiny of the links between the neighbourhood and the wider urban system;
-- *Local services and facilities*: analysis of the appropriate quantity and mix of public and private facilities and services;
-- *Ecological sustainability*: detailed investigation of environmental effects.

Pre-requisites

When housing investment is intended to promote self-sustaining change and community momentum, and not merely the rehabilitation of dwellings, the following actions are likely to be required:

-- social work programmes to deal with issues such as alcohol and drug dependency and their consequences;
-- educational programmes to shift expectations and counter any tendencies towards "underclass" culture;

-- active policies to develop community groups and expertise of residents in dealing with the bureaucracy;
-- early training policies for unemployed residents who could become involved in downstream investment (though if this training is too early successful trainees may relocate);
-- environmental upgrading for sites requiring private investment;
-- strategic but, intendedly, temporary agency purchase of land and property in order to capture regeneration gains for local residents and to assemble land.

If these actions are ignored investment may have only an ephemeral effect and the neighbourhood's role is unlikely to change.

Thus, before resources are used for housing renovation, extensive inputs are required from education, social work, participation and economic development agencies.

Housing action integration

Housing policies are, in many countries, diverse and sometimes conflicting components of urban policy, operated by different agencies. In areas of predominantly social housing, for example, it is essential to establish the appropriate tenure mix for the future and the desired quality of management service provision. The actions of the municipality (especially where it is the major housing provider as well as planning authority), other public and voluntary housing agencies and co-operatives and the private sector all need to be co-ordinated. The housing component of the policy needs to be linked to more general strategies towards the property market and land use planning, not least because one major issue in many post-war social housing schemes is how to reduce the level of on-site demand and densities. For the renovation and demolition of outworn social housing to be strategically successful, a coherent local and city-wide land market policy is essential. Previous OECD reports have demonstrated how land regeneration agencies can in this connection make important contributions to urban change, for example, in France.

Transport links and circulation

In many cities neighbourhood residents are disadvantaged in relation to labour market and general urban access by badly structured and expensive transportation arrangements. This may reduce full and part-time employment by local residents and restrict service choices. Social exclusion is reinforced by spatial exclusion. Transport links need to be examined. At the same time some micro-neighbourhoods may suffer in the opposite sense from unnecessary traffic flows and noise, emphasising the importance of traffic calming.

Local services and facilities

Surveys designed to elucidate why households dislike their homes often find that are particularly concerned about the lack of non-housing amenities, *e.g.* shops and sports facilities, or about the inadequacy of services, such as refuse disposal, policing, etc. Most residents in fact adopt a holistic perspective which it would be well for agencies and governments to emulate. Housing choices are inextricably linked to such valued neighbourhood characteristics.

Where this type of "non-housing" problem occurs, a number of "housing" consequences may arise:

-- more affluent households will refuse tenancies in such localities;
-- tenants who are doing relatively well in the labour market are likely to move elsewhere;
-- increasing numbers of residents may become discouraged from looking after their homes and environs.

Housing dominated projects which ignore such factors as school quality, security, shopping access and so on may in fact be wasting resources on expensive capital works. In many cases, to stabilise such neighbourhoods, it may be wiser to improve services and amenities and undertake only modest housing renovation than to build new homes for the poorest households. Often the homes are tolerable but the environs, facilities and services are not.

Once housing investment is ongoing, the links to health, education, policing, shopping and employment initiatives, to name only the most basic, must be made and maintained. Those responsible for these services need to share the "vision", in order to maximise linkages and to develop new inter-sectoral perspectives on neighbourhood change. The key is likely to lie with the nature of the "partnership" formed between the relevant agencies.

Ecological sustainability

A further, important, series of interconnections needs to be added to the agenda: those that relate to ecological sustainability. In many countries, urban regeneration policies of the kind noted above will have a greater impact on the urban poor and, arguably, on city structure than any other thrusts of public policy in the 1990s. It is therefore essential not only that housing policy fulfils its key role in the process of urban regeneration but also that regeneration policies support policies to enhance environmental "sustainability". In selecting areas for regeneration and demolition, especially in declining cities, the impacts on nature and traffic flows must be considered, in the context of more compact, locally multi-functional patterns of land use. Similarly the environmental consequences of ignoring urban regeneration and consolidation and encouraging the movement of households to peripheral suburbs must be addressed.

Linking the partners: new governance issues

The widening experience of urban regeneration during the last decade have highlighted the need for new temporal, spatial and sectoral integrations in planning and implementing policy and projects. At the same time, *ad hoc* innovations in policy style -- notably the attention paid to the three "p's", participation, private sector involvement and partnership -- have changed the ways in which regeneration policies are managed. These evolving governance arrangements need to be scrutinised carefully to establish their likely effectiveness in large scale, multi-sector policies. Not all the measures relevant at the neighbourhood or specific sector level are appropriate in formulating and governing city-wide regeneration strategies.

Participation

Resident participation and community involvement have played a critical and growing role in stimulating, developing and now managing, housing and neighbourhood-based regeneration programmes. There has been much success in this regard, although tenant groups are often too under-trained and poorly funded to make an effective contribution.

Such participation requires to be fostered. It is best aimed at specific sectors and neighbourhood level issues. Arguably "representative government" has been weak in recognising *local* preferences and potential. But, as projects become multi-sectoral and strategic, involving difficult inter-area and inter-sectoral resource re-allocations, it may become necessary to set limits to the role of tenant and neighbourhood participation in city-wide strategy formation. A clear balance has to be struck between representative democracy and participation. There may be merit in the former focusing more sharply on city-wide strategy and enabling roles, and in the process consulting local communities. Local communities, on the other hand, should have a clearer say in multi-sectoral service provision and planning within their neighbourhoods. This may in effect require the decentralisation of service provision to neighbourhood levels.

This approach would in effect extend the notion of "subsidiarity" to intra-urban governance roles. However, if municipal governments are to be persuaded that service delivery and integration should be decentralised and devolved to communities, they may expect national and provincial governments to apply the principle consistently and give a clear, positive role to municipal governments.

The private sector

There has been much benefit in increasing private ownership and private finance in urban regeneration schemes. The provision of owner occupied homes can diversify the socio-economic mix of previously homogeneous neighbourhoods and can bring into use otherwise vacant land and buildings. The use of private finance in public projects helps to sharpen the processes of evaluation and risk appraisal, though the private sector has not demonstrated any particular acumen in understanding future market trends in recent years. In many cases the financial gains from regeneration projects have arisen from public accounting conventions and the desire to cut government spending. The real economic gains from this process are often more modest.

Corporate skills and business acumen can also represent an important contribution from firms to local communities. But the real benefit from private sector involvement in urban regeneration activity over the longer term will probably flow not from corporate altruism in specific projects, but the incorporation of a city's "vision" into the corporate strategies of major enterprises. That is, in planning for the future, firms may become less "footloose" in their behaviour and more inclined to contribute to a local developmental milieu to which they have some degree of intrinsic loyalty. International competition naturally limits such managerial discretion; but there is some margin to be tapped.

The role of both the private sector and community participation need to be rethought, so that they, like government, can contribute what they do most effectively.

Partnerships

Nonetheless, however great the contributions of local communities and the private sector, governments -- national, provincial or local -- have the key roles to play in shaping, managing and monitoring urban partnerships. The experience of the last decade indicates that many different forms of inter-programme, inter-sectoral co-ordination can be successful. Each is a form of partnership; and this applies to city-wide, large area schemes as much as to local neighbourhood scale initiatives. For example, in Glasgow (Scotland) during the 1980s, three or four different styles of partnership operated, apparently effectively, in different parts of the city.

In general, "partnerships" tend to be formed after one agency or government department has identified the specific area for action. This is undesirable. City-wide strategies need to involve joint strategic planning and this should involve all "partners". At the local operational scale, most partnerships evolve effective leadership and co-ordination arrangements and are an effective method of forming good working relations with communities and firms.

Local teams appear to be particularly good at breaking down interdisciplinary barriers and at developing holistic perspectives. Shared inter-agency objectives for areas appear to emerge rapidly in the process. However, government budgetary processes which give departments, municipalities or agencies fixed period budgets as a basis for longer term regeneration projects make this process more difficult. Public expenditure programmes, over time, put different pressures on the partners involved and, in the absence of dedicated project budgets, the commitment of the various partners is likely to reveal differing degrees of strain. Smooth project phasing may then be disrupted.

At the local scale, the governance of urban policy has improved greatly over the last decade in a large number of countries, at least where specific regeneration projects have taken place. But as urban regeneration becomes a city-wide task, on the centre stage of national as well as local policies, a new coherence of national governments, local authorities, agencies, citizens and firms will be required.

Chapter 4

Social Renewal and Livable Environments
by Dr. Satya Brink

Can societies afford the costs of social exclusion? The costs were once considered the burden of the excluded; but the true costs are now becoming evident in the urban system. The inability of individuals to contribute to and participate in economic, social and environmental urban activities is obviously a waste of human resources. But the unaccounted price is insidious and hidden. The many externalities resulting from inequalities hamper future economic growth.

Economic and social disadvantage diminishes future prospects for those entrapped in poverty. The culture of poverty and exclusion focuses on survival, with decisions that are oriented to the present, rather than the future. The link between poverty and environmental degradation, due to this view, was established at the Stockholm conference on the Environment (1972). The widening of the gap between the haves and the have-nots within the confines of the city can give rise to potential social divisions, conflicts, social unrest and even riots. Expensive welfare programmes have had questionable success as poverty and marginalisation remain intractable. The costs of social exclusion are therefore paid by all urban residents, and eventually by the country as a whole.

Though the reasons for action vary among the OECD countries, there is increasing support for the social renewal of cities. In addition to traditional strategies to redistribute income and to reduce unequal outcomes from policy implementation, a number of proactive approaches for social renewal are being attempted in Member countries. These strategies tend to be multi-sectoral in nature and address multiple goals and objectives. Despite this convergence, the strategies launched by each country have their own characteristics.

Links between the components of social renewal

The concept of social renewal arose from the need to recognise the multiple causes for social deprivation in cities. Social renewal strategies have three major thrusts: first, they deal with the multiple inter-related sources of disadvantage, second, they attempt to prevent social problems and third, they support resident initiatives and good citizenship. All three require multi-sectoral approaches.

The need to address the chain of causality through social renewal required a better understanding of the processes of poverty and social exclusion. Co-located problems such as neighbourhoods inhabited by poor households, with low education, lack of marketable skills, little job experience led to social renewal strategies linking education, skill training, job placement and job creation. To break the cycle of deprivation, strategies for children included, day care, preschool education, sports and recreation, nutrition programmes and after school programmes. The growing number of women in poverty has led to strategies that include shelters for battered women, job training and apprenticeship programmes, opportunities for self employment and small business, family counselling and information on eligible benefits.

The emphasis on prevention of urban problems of unemployment, poverty, crime and homelessness led to a systematic examination of the nature of the problems. The trails for individual problems tended to join together, signifying similar origins. When long term multi-sectoral policies are designed, they must address the cluster of problems. This approach is more cost-effective, avoiding costly duplication. Income security programmes should be consolidated, rather than offering separate programmes for food, shelter and income. A portion of the assistance should be directed to education, training and job search.

Good citizenship requires confidence and the ability to participate in society. Social renewal strategies include capacity building and empowerment. Residents are encouraged to undertake initiatives that meet their own priorities. Local networks are used for community action. Social renewal is a long term process of shifting from individual concern for survival to working cohesively for the betterment of the entire community.

The process of social renewal recognises the key role of housing. In the extreme case, urban residents without housing are rendered dysfunctional if they do not have a fixed address. Therefore, security of tenure is important for social integration, job applications, credit and government assistance. Residential areas must include social and recreational services for the support and well-being of residents. For these reasons, housing is a fundamental condition for any other programme of assistance. When housing is secured, individuals are able to focus their efforts to meeting other needs, rather than the seeking of temporary shelter each night.

Cities also need to protect their investment in housing and infrastructure. Early attempts at urban renewal were first directed to the improvement of single houses. The need to focus funds for renovation in neighbourhoods were evident when there were important spin-off effects. However, such neighbourhoods attracted little private investment and urban renewal funds were soon squandered as the neighbourhoods continued to lose ground. It became necessary to empower residents but to also give them the urban supports required to better themselves. It has proved extremely difficult to reverse dysfunctional communities, occupied by residents in difficulty. Neighbourhoods need to be stable, with essential commerce and amenities, to function successfully. Road and transportation networks are important links to jobs, essential services such as hospitals and green spaces. Citizens need to be able to traverse the city in safety, at affordable cost.

There are still important questions that remain to be answered. While the negative links between the problems have been identified, the positive links within the urban system are still unclear. Which are the critical links in the chain of disadvantage, that when broken, allow households to rehabilitate themselves? Should social renewal activities be pursued, while keeping households in disadvantaged neighbourhoods or should they be dispersed into communities that have a rich array of supports that can help boot strap them out of their predicaments? Since the costs of social and urban renewal are so high, will other city residents support large scale investments in problem areas which are slow to recover? Is social renewal sufficient to integrate low income neighbourhoods into the fabric of the city?

The project addressed specifically the following aspects of achieving social renewal and more livable environments: housing, education, training and unemployment in the community; housing the homeless: towards social and economic integration; the residential environment: ensuring a positive focus for health, prosperity and quality of life; involving and empowering residents; improving social cohesion in neighbourhoods; integrating the young: the role of social services, cultural and leisure activities and education; and safer cities: a prerequisite for sustainable urban development.

Housing, education, training and unemployment in the community

Main issues

There is widespread agreement that continued economic growth in OECD countries is, by itself, unlikely to alleviate the problem of long term structural unemployment now adversely affecting cities. In general, it is believed that it takes 2.5 to 3 per cent growth, ceteris paribus, to reduce unemployment. The phenomenon of "jobless growth" is thus increasingly common in OECD countries, as is the realisation that a proportion of the population is now being adjusted into unemployment rather than into new jobs. Table 4.1 shows the average unemployment rates, inactivity rates and the total non-employed for 25-54 year old males in selected OECD countries, averaged for the 1980s. The pattern of unemployment and non-employment rates is worthy of note. Total non-employment rose in almost all cases between 1980 and 1989. In continental Europe the rise during this period can be largely explained by the growth in unemployment; in the United Kingdom, Canada, Sweden and Australia, it is the rise in inactivity which is at least as important. Only in the United States did the non-employment rate fall slightly (*Cf.* Balls and Gregg, 1993). However, since 1989 the rate of unemployment has risen sharply in most of Europe and Australasia. Moreover, the picture for women is notably different with rising participation in the labour force.

The difference between the experience of the United States and many European countries is notable. In the United States, the overall rate of unemployment (and in particular the rate of long-term unemployment) has been kept down; but large numbers of workers are only able to find part-time or occasional employment. In many parts of Europe, where the overall rate of new job creation has been much lower, labour force participation is lower, unemployment is higher but those in work have tended to enjoy more stable and secure employment.

The tenacious grip of poverty can be due either to low wages in employment or to the lack of jobs that provide steady income. Many people survive by working in the shadow economy. In tight economic situations, where there is keen competition for jobs, the unskilled and the poorly educated have difficulty finding permanent jobs. When such jobs are available, they are often poorly paid or short term resulting in sporadic or insufficient income. Housing is one of the greatest difficulties for those without steady income. The rental market discriminates against those without reserves and a reliable source of income. There are few alternatives to monthly rent. The consequences for the poor and the unemployed can be severe. They may concentrate in poor neighbourhoods, crowding into shared accommodation or they may seek public housing assistance. Those that are unable to negotiate either route may become homeless, victims of the no-home, no-job cycle.

Table 4.1 **Unemployment and inactivity rates (averages) 1980-89, percentage of the male population (25-54)**

Country	(a) Unemployment rate	(b) Inactivity rate	(c) Non-employment
Spain	11	6	17
United Kingdom	9	6	15
Canada	7	6	13
United States	5	7	12
France	5	4	9
Australia	4	7	11
Germany	4	8	12
Italy	3	9	12
Japan	2	3	5
Sweden	2	5	7

(a)   not employed but seeking employment
(b)   not employed or seeking employment
(c)   (a) + (b)

Source: OECD Employment Outlook 1992.

Traditional approaches to poverty relief relied on unemployment insurance to tide people over the time of job search. When this period elapsed and unemployment led to poverty, income support payments were paid. These two types of assistance have in many cases proved inadequate to deal with the present economic challenges. Some countries, such as Sweden, where there is a strong interventionist labour market policy, have complementary job training or apprenticeship programmes; and they are better able to respond to the needs of the economy and the labour pool.

The trend for industrial activity to relocate to countries where labour costs and overheads are lower is likely to intensify meaning that many jobs lost today in OECD Member countries are permanently lost: jobs that disappear in recession increasingly never return to developed economies. It is therefore crucial that OECD governments develop policies to encourage alternative forms of beneficial activities and occupations of an economic, social and environmental nature. Those persons who, in recent years, have been excluded from economic life must be given a chance to reintegrate into society through the creation of jobs, occupations or services which allow them to actively earn a living and to lead useful and satisfying lives.

The problem is particularly acute where it concerns young people with the major share of their working life ahead of them. It is therefore important that those responsible for cities take fully into account the likely future impact of macroeconomic trends at city level. Sensitive planning can encourage structures which assist communities in adapting to new life-styles and favour innovative forms of employment creation.

Poor housing conditions and high unemployment co-exist in disadvantaged areas. The structural problem is presently heightened by the negative effects of global economic restructuring and recession. In turn, these factors are compounded by the lack of educational and vocational attributes of inhabitants, a lack of local jobs and limited connections to the wider labour market. Such areas become stigmatised in the perceptions of employers and a poverty culture can emerge.

The connection between housing and employment opportunities, in the community or the wider regional economy, begins with education which is the first step out of disadvantage. Those that are illiterate or innumerate have the greatest difficulties to overcome in the labour market. Immigrants often face considerable job search difficulties because they are not fluent in the local language. Children from poverty backgrounds have several barriers to negotiate. In run-down areas, local schooling resources and educational quality are often inadequate and not well adapted to the very specific needs of residents. The intrinsic value of education for the poor is often a luxury. The instrumental value of education, therefore, has to be stressed and its direct benefits made more clear, and thus the long term value of education and job training has to be made evident in programmes. It is essential that educational quality is improved in disadvantaged neighbourhoods with particular attention paid to attacking illiteracy and innumeracy.

Unemployment is also greatly affected by the interaction of female participation in the labour market. Urban planning has encouraged suburban single family housing designed for nuclear families and large peripheral housing estates. Single women and one parent families are often consequently disadvantaged in the labour market by poor public transport, lack of access to cars and child care facilities. A related problem in many countries is that social security systems were designed at a time when the labour market mainly dealt with questions of full-time (predominantly male) employment and unemployment. With the increasing proportions of part-time, temporary and other forms of insecure employment, particularly prevalent in the United States, Canada and the United Kingdom, there is a wedge being driven between the labour market and the social security safety net.

The challenge for national and local economies is both to weather the process of economic restructuring and to adapt to conditions of increased competitiveness on world markets, while, at the same time, developing local policies that tackle employment-related problems, often through the creation of innovative forms of occupations and services. The prevention of persistent unemployment is crucial. This requires building pathways or ladders of assistance, beginning with improved basic education, relevant training opportunities and skill-learning to facilitate entry into the labour market (see Inset 1).

It takes a long time for areas and local populations to become disadvantaged when multiple and complex causal forces are at play. In the same way, it will take time, resources and a multi-sectoral approach to bring about reintegration. Policies aimed at such a process of change therefore need to prioritise the balance of effort between different sectoral responses and must consider the phasing or timing of each response. Thus, labour market policies have to consider the balance and timing of measures to support education and other pre-entry labour market instruments, as against vocational training and enterprise development. At another level, policy has to weigh up the development of general and transferable labour market skills and the development of employer-specific skills that target specific sectors of the local labour market. A similar type of question considers whether new employment opportunities should be created within the disadvantaged area or whether there should be more connections with existing employment within and beyond the neighbourhood. In many cases the intended beneficiaries may be local residents; but, as their circumstances improve, they simply move to better areas to be replaced by equally disadvantaged households. The dynamics of the process are critical.

Policy strategies and instruments

The options open to governments if they are to redress the local unemployment problems in disadvantaged neighbourhoods include: creating local employment opportunities (see Inset 2); using the physical regeneration of an area to create employment; the creation of housing agencies and local employment and training opportunities; and, alternatively, fostering links with the wider labour market.

Inset 2. Creating Local Employment Opportunities

There is a tendency to attribute the origins of an area's unemployment problems to the loss of local employment opportunities at some time in the past; and so effort goes into trying to replace these lost jobs. There are many difficulties with such an approach. Exclusion from the labour market is not a symmetrical process. The barriers experienced by residents in the low income neighbourhood are not necessarily the ones faced by the unemployed elsewhere. For every 100 jobs created in a low income neighbourhood, fewer than 50 will go to local residents. Unfortunately, each generation of economic development organisations needs to re-learn this lesson.

Unconventional forms of enterprise such as community businesses can be successful in targeting jobs to local residents. However, they create relatively few jobs at a high cost in public funds; and very few have proven to be sustainable businesses.

In an economic recession, it is difficult to attract conventional businesses to disadvantaged neighbourhoods which tend to be in poor locations. These areas are often not good environments to start up small businesses, reflecting the lack of local purchasing power, limited business skills and lack of access to credit.

On the other hand local jobs have wider benefits:

- by providing training and other support services to local people it should be possible to raise the share of local jobs going to local people;
- local residents themselves want to see this happening as it is evidence of external support for, and belief, in the area which can mutually reinforce confidence about the area's future;
- diversification of land and property use in predominantly residential areas does more than break down economic exclusion: the growth of local employment breaks down the perception and reality of that exclusion.

The physical regeneration of areas through investment in the housing stock, environmental improvements and the development of non-residential land uses can lead to substantial injections of resources into relatively small areas. This may be the only major investment in the area over a period of decades and is a highly visible process, something which local residents tend to feel very strongly about and over which they would seek some degree of user control. In Southern Kirchdorf (Germany), in the south of Hamburg, for example, low quality housing blocks are being renovated through the use of employment subsidy programmes to create jobs for the unemployed. The evidence about the effects of such programmes is, however, mixed. It can make small but significant contributions to local employment, but to work it needs to be locally-based and requires to champion local residents in the fight to secure work from relevant builders. Not surprisingly, those areas where there is a pre-existing network of small businesses, tend to retain more benefit within the community. Finally, such physical regeneration can inspire confidence and act as a springboard for a range of other activities (see Inset 3).

Inset 3. **Training for Small Enterprise**

The British Enterprise Allowance Scheme and the Australian Enterprise Incentive Scheme are two examples of programmes which aim to encourage unemployed people to become self-employed by offering business training for a year. Trainees receive social security during this time so that loss of unemployment benefit is not a disincentive and so that they are not obliged to divert time or money away from their businesses to pay for living expenses. Evaluations have shown that those who were long-term unemployed were as likely to do well as others in these programmes. In Australia the scheme is federally funded but operates in concert with State-level aid for small business. The two levels of government jointly set eligibility criteria for trainees.

Special measures can be introduced to increase the internalisation of these benefits from housing-led initiatives: for example:

- training programmes set up in advance of the regeneration process can provide skilled labour; this would include finding training opportunities for school leavers with some of the larger companies winning contracts;

- support for community enterprises, co-operatives or other business developments to provide the economic infrastructure to sell security, environmental and other services to the big developers and builders on site;

- encouragement for community-based and other local housing bodies to set up their own "stand alone" companies to do some of the building and environmental works, directly employing local people;

- creating manufacturing and training opportunities in the same way and providing the same service for other disadvantaged areas.

Another housing-led option involves special capital programmes to renovate the housing stock. These can be very substantial programmes over short periods of time but there are, nonetheless, problems in extracting benefits from such programmes. A large proportion of such expenditures are non-labour items (material and capital equipment). Of the direct labour input, a large proportion tends to be siphoned off by the professions: only where trainees from local areas can be employed in such architectural practices, etc., will there be much scope for local employment gains. Larger builders, moreover, tend to have their own work-forces which are moved from other sites to do the work. Finally, in many OECD countries, there are legal constraints on the process of tendering which limit the possibility of extracting specifically local employment benefits.

Inset 4. **Promoting Education in Social Housing, Omaha, United States**

The Omaha Housing Authority, in the United States, stresses the education of children living in their public housing. Children are encouraged to build perfect attendance in primary and secondary school. Every child that has a perfect attendance record during the academic year is presented with $100 savings bond, rewarding the child and encouraging saving. Funding for this project comes from the Omaha Housing Authority Foundation Inc., supported through private donations. Each summer, the foundation awards at least one scholarship to a public housing high school graduate who has achieved academic excellence. Agreements have also been reached with three universities in Omaha to offer additional scholarships.

Study centres have been established in each family housing project. These centres are equipped by the school system and staffed by community volunteers. They provide individual tutoring for young scholars, many of whom have performed better scholastically and have improved their classroom behaviour since the programme was instituted.

Because the private sector ethos is not always supportive to disadvantaged local economies, agencies set up to tackle recurrent problems, such as regular repair and maintenance contracts, may be a better, if less dramatic, approach. There is a steady demand for work of this type, which has a higher labour content than large capital programmes. In San Francisco, under a public works project, local workers carry out repairs for the elderly and disabled.

An alternative, yet complementary approach is to develop links between those in the excluded neighbourhood and the wider labour market (see Insets 4 and 5). However, early attempts in the 1980s to target skill-training in occupations that are in strong demand were not always successful for a number of reasons, including: high percentages failing to complete courses; very low percentages actually finding work at the end of the training; some trainees only remaining in work temporarily; low pay making the work option unattractive; some trainees finding the hidden costs of working too high -- for instance, child care, transport and related costs.

Inset 5. The Tosach Training and Development Scheme in Dublin, Ireland

Tosach Training and Development is located in inner city Dublin and offers training, counselling, social support and work experience. It is aimed at young, long term unemployed persons, mostly women, who are unable to reach the standard required by the formal education system. Training is offered in light engineering, hairdressing and office work. There is also a sewing co-operative. A part-time literacy teacher helps participants. Funding is channelled from several government departments.

Out of this experience, a multiplicity of new programmes have emerged, which, in broad terms, involve widening and deepening the commitment of both the residents of excluded neighbourhoods and their potential employers. These include:

- Education-Business Partnerships;
- Home-School Support Schemes;
- Raising the Quality of Vocational Guidance to School Leavers;
- Counselling the Long-term Unemployed;
- Personal Development Programmes;
- Vocational Training Programmes;
- Directly Accessing Jobs;
- After-Care Schemes.

From schooling to the after-care activities, reintegration is a process or a pathway to work: the investment in an individual has to be nurtured and then reinforced and safeguarded. There are now well-established techniques for re-establishing these pathways. These include several essential components: a strong element of local control involving local organisations for training and employment; making the most of all local expenditure possibilities; recognising that success with a small number of individuals may be more important than a larger but badly-resourced programme; recognising also that working in schools, and with the short-term unemployed, and getting at the problem before it becomes long-term may be the most effective approach in the long run; safeguarding advances already made; and ensuring that housing and labour market improvements go together. A multi-sectoral approach is in fact critical to the success of these programmes (see Insets 6 and 7).

Inset 6. The Learning Shop in Dundee, Scotland

In Dundee, education is a key component of the area-based renewal activities. "The Learning Shop" developed an educational curriculum for use within the community, based on listening and talking. The main emphasis is the delivery of basic education for adults. Courses on return to study help adults who have spent time away from education to return to it. Remedial courses in spelling and arithmetic are also available. Tutors work with individual clients on self study programmes.

Pre- and after school education is available for children up to the age of eleven, whose parents are taking up work or training. The enriched programme enhances the growth and development of children and regular meetings are held with parents. Parents are also counselled on how to work with their children and to help them with their school work. This has the additional advantage of stimulating parents to continue their education.

The Dundee Compact is a partnership between employers, schools, young people and parents. At selected high schools, young people agree to work to agreed goals, which include academic achievement, punctuality, attendance and motivation. In return, employers guarantee jobs with training and training leads to jobs. A range of activities to prepare young people for the world of work, such as work experience, practice interviews and site visits, is included. Employers work with high schools to develop the programmes and staff some of them.

Policy analysis and guidelines

There remains a lack of conceptual understanding about the process of neighbourhood change and the most appropriate phasing of different types of programmes. Programmes of reintegration usually follow the order: *i)* physical regeneration; *ii)* training programmes; *iii)* education policy. Yet this is often the reverse of the necessary order of priority in terms of timing. Analysis of these processes and their interrelationships suggests, with the benefit of hindsight at least, that the appropriate scale for intervention is much smaller than would have been thought in the past. The evidence is beginning to grow that highly localised populations of 1 000-2 000 may be the most effective grouping for the delivery of the required labour market and training packages.

77

The re-establishment of pathways between excluded neighbourhoods and the wider urban economy requires well-known strategies, based on local control and organisations working for the area within the area.   These should focus expenditure on long-term benefits: hence the importance of basic education, training and vocational-skills building, as well as labour market counselling. Education is the first step to economic independence, and opportunities, especially for adults, must be made available in areas of disadvantage. Partnerships between employers and schools will encourage the development of a more appropriate work force for the region.   For those who cannot function within the formal education system, specific skills training and on-the-job training should be designed.

It is highly unlikely that the resources required for these policies will be available from traditional public sector sources in the 1990s. As a result, it is critically important to bring a range of governmental agencies into play to tackle specific areas' problems, and to engage the private sector as a co-investor in the regeneration of economically and socially excluded areas. This is the biggest challenge in resourcing reintegration in the years to come. The resourcing issue is one of the main reasons for supporting the partnership approach.

The limitations placed on government budgets suggest that public sector employment will at best stagnate in the years to come. This places the onus squarely on the private sector as the source of employment opportunities for the residents of disadvantaged neighbourhoods. Unfortunately, to date, there is little evidence that it is willing or able to take on this role. A key question for the future, therefore, is how the private sector can be brought more effectively into multi-sectoral partnerships.

Multi-lateral action to make changes come about is also essential. Economic policy is steered by national governments. Labour policy tends also to be national in scope. Urban regeneration, however, requires collaboration with local or regional governments, and with private sector employers, to facilitate micro-policies framed in the partnership model which has been determined to be appropriate to neighbourhood reintegration. It is only through this "local sensitivity" that job training policies, linked to the community and to housing, can accommodate the special needs of specific groups in terms of job placement such as: women with children, ethnic minorities, the young and the disabled.

A further dilemma for these area-based policies is that they have both competitive and spill-over effects to the detriment of the rest of the urban area. Where national or regional unemployment is rising, it is difficult to see how this can be avoided. The challenge for policy makers is to manage this inevitable process fairly and effectively.

Innovative approaches to employment creation need to be developed, based on new concepts of employment which replace the traditional jobs lost in industry. Such occupations, activities or services should be developed to make cities more livable places from a social and environmental perspective. Innumerable tasks which improve the quality of life in cities can be powerful tools in reintegrating those who no longer have access to a labour market which corresponds to their level of skills.

There are three specific national-level policy areas that need to be addressed (among others). First, the increasing reliance on the market for transport services

79

severely disadvantages communities with low car ownership figures or who have become spatially excluded (as with many peripheral estates). Second, there is the issue of child care facilities, a major barrier to labour market reintegration. Government-funded support for nursery provision varies widely across the OECD. Finally, many benefit, welfare and income support systems are a major barrier to full participation in the labour market because of very high marginal tax rates. In socially and economically disadvantaged neighbourhoods, it is not uncommon to find that the majority of households are dependent on state income. But many measures designed to circumvent the poverty trap tend in turn either to be Draconian (for example, variations on the principle of work-fare) or too expensive (for example, basic income support or negative income tax schemes). A bolder approach would involve taking a number of run-down neighbourhoods and trying to use some of the welfare benefits in a series of more constructive schemes, such as financing work which otherwise would not take place but is socially worthwhile. This could then be monitored for effectiveness, the basic objective being to change welfare benefits from a trap into an opportunity.

The following guidelines for policy are therefore suggested by the conclusions of the project:

- **The aim of programmes for social renewal and integration should be to re-establish the pathways between excluded neighbourhoods and the wider urban economy.**

- **Education and training should be an integral part of any programme designed to re-integrate disadvantaged areas or groups into the urban mainstream.**

- **Employment-oriented programmes for social renewal should usually be directed to highly localised areas of no more than 1 000-2 000 persons.**

- **Job-training policies, linked to community action and housing renewal, need to display "local sensitivity" to accommodate the special needs of specific groups: such as women with children, ethnic minorities, the young and the disabled.**

- **Multi-lateral action through local partnerships is essential to make the required changes come about.**

- **The methods by which resources for increasing employment are organised, accessed and evaluated are as important as the funds allocated.**

Recommended approaches include:

i) the promotion of a "lean" organisation;

ii) the reliance on neighbourhood-based facilitators within a co-ordinated city-wide programme;

iii) the recognition of multiple ways in which private sector companies might relate to a social need in a city;

iv) the recognition of the different needs of different city neighbourhoods;

v) the concept of a one-stop shop where a needy individual can have his or her problems assessed in one location;

vi) the follow-through of cases over a certain period;

vii) the search for linkages and sub-programmes which will open blockages in the path of reaching objectives.

- Innovative approaches to employment creation need to be developed, based on new concepts of employment which replace the traditional jobs lost in industry.

- Specific measures need to be introduced:

i) to ensure adequate public transportation for disadvantaged groups and areas to encourage labour market participation and widen the range of opportunity;

ii) to provide adequate child-care; and

iii) to eliminate high marginal tax rates within the social security system which might act as a disincentive to labour market participation.

Housing the homeless: towards social and economic integration

Main issues

The most extreme manifestation of marginality and social exclusion in the midst of affluence and economic growth is the phenomenon of homelessness which is found to exist to differing degrees in all developed countries and is growing at worrying rates; for example, more than one per cent of households are homeless by national definitions in Germany, the United Kingdom and France. The problem was underscored in 1987 when the United Nations declared that year to be the International Year of the Homeless. According to FEANTSA (the European Federation of National Organisations Working with the Homeless), there are at least 2.5 million homeless people in the European Union (7.5 persons per 1 000), defined as without shelter or in receipt of public or voluntary/social accommodation services in 1991 or 1992. They point out that such estimates do not include those unknown to be homeless, those who have received alternative and /or informal assistance and the many households across Europe who are potentially homeless because of insecure forms of accommodation. Importantly, the evidence suggests that homelessness as a social and economic problem is getting worse.   With the turbulence of large scale immigration returning to western Europe, plus the economic recession and global restructuring, FEANTSA believes that the true level of homelessness in Europe may be 5 million.

The emergence of homelessness as a major problem throughout the major cities of the United States in the course of the 1980s has also been well documented (*Cf.* Loveland, 1988; Caton, 1990).

Table 4.2 indicates that in the European Union there are three levels of homelessness.   Britain, France and Germany have the highest known homelessness levels; Belgium, Italy, Luxembourg, the Netherlands and Ireland have moderate levels of recorded homelessness; and Denmark, Portugal and Spain have the quantitatively lowest levels.

A particularly important problem concerns youth homelessness.   It is estimated that as much as 70 per cent of the European homeless are aged below 20. A similar pattern is found in the United States. For the young, a key constraint is the vicious cycle of problems created by the "no-home, no-job" syndrome which effectively prevents vulnerable young men and women from fully participating in work and life in the community. Access to social security may also be restricted without an address. It is also difficult to store belongings, keep clean and to launder clothes, all factors that make getting a job all the more difficult.

Table 4.2 **Estimated homelessness in the European Union, 1991-92**

Country	Total population	No. of homeless	Homeless per 1 000
Belgium	9 987 000	26 000	2.6
Denmark[1]	5 135 000	2 800	0.5
France	56 614 000	627 000	11.1
Germany	80 440 000	1 030 000	12.8
Greece	10 269 000	N.A.	N.A.
Ireland	3 536 000	5 000	1.4
Italy	57 739 000	90 000	1.6
Luxembourg	378 000	500	1.3
Netherlands	14 891 000	30 000	2.0
Portugal	10 497 000	2 500	0.2
Spain	39 322 000	30 000	0.8
United Kingdom	56 490 000	688 000	12.2
Total (excluding Greece)	**335 029 000**	**2 531 000**	**7.5**

1.   Danish data from 1989 from a one day census.

Source: Daly M. (1993), *Abandoned: Profile of Europe's Homeless People.* FEANTSA.

Homelessness is closely associated with insufficient quantities of affordable, rental housing, particularly hostel accommodation for single people who lack "home-making" skills or inclination. This is a problem which has been intensified by processes of gentrification and policies of substandard housing clearance which have subsequently not been replaced by new provision of affordable social housing. As a consequence, there is increased pressure on the existing stock of social and affordable rented housing. (This is discussed further in Chapter 5: Housing Affordability). (See inset 8).

How do people become homeless? Generally speaking, one can imagine a slow decline ending in the sudden crisis of homelessness (broadly defined as a lack of secure, permanent accommodation). There are indications that this eventual plunge into homelessness arises from the confluence of a range of economic, social, political and physical factors. One or more of these factors may trigger the actual descent into homelessness. Four key factors have been identified by FEANTSA in their cross-Europe study. They are, in order of importance:

--   **material** factors, such as loss of housing or financial problems;

--   **relationship** factors, such as family difficulties, violence in the home or isolation;

--   **personal** factors, relating to physical or mental health;

--   **institutional** factors, such as detention in prisons, refugees and so on.

If these factors are then reinforced by problems in the support system, for instance, the specifics of adequate affordable housing, inadequate social security support, lack of effective community care facilities or the more general problems created by unemployment and local economic decline, then family-scale crises can no longer be contained and homelessness can emerge. Marginalised groups in cities risk being homeless, if social security provisions do not protect them. But it is important to realise that the problem is multi-faceted and that, as a result, there will be no simple solution. Providing more affordable housing, without tackling the domestic or the employment roots of the difficulties that led to homelessness may simply defer recurring problems. Policy and programme strategies must therefore consider a number of issues and different agencies must work horizontally to tackle homelessness, which is a paradigm of the partnership and multi-sectoral approach to urban problems.

Misperceptions regarding the condition of homelessness is a major obstacle. In the past, there was a pool of itinerant cheap labour that were variously called hoboes, drifters or vagrants. Public policy was not directed to this group since it was perceived to "remain homeless by choice". The current homeless population, which does not fit this stereotype, is heterogeneous, consisting of a number of groups who, unable to operate at the margins of the economic, social and residential life of the city, become victims of "the new poverty".

Housing policies can exacerbate the problem of homelessness. Many cities have rigorously eliminated sub-standard housing, single room occupancy lodgings and cheap hotels. This process, augmented by the gentrification and filtering up of inner area neighbourhoods, has drastically reduced the available urban low income low cost dwelling stock. This process is, in many places, further intensified by the land use planning and zoning systems that operate in many OECD cities. In the public or social housing sector, waiting lists are often long and move very slowly. Mortgage defaulters rarely receive the support that lenders receive from mortgage insurance.

In many countries the policy towards homelessness used to rely on outdated vagrancy laws. It soon became clear that criminalising homelessness was not the solution. Voluntary organisations were the first to take purposeful action, organising emergency shelter and food. Whereas many of the homeless themselves had no political constituency, as soon as householders became worried for their safety, property and the security of their children, national governments began to pass legislation. For example, in the United States, the Comprehensive Homeless Assistance Act offers federal grants to state and local governments with matching funds on programmes for shelter rehabilitation, emergency food, medical provision and job training.

Inset 9. The Foyer System in the United Kingdom and France

Foyers are hostels aimed at young people aged between 16 and 25 years old, with an integrated approach to their training, employment and accommodation needs. Foyers have been operating in France for more than 60 years, with a national network of 450 schemes providing bed spaces for 50 000 young people at any one time, and services provided over the year for 100 000 young people.

Foyers have a number of specific aspects. They get away from the bad image associated with hostels, and do this by providing high standard accommodation and treat young people as responsible adults and not as problem cases. In return they expect young people to be committed to work or training. Another important aspect of the Foyer system is that it is based on affordable rents, even though they are located in the larger cities where accommodation is more expensive. Although Foyers are not aimed at young people with special needs, at any one time 20-25 per cent may have special needs. Foyers are a national network; so they provide young people with scope to move around.

The Foyer system in the United Kingdom is needed because of very high youth unemployment rates which co-exist with the worst youth homelessness problem in western Europe. The foyer is a pivotal way to break out of the "no-job, no-home" vicious cycle. Foyers are seen as one of the possible solutions because of the distinctive relationship with the private sector who are both keen to do something about youth homelessness and increase the level of training skills.

Presently, there are nine schemes in operation in the United Kingdom; but by the end of 1994 another 12 new build schemes will open and by the end of 1995 another 10 will open; (the YMCA and YWCA are also expected to join the network). There is now a European network of foyers (OEIL) which is not simply an Anglo-French venture but also involves Ireland, Denmark, Germany, Portugal and the Netherlands.

The foyer experience has demonstrated that such a network can grow very quickly because of the strength of the voluntary organisations that underpin it. The transnational approach has also been very stimulating for all concerned and can only be of benefit in terms of services to young people.

Early policies fell into three types: the provision of emergency shelters, the provision of temporary shelters and longer term solutions. Emergency shelters were usually the most basic dormitory type accommodation. Temporary shelters were typically of two types: either housing vouchers were provided for a few months or families were lodged in bed and breakfast accommodation intended for short periods of time. Some services such as detoxification, counselling and health care were available along with facilities such as a laundry or kitchen. Longer term solutions involved the building of affordable housing. In the best cases, housing at subsidised rates was made available from which the person would move only when rehabilitated. Services that facilitated integration to society such as child care, literacy or job training and job placement were part of the package in these programmes. Housing-led policies co-ordinated with health and social policies seem to have been the most effective (see Inset 9).

Public policy often distinguished between those in need of shelter, assisting the "deserving" while screening out the "undeserving". In some cases, priority was given to those who exercised some personal responsibility or showed some initiative in solving their homelessness. In the United Kingdom, some local authorities, identified the "intentionally homeless" as those who had moved seeking employment or those not pursuing their right to the marital home. In most countries families are given priority treatment. Many voluntary organisations working with the homeless are not eligible for public funds because they are not formally organised or incorporated. Partnerships are only possible when organisations are recognised and in touch with the public organisations responsible for housing, health and social services.

Policy strategies and instruments

Homelessness appears to be a largely urban problem and municipalities are trying a wide range of approaches that combine multi-sectoral and multi-lateral approaches (see Insets 10 to 14). In many countries, partnerships have been formed with the voluntary sector that have been actively working to help the homeless without public support. Policies to address homelessness tend to have one or more of three objectives:

-- to prevent homelessness;

-- to reduce the incidence of homelessness in the future;

-- where possible, to rehabilitate the homeless.

These objectives are achieved by policies to prevent homelessness, to provide emergency shelter or to increase low cost housing stock, by policies that combine social and housing assistance and by policies that aid re-integration into society by combining housing and work opportunities.

Policies to prevent homelessness

Tenant protection measures are important in this regard. Regulations for the security of tenure have been strengthened and relocation assistance made available to vulnerable groups. In other cases, procedures have been instituted to move homeless households quickly into vacant publicly managed stock. In countries like Sweden, rental management programmes prevail: a central registry allocates vacant rental units to households seeking housing.

Inset 10. Good Practice in Homelessness Policies in the European Union

The first Report of the European Observatory on Homelessness (FEANTSA, 1992) identified several positive (and diverse) elements in homelessness policies when it surveyed national policies:

- the early warning mechanisms operating in certain cases in Denmark, for instance, whereby the social services must be notified in advance about the likely eviction of a family with children;
- the partnerships that are built into French policy between national and local authorities, the statutory and voluntary sectors and between landlords and tenants;
- the power of the municipal authorities to take over every fourth apartment that becomes vacant in Denmark thereby ensuring an adequate supply of housing so as to fulfil statutory obligations towards homeless people;
- the codification of the rights of people to housing and to a guaranteed minimum income as in France;
- the integrated nature of the French national response which attempts not only to meet the housing needs of homeless people but also prioritises their long term reintegration into employment.

Source: Daly, M. (1992), *European Homelessness: The Rising Tide.* FEANTSA.

Policies for emergency shelters or low cost rental housing

When it becomes apparent that emergency shelters are short term solutions and insufficient, such policies can be combined with policies to increase the supply of low cost housing. Some policies are as simple as calling a moratorium on demolition or conversion of single room occupancy dwellings or the renovation of cheap hotels and boarding houses. Others require that older low cost rental stock should only be lost when newer stock is available. Steps can be taken by cities to protect the low cost rental stock by maintaining an inventory of such housing and monitoring losses. Some cities include preferential property tax treatment for residential hotels. Other policies, however, are more complex. They run the gamut from establishing a system to directly fund permanent housing for homeless families to investing in the development of new stock in partnership with organisations that help the homeless (see Inset 13).

Inset 13. **Facilities for the Homeless in Rotterdam, Netherlands**

Both the national and local level of government finance the cost of beds in shelters for the homeless. However, the shelters are inadequate to meet the demand. In addition, some groups such as drug addicts and psychiatric patients are not well served by these shelters. To be more effective, a client registration system has been set up. The Havenzicht Night Lodging was established with a "low threshold" policy to house homeless drug addicts and psychiatric patients for an unlimited number of stays. In addition, Van Speyk Day Centre has an open entrance and exit policy, attracting a number of drug users, psychiatric patients and immigrant homeless persons for an average of six hours. The Housing-Working-Living Centre offers opportunities for homeless people to become fully self-sufficient. Collaboration with health and social service departments ensures that necessary supports are provided for the residents. Fourteen out of 35 clients were successful in entering the mainstream a year after they were rehabilitated.

Policies that combine housing and social policies

Homelessness is a housing problem with distinct social dimensions. Co-ordination between health, housing and social services is essential. Because of the heterogeneity of homeless groups, each group may have special problems. Single women are reluctant to enter mixed sex shelters. Psychiatric patients with disruptive behaviour are frequently not admitted into shelters. Such groups may therefore require specialist shelters and support, specifically designed to meet their needs. Policies that offer "shelter plus care" are essential to reverse the downward spiral.

In some cities, a spectrum of solutions is available to give help to homeless persons when they are ready and willing to re-enter the mainstream. Progressively, the instinct for survival is harnessed for self-help. Residents may begin by taking some responsibility within the project and slowly move to greater responsibilities outside the residence.

Inset 14. Job Placement and Employment Training Programme, Australia

In response to the established strong association between homelessness and unemployment, the Australian government established the JPET programme to fund a series of pilot projects over two years to provide employment and training assistance specifically designed to increase the opportunities, skills and independence of homeless young people.

JPET links with existing health, social security, supported accommodation, training and employment programmes for young people. The objectives of JPET are to achieve full open market employment for young homeless aged between 15 and 19; and to establish working strategies for appropriate employment and training programmes with voluntary and government agencies, consistent with existing programmes of assistance.

Priority areas for assistance were assessed on the basis of high rates of youth unemployment and homelessness; the job opportunities in the region's labour market; and the amount of supported accommodation and related services that existed in each region. JPET projects are managed on a decentralised basis and the services it provides ensure that the young person is accessing appropriate housing, income, health and counselling services. The major role of the JPET worker is to help each young person develop a personal plan which involves options for training and employment opportunities. Each project has undertaken to find local employment and is working closely with small businesses, major companies operating in the area and with employer groups.

The main objective for the pilot is employment for up to 1 000 young homeless people. As JPET is a pilot programme it will also be able to test and evaluate different models for providing support and special assistance which homeless people need when seeking entry to the labour market. A comprehensive evaluation strategy is underway to assess the success of JPET.

Policy analysis and guidelines

There is a need for an internationally defined and agreed measurable concept of homelessness. To facilitate better understanding, homelessness counts should become a mandatory part of population-information gathering exercises.

The legal rights of the homeless also need to be fully considered. For instance, the right to accommodation contained in the United Kingdom's homelessness legislation has had a major quantitative impact on the problem by making local government responsible for housing homeless people.

It is also necessary to acknowledge the complex causes of homelessness. A well co-ordinated strategy involving housing, health, employment, training and social services is essential in the design of programmes to recognise the interrelated problems of homelessness. Co-operation and co-ordination between service providers is also essential if the problems of homelessness are to be dealt with. The issue of the cause and effect of homelessness varies on an individual basis and therefore innovative and flexible arrangements are necessary. Equally, it must be recognised that shelter is a necessary, short run solution to a longer term problem of social exclusion, and if measures are confined to bed-space or crisis solutions, the longer term problem will remain. Some countries have been successful in making these linkages.

Community support is an essential ingredient: criminalisation and medicalisation, on the other hand, tend to be unproductive strategies. Socially isolated facilities are not successful either. Homeless people must find constructive models of social and community responsibility before they make the transition into the mainstream of society.

Opportunities for progressive rehabilitation are of the utmost importance, since homelessness is a traumatic experience. Successful policies offer opportunities gradually to enter or re-enter the labour and housing markets. Assistance may be required to find and keep gainful employment and housing. Personalised support and guidance are required on this road to self-sufficiency.

Housing-led policies to address the problem of homelessness are essential: the primary, immediate need is sufficient housing. But in the longer term assistance needs to be multi-sectoral. Steps must be taken to ensure that an inventory of low cost housing is available. If not, such stock must be developed.

Partnerships and joint ventures with the voluntary and non-profit sectors show promise and should be encouraged, including the use of innovative administrative arrangements. The public sector may make capital investments but benefits from the administrative expertise and work experience of the voluntary sector that can be charged with operating facilities and running programmes. Voluntary organisations are more successful than large public organisations in gaining the confidence of homeless people.

The following guidelines for policy are therefore suggested by the conclusions of the project:

- **Governments should establish a clear definition of homelessness which is easy to apply and to use as a basis for measuring the extent of the need for shelter.**

- **The legal rights of the homeless should be clearly codified and applied on a uniform national basis.**

- **A variety of programmes should be developed to take account of the wide range of circumstances that can result in homelessness.**

- **Similarly a variety of types of shelter, ranging from crisis accommodation to long term affordable housing, should be made available to meet housing needs.**

- **Homelessness programmes should be integrated with other initiatives, such as employment and training programmes, to encourage the progressive rehabilitation of the homeless and their re-integration into the mainstream.**

- **Voluntary organisations should be encouraged to play a central role in the process in partnership with local and national governmental agencies.**

The residential environment: ensuring a positive focus for health, prosperity and quality of life

Main issues

The residential environment acts both as a setting for and as an important influence on the health, prosperity and quality of life of residents. A good environment is one that facilitates all desirable human activity and promotes well being. Environments that cause stress to urban residents or that hinder economic or social activity during the life course are unsatisfactory. Stressful elements can be present in the overall environment of the city or in the micro-environment of the home. They may be physical, social or economic. Physical sources of stress include poor housing, noise, unsanitary facilities, lack of sunlight and distance from nature. Social sources of stress include lack of social networks, crime and lack of safety or security. Economic sources of stress can include the high cost of housing compared to income and unaffordable costs for heating fuel and high costs of commuting.

The most visible aspect of a blighted neighbourhood is the preponderance of substandard housing in disrepair. However, this is usually just a symptom of more complex disorders. The scale and speed of the degeneration brought about by the recent economic recession have had a serious impact on the residents of many low-income neighbourhoods. There is evidence to show that the larger the concentration of disadvantaged people or households, the less their chances are of breaking out of the poverty trap. The trap is particularly pernicious because of the inter-generational effects of unemployment and disadvantage.

Unfortunately, there are constraints on collective action by the residents of declining neighbourhoods. They are often unable to improve their neighbourhood by their own efforts; nor are they able to exert sufficient power to demand their rightful share of public expenditure within the city to raise the standard of the residential environment. In the competition for scarce resources, they are powerless because of their lack of economic resources, allies or political influence. However, the existence of insalubrious neighbourhoods affects not only the residents but the larger city as well. Some of the impacts are reduced city revenue, threats to public health, potential fire hazards, reduced safety and social tensions.

In the past public policy responses have often not been based on a good understanding of the forces of disintegration and re-integration. Indeed, some of the forces of change leading to renewal or decline have been directly due to the actions of public, private and non-profit agencies. Large peripheral projects built rapidly in the decades of housing shortage, for example, have become arenas of disintegration despite good intentions. This problem is now generally recognised in a variety of Member countries, including Sweden, France and Germany. The choice and design of urban amenities may also favour one type of benefit to the detriment of another type of benefit. In the process of trade-off, social and environmental benefits may be subordinate to economic benefits. For example, a lack of good public transportation may result in the development of a vast network of highways that divide neighbourhoods and in the process destroy social networks and consume large tracts of central city land. These highways increase the volume and speed of the traffic moving people to and within the city, resulting in increased pollution and noxious emissions. Economic benefits for a few are bought at the cost of widespread disruption of neighbourhoods and environmental degradation.

Re-integration, based primarily on housing and neighbourhood renovation, has proved to be insufficient unless cities incorporate welfare and job creation programmes with them. However, inadequate policy results have also shown that re-integration requires more than basic education, skill training or income support when low skill manufacturing jobs are disappearing and the basic requirements for earning an income are rising. Solutions should therefore focus on addressing not only the immediate problems but also the longer-term impacts of large-scale socio-economic exclusion in residential communities. This requires investment in human capital, as well as in the housing stock and urban infrastructure, with a focus on the future rather than the past.

Policy strategies and instruments

Neighbourhood rehabilitation

As a first step to rehabilitation, cities should take action to improve the physical appearance of residential neighbourhoods. There are many examples of successful housing renovation initiatives in Member countries (see Inset 15 for an example from the United States). Another interesting programme is the "main street programme" in Canada where grants are made available to municipalities to improve the central core while renovating city landmarks and heritage buildings. France has major central government assistance for the improvement of HLM (social housing) properties and rental properties in cities (programmes called ANAH and PAULOS).

But traditional approaches based on providing assistance to individual home owners may not work in severely disadvantaged neighbourhoods. Most residents are tenants and slum landlords are not anxious to renovate buildings which will raise rents to unaffordable limits for their clientele. Low-income owners may not wish to accept further economic burdens to improve their home. In the longer run the only means of improving the environment is to improve integration of these neighbourhoods into the economic life of the city through employment and retail opportunities.

Environmental controls

Environmental controls can contribute significantly to improving the quality of life for urban residents, even at a time when de-regulation is current. These environmental regulations may be justifiable on grounds of public benefit. Most Member countries now recognise as a new dimension to public policy the notion of stewardship of the environment for the purposes of inter-generational equity. The range of possible measures is very large; it goes beyond the scope of this report, many being highly specialised. Some examples are summarised in Inset 16.

Environmental policy can, however, also be proactive, for example in Norway the central government has engaged five cities to participate in a project to develop environmental cities. The project will focus on the important links between the physical environment (housing, infrastructure, historical and heritage sites, etc.) and the livability and integration of cities.

Allocating access to urban services

Improving access to urban services and amenities is an important adjunct to improving employment and economic opportunities in neighbourhoods. Retail, service and small industries require adequate access to public goods and services. Spatial disparities and imbalances may require corrective action. For example, more resources may be needed in some areas to provide a given standard of service or to achieve social objectives, because of the nature of the population, the physical characteristics of the area and the local price of resources.

This type of micro-scale action can be achieved through the decentralisation of services to sub-municipal units, which understand the needs of local residents and the locality. However, the central allocation of budgets will still be critical in determining to what extent differences in local needs and resources can be, or should be, equalised (see Inset 17).

97

Cross sectoral activities

Joint activity by government departments engaged in policies that impact on the environment enables better decision making based on outcomes in economic, social and environmental terms. At the same time the reasons for public action must be carefully explained to the public so that there is general support and widespread benefit (see Inset 18).

Integrating energy conservation goals in community design

Though there is considerable scope in Member countries to incorporate energy conservation and other ecologically sound practices into the design of new housing, it is not common yet to incorporate such measures into subsidised housing. Low-income households, and government ministries that provide income support, would save resources if such measures were undertaken, (although in some cases initial costs may be higher). Partnerships are critical for the successful implementation of ecologically sound and energy saving community design (see Inset 19).

Inset 19. Solar Village in Greece

In Lykovryssi, a suburb of Athens, a small community was built around a main square. The community has a small shopping centre, a cafeteria, an information centre, a multipurpose hall, a library and an energy centre. The village houses 534 families eligible for subsidised housing from the Workers' Housing Association. A major goal of the settlement was to make intensive use of active and passive solar and other advanced energy systems in the design of the housing. Measures were taken to ensure quality of life as well as acceptance and utilisation of the energy saving systems by the residents. Since the project was an experiment, a variety of heating systems serve the homes and these are due to be evaluated to determine the most appropriate and cost effective solution.

Policy analysis and guidelines

Housing is a vital part of the city environment but its value depends on its integration with the environment as a whole. The quality of the urban environment depends to a large degree on the manner in which the individual experiences both the natural and the man-made environment. The impacts of the factors responsible for economic, social and environmental stress must be considered in public policy.

Long term and short term urban impacts on city living should be considered. The impacts of dysfunction are experienced in the short term by the residents of blighted neighbourhoods but also by the city as a whole. There are grave long term consequences as well, due to the inter-generational aspects of poverty, unemployment and disadvantage resulting in a growing segment of the city population who have never experienced prosperity or who can ever act on hope. Such intractable poverty and exclusion is a drag on economic functionality and city competitiveness.

More social and policy research on the factors of disintegration and re-integration is required. The complex inter-relationships between the economic, social and environmental factors under the present conditions of rapid change are imperfectly understood. Some of the impacts on human health and the environment may be long term or even irreversible.

The costs to the urban environment must be better assessed when trade-offs are made. The intended and unintended consequences of actions by public, private and non-profit agencies within the urban setting for the achievement of economic and social goals must be evaluated.

Cross sectoral planning is essential. Actions by all urban actors must be aligned through a shared vision of the city. Organised implementation and cost effective use of resources is possible only through cross sectoral planning resulting in multi-sectoral policies.

The following guidelines for policy are therefore suggested by the conclusions of the project:

- **The links between the economic, social and environmental dimensions of living in disadvantaged neighbourhoods need to be recognised: the need for employment, income security and improvements to community facilities goes hand in hand with the need for improvements to the physical quality of the local environment.**

- **The short-term and long-term costs of deteriorated residential environments in terms of health, social dysfunction and criminality and environmental degradation need to be assessed and made clear to the wider community.**

- **The potential consequences of actions taken elsewhere in the urban context -- for example, in relation to highway construction or industrial restructuring -- for the quality of the environment and the health of residents in disadvantaged neighbourhoods need to be kept under continuous review.**

- Multi-sectoral partnerships between agencies and organisations, such as area health authorities, private sector employers and community groups, need to be established to devise co-ordinated measures to improve the quality of local residential environments and local public health.

Involving and empowering residents

Main issues

The "two-tier" society describes the division between the citizens comprising the mainstream, who contribute to and benefit from economic, social and environmental urban activities, and the citizens who are excluded. Those in the second tier are often marginalised by external economic, social and environmental conditions that cannot easily be overcome by individual action. Deprived of access to wealth, status and power, individuals languish under conditions of poverty, alienation and powerlessness which prevent them from relying on personal initiative. With no prospects and incapacitated by the hopelessness of personal effort, these people have little self-esteem, real choice of options or opportunities to be independent. Unable to compete, they may become concentrated in cheap housing in declining neighbourhoods or in social housing estates. Entrenched among certain groups or urban neighbourhoods, this situation encourages a culture of poverty and a dependency on public or charitable programmes.

Early ideas tended to blame those excluded from societies by describing them as lacking the work ethic or the ambition to better themselves to ascend the "ladder of citizenship". Indeed, the "undeserving" were penalised by spatial exclusion which isolated them from the developing areas of the city. When policies were first developed, they were directed to the most visible symptom of decline, the housing, rather than the spiralling inter-related problems that led them to declining neighbourhoods. Greater understanding of the complex mechanisms of socio-economic deprivation has led to increasing support "rescue" programmes or policies to reverse the process of decline. Well-intentioned as these programmes were, they have had mixed results because they have not dealt with the underlying condition of powerlessness. Deprived neighbourhoods and their residents are more dependent than ever on mainstream structures, services and cash which continue to confirm their lack of power.

Powerlessness arises from three major types of obstacles: first, externally imposed factors such as economic restructuring, unequal political representation,

101

ghetto creating policies and competition for scarce public and private funds; and second, internal characteristics of people and place. Factors associated with people describe the lack of personal resources due to poverty, lack of skills or education, disabilities and poor social or family support. Factors associated with place include, poor reputation or stigma, isolation, lack of transport, amenities and shopping and poor conditions. In addition, the sense of powerlessness can be reinforced by disabling support, such as low standard or inappropriate services, short term or erratic interventions and few preventive programmes but heavy social service or police action. For example, the impact of the lack of telephone service has been especially identified as a barrier in the study undertaken by the European Foundation for the Improvement of Living and Working Conditions (*Out of the Shadows*, 1992).

Empowering residents implies a positive attempt to equalise conditions by removing these three types of obstacles to allow them to participate as equals in economic, social and political activities. In public policy terms, empowerment can be defined as enabling low-income households, living in marginal areas to affect conditions, influence decisions and play a role in improving the local area. The results of such enablement have been described as the "residents own pathways to success".

There is increasing support for empowerment as a means for integrating disadvantaged groups into social, economic and political life. The economic arguments are to reduce dependence on public programmes, to better use human resources by preventing withdrawal, to avoid the risks of disorder and to reduce the costs of containment. Social benefits include motivating people to influence personally the outcomes of their lives while working collectively to transform their communities. The aim is to ensure that dependence should become interdependence and that withdrawal should be replaced by engagement. Politically, the strategy is attractive. The well-to-do majorities have few incentives to pay for rescue programmes that do not benefit them. However, empowerment implies a reciprocity, because beneficiaries contribute as well as receive, while tax payers pay as well as benefit from spin-off effects. The pay back over time for all these reasons can be considerable.

Three conditions have been identified for success. The first, requires the optimum use of the resources of the neighbourhood and its residents. Local action should be in tune with the needs and resources of the community, requiring a bottom-up approach. The land, buildings and amenities of the neighbourhood should be used efficiently. People should be consulted, enabled through education and facilitated to act for tangible rewards. A simple local administrative structure is preferable, involving partnerships with neighbourhood and government agencies. The second, requires the construction of bridges that link the neighbourhood to the wider urban system. These bridges will facilitate the development of a local base from which residents can tap into opportunities in the larger society. The third requires the effective use of external resources. Earlier financial and programme supports were fragmented, short term and inappropriate. Long term commitment and flexible resources are essential. Outsiders from agencies or government must work to meet local goals and to foster local leadership.

The approaches taken in Member countries have varied depending on the nature and intensity of the problems and the political approach adopted. In some countries, the existing institutional dysfunction suggested a more functional local, consultative approach. This has led to policies which improved the access to opportunities but still relied on personal initiative. In other countries, political disenfranchisement has been judged to be the main problem, resulting in programmes designed to place the tools and resources for neighbourhood regeneration more directly in the hands of the residents.

Opinions regarding the motives for empowerment differ. On the one hand, supporters claim that empowerment is a means to harness efficiently individual and public financial and other resources and to develop the untapped or latent capacities of the disadvantaged so that the nation's productive potential can be utilised. This is the basis for the "active society" principles pushing for full employment and a balance between rights and responsibilities. On the other hand, critics claim that governments are quick to relinquish collective responsibilities and that the initiatives are driven by the need to reduce public expenditures. In the long term, it is alleged that some groups will be overwhelmed by forces beyond their control and be relegated to more persistent poverty and disadvantage. In many Member countries, however, there is a ground swell movement for the adoption of empowerment for its own merits regardless of the interests of the public sector.

Policy strategies and instruments

Empowerment through resident participation, management and control of public/social housing

Though widely adopted in many countries, the principle of empowerment has become a linchpin in the housing policies of the United States and United

Kingdom. Tenants are empowered through a range of devices stretching from involvement in management decisions to outright ownership of the housing project. In the United States and the United Kingdom, a progression of increasing responsibility is envisaged in the design of programme assistance.

Inset 20. The Resident Management Corporations of the United States

The United States Department of Housing and Urban Development Programme for the development of Resident Management Corporations has seven steps. First, the housing project must have a Resident Council backed by a strong resident organisation. Second, the Council with the assistance of a management specialist, undertakes a feasibility study of a resident management system assessing the real interests and abilities of tenants. Third, an education programme is provided to residents through meetings, written materials and face to face contacts. The fourth step is incorporation, where specific contract provisions for resident screening, rent collection, budgetary authority, subsidy allowance, operating reserve investments, maintenance staff, procurement and modernisation are detailed. Corporate functions including the services to be provided such as day care and counselling are noted. The organisation is created with a Board of Directors and Working Committees.

During the fifth step, training and assistance in real estate management is tapped. HUD has initiated a Resident Management Certificate Programme in collaboration with the National Association of Resident Management Corporations. Sixth, a management contract plan and budget are developed for the transferral of authority from the local Public Housing Authority to the Resident Management Council. During the seventh step, the council becomes operational. This carefully designed process allows the grass roots power to mature while providing the required training and support.

Tenant organisations may also run small business with the housing estate as the client, providing maintenance services, repairs and janitorial services. They may also run laundries, corner shops and postal stations which service local residents.

In the United States, empowerment has ben described as the process of energising individuals, either by putting certain kinds of power into their hands which they do not have, or by activating the power which they already have but which for various reasons they refuse to use or are inhibited from using. Empowerment in economic, social and political arenas can be gained through control of one's housing and this is therefore a powerful argument for empowerment to be an overt objective of housing policies.

In the United States, over 100 resident participation programmes are in the process of development and the hope is to increase the number to at least 250. Considerable success is claimed due to substantial improvement in the quality of life of residents, measures in terms of declining crime and violence, rising education and morale (see Inset 20). Similarly, the Priority Estates Project (PEP) in the United Kingdom relies on a non-profit organisation to assist tenant councils to assume various degrees of control over their housing estates. The tenants may form a management co-operative or estate management board. They may also negotiate to have ownership transferred to another landlord or assume ownership as a tenant ownership co-operative. In both cases, grants are available from the central government and costs may be shared with local agencies. The tenants do not incur additional expenditures.

Empowerment through multi-sectoral community action

An example from Spain illustrates the scope for a multi-sectoral approach to the empowerment of disadvantaged communities. The city of Huelva has on its outskirts a squatter community called Marismas del Odiel, located on unserviced swampy land. In-migration has increased the population to over 1 000 families. The community is characterised by illiteracy, illegal status of individuals, unemployment, lack of amenities such as schools and health facilities and a hidden economy. The community was marginalised and isolated. The city launched a phased programme to combat socio-economic exclusion of the residents. This programme gives legitimacy to the people and the neighbourhood after years of neglect while empowering them to improve their own lot (see Inset 21).

Inset 21. **Empowering the Disadvantaged in Huelva, Spain, through Global and Multi-sectoral Action**

The programme undertaken in Huelva relies on six principles: Participation of residents, co-ordination of institutional effort, global and multi-sectoral action, integration of the most disadvantaged, visible and transferable strategies and evaluation of results. The implementation of the programme was phased. During the first phase, the organisational structure with all the key actors was put in place and the needs of the residents were studied. During the second phase, actions were taken to improve the residential environment, jobs, health, social services, education and cultural activities. During the third phase, the activities focused around the improvement of housing and local development. As the project has evolved, the residents have been empowered to take action themselves in partnerships with other agencies. For example, groups of youth, long term unemployed and women have set up task forces to deal with employment issues important to them.

An alternative approach to empowerment is through resident-defined programmes of social renewal. A good example of this approach comes from the Netherlands. The stated objective for social renewal is "to improve the position of people who are socially disadvantaged or who are in danger of becoming so". Social renewal has been pioneered by the city of Rotterdam as a means to link economic recovery with the resolution of social problems. The process now begins with the setting of concrete targets and the delineation of multi-sectoral municipal policy. These policies are carried out by different levels of government, non-government bodies and by trade and industry. The process is considered as important as the results. Social renewal has now been adopted by the national government as well as by a majority of Dutch municipalities.

Inset 22. **Social Renewal in Rotterdam, Netherlands**

The local government served as the activator but is no longer in sole charge of social renewal. The process is shaped from above, below and from the side. A Social Renewal Project Office was established for communication, programming, political support, co-ordination between components and monitoring results. Five areas were of special concern to the residents: integration of minorities, education, work, dirt and lack of safety in residential areas and greater coherence in care services. Objectives and targets were set up. Illiteracy was identified as a major problem for integration, education and work. The Foundation for Basic Adult Education will carry out literacy training with funding from the district councils. To meet the twin objectives of creating jobs for the long term unemployed and accomplishing socially useful tasks, a job pool was set up by the New Jobs, Rotterdam Works Foundation.

Persons who have been unemployed for over three years are eligible for the jobs which pay a minimum wage (slightly higher than welfare benefit). For example, the Slinge metro station was dirty and unsafe. Now, 30 people from the job pool work there as car park attendants. The area is safe and is rarely vandalised. Garage services are provided while the car is parked. These jobs can serve as stepping stones to others in the job market. Residents themselves took matters into their own hands to improve their neighbourhood. In the Nieuwe Westen area, residents provided their houses with outdoor *"Opzoomer"* lighting to make the streets safe. They installed flower tubs and each Thursday evening all the residents swept the street. The success of this resident initiative led to the verb *"opzoomeren"* entering the Dutch vocabulary and the municipality established the *"opzoomer* prize".

Three guidelines were specified. The first was concerned with reassessing policies to combat social disadvantage. The objectives are: to utilise latent potential of people; to concentrate on the right to meaningful work rather than benefits; to reformulate rights and responsibilities of individuals; to deviate from general policies to specific policies only when necessary. The second is intended to encourage the re-evaluation of services in order to reduce dependence and social divisions. Four criteria are applied covering activation, client orientation, prevention and co-operation. The third guideline involves a re-ordering of responsibilities. This is designed to achieve decentralisation from central organisations to municipalities, working through district councils, consultations with residents, partnerships with private and non-profit organisations and openness to initiatives from the public (see Inset 22).

Policy analysis and guidelines

In many countries strategies for empowerment are relatively recent and comprehensive evaluations are not widely available. However, initial programme evaluations have been successful despite some problems. For example, involving residents that are alienated is not easy. The reality must be recognised that there will always be a residual group that does not have the ability to become self sufficient due to negative pressures, such as discrimination, which are beyond their control.

A study has been conducted by the European Foundation for the Improvement of Living and Working Conditions to examine how disadvantaged people coped with economic and social change in seven countries. Among the recommendations that arose from that work are: local action is an indispensable strategy for social cohesion; non-controlling, arm's-length arrangements provide flexibility and room for independent action; the economic value of unpaid work should be recognised; key partners, such as national voluntary organisations and local groups, should be encouraged to play appropriate roles. Residents rely greatly on family networks and are most satisfied with such actions (*Out of the Shadows*, 1992).

Recent European experience has led some commentators to the following conclusions:

--   It has not been proven that bottom-up processes are cheaper. They are, however, more likely to result in customised relevant solutions. A combination of the "bottom-up" and "top-down" approaches is likely to be most successful.

--   Most strategies are too complex, bureaucratic and administratively heavy to be successful. Systems should be simple and legible for use by disadvantaged people.

--   To be successful, the programme should be based on a long term perspective and commitment. The programme should be well resourced, with a training component for staff as well as groups.

--   Private financing is subject to market forces, therefore it may be time limited. Though some social investments are possible, they are still business rather than altruistic decisions.

--   A balance must be struck between representative democracy and local action. Local action should take place within a strategic view of the broad urban context.

The following guidelines for policy are therefore suggested by the conclusions of the project:

•   **A local focus should be established for dealing with problems to draw on local knowledge and to establish better co-ordination of services, direct communication and consultation with residents and a focal point for generating solutions.**

•   **Multi-sectoral action, concentrated locally, is essential but the aim should also be to influence the wider community. Failure to approach problems as multi-faceted and to build bridges to wider community needs and perspectives may generate despair and a greater sense of alienation and powerlessness.**

•   **Resources should be allocated directly to local programmes and initiatives. To redirect wasted resources and maximise local impacts, this may be assisted by localising both decision-making and service delivery.**

•   **The latent potential of residents and local resources of the neighbourhood should be harnessed, based on the involvement of** neighbourhood agencies and spontaneous networks and partnerships between public, private and non-profit agencies in the neighbourhood.

- Links to the mainstream community should be fostered. Concentrated neighbourhoods of disempowered persons should not be permitted to become isolated or stigmatised through outside pressures.

- The responsible authorities should enter into long term policy commitments and be patient about resource investments. Fragmented policy approaches, under-resourcing and *ad hoc* funding have been major problems in developing empowered neighbourhoods and residents.

Improving social cohesion in neighbourhoods

Main issues

As the population of Member countries has become more diverse mainly through immigration flows, a debate on the merits of concentration as opposed to dispersal has emerged. While this was regarded as an important issue in the United States in the 1960s, the same questions are being asked again in many European countries.

The diverse populations of modern cities can be a positive or negative force. Dynamic ethnic communities may be characterised by social cohesion and community spirit while other neighbourhoods may be riven by parochial ethnic interests or may concentrate minorities in ghettos due to discrimination, poverty or race. Policies of dispersal which were ostensibly to achieve real or notional assimilation or acculturation were sometimes implemented at the expense of social support and ethnic identity. In consequence -- to take one recent example -- the Netherlands has directives that do not favour either concentration or dispersal of minorities; rather these directives promote equal treatment between groups of diverse origins, allowing them the greatest possible choice with respect to location.

The degree of locational choice appears to influence the outcome for residents. When inner cities exhibit urban problems, middle class households and businesses tend to leave declining inner city neighbourhoods and move to the suburbs. Public policy has facilitated this process since in many countries residents were able to escape high local taxes and the costs of servicing the low-income residents of cities. As a result these suburbs often became economically and racially segregated. The low-income households, on the other hand, had limited choice with respect to location, social mix or ethnic diversity. While this pattern of polarisation is especially evident in the United States, it has recently become manifest also in a number of European countries.

Social cohesion can be a positive force where neighbourhood residents share a sense of community, exchange informal social support, provide organised community services (*e.g.* Neighbourhood Watch) and collectively act to protect and improve their community. It is reflected in a spirit of empowerment and a community's confidence to act on its own behalf. Latent talents and hidden skills are used for the benefit of the contributing individual and the sharing community. Socially cohesive neighbourhoods can be "caring communities" adding value through activities that are outside the normal activities of production.

But in practice social cohesion is noted often by its absence. Two such negative conditions are the lack of integration and social exclusion and they can be separately examined.

First, integration of different socio-economic segments, ethnic groups or racial populations into the urban mainstream has many positive benefits. Therefore, a social neighbourhood mix has been seen as a positive goal for public policy. However, it is not clear that congregation of similar individuals or households in a homogeneous neighbourhood is necessarily deleterious, particularly if it is voluntarily chosen. There are examples of culturally rich ethnic communities, vibrant racial neighbourhoods and residential areas housing one discernible class with a strong identity. Furthermore, some imposed social mixing through misguided policies of social engineering have resulted in highlighting the differences in class and race and creating neighbourhood tensions. However, it is abundantly clear that, when economically disadvantaged households are trapped in declining neighbourhoods, powerless to improve their lot and lacking economic, social and residential mobility, social cohesion is not evident. In fact, such communities may be relatively mixed, containing a variety of demographic groups such as the young, the old and immigrants from various countries but all sharing the condition of poverty.

Secondly, social exclusion expresses the nature of the relationship between the economically disadvantaged areas and other parts of the city. The flow of goods, services, capital and people in and out of such areas is limited, increasing

110

economic and social deprivation. Under such conditions of alienation and deprivation, social cohesion does not develop naturally. Nor is it easy to promote through external interventions unless the root causes of the problems of disadvantage are addressed.

Social cohesion can be assisted by building on the existing strengths of the residents and community, relying on existing social networks and promoting co-operation and community development. The appropriate policy responses to achieve such aims would be to empower and to improve opportunities through community building initiatives. Steps should be taken for "capacity building" and increasing community confidence to act in their own interest, selecting alternatives that meet their needs. Community development can be aided by access to expertise, having experts of various professions "on tap rather than on top". Community education includes a process of developing critical awareness of issues and developing residents' abilities to undertake demanding responsibilities. These responsibilities may range from community lobbying to tenant management. Grass roots efforts can capture community energy and build economic and social momentum, which are indicative of social cohesion.

Policy strategies and instruments

Bottom-up approach to community development

Community planning and capacity building can make effective use of local resident participation, tapping resources and expertise from various sources as they become necessary. Working together, the community can determine their own priorities for action, for resource expenditures and for the allocation of benefits.

Typically, tenants are allocated dwellings in social housing projects. Because of the transient nature of residents and the lack of social or political mechanisms, the natural growth of the community spirit is hindered. Yet, tenants in such communities need the social supports and networks to function in the urban setting. Sensitive pre-planning and programming can overcome these difficulties (see Inset 23).

The support of various levels of government and other appropriate organisations is necessary for the success of community development projects. This was shown in a multi-sectoral programme which was launched by the municipal authorities of the peripheral housing district of Loddefjord/Vadmyra in the city of Bergen, Norway. The three year programme was initiated in 1990 and combined forty objectives for action in the fields of housing, social services, crime and drug prevention and child welfare.

A project group was established to co-ordinate the delivery of services to targeted groups in need and this was overseen by the local authorities. It was established that the project should improve services within the level of resources already applied by municipal authorities in the district. The project received funding from the central government, however, all resources were combined in a deliberate partnership with the voluntary sector to increase efficiency and accountability. The co-operative housing estates also invested in the refurbishment of their estates and commercial and service centres.

Inset 23. **Two Community Projects in Ireland**

The Finglas Enlivenment Project in the Dublin area relied on a community planning approach. The underlying concepts were to enable community participation, by a sensitive use of external resources and experts. Consultation meant listening, networking and creating a wide range of partnerships. The owning role of inhabitants in shaping their environment was stressed. It began by creating awareness of community resources, by selecting positive community elements on which to build and by facilitating a wide range of initiatives for sustainable long-term change in the community. The proactive approach taken encouraged pride in the community, community gain and action on community priorities. Through community and participation actions, shop fronts were refurbished, public spaces were improved with street furniture and public sculptures, historic buildings were restored and community festivals were held. Large future projects such as the creation of a sculpture park continues to mobilise the community.

RESPOND, a voluntary charitable organisation, creates innovative social housing environments for households on the lowest economic rung. But the objective is to not only provide good quality housing but also to foster community development. Each resident is invited to play a full and active part in the creation of "community ownership". This is accomplished by several steps: a training programme for prospective tenants includes sessions on community responsibility; resolution of community conflict; estate management; and tenant control of resources, possibly leading to eventual ownership of the project; establishing links with residents of adjoining public and private housing estates; providing amenity services such as a creche or social services to the full community. Several successful communities have been created.

A thorough evaluation of the project has not yet been undertaken however obvious results such as a reduction in crime rates, increased social stability, strengthening of the identity of the district and pride of the local residents indicates that positive results have been achieved.

Policy analysis and guidelines

Social cohesion is recognised as an important urban goal. Social cohesion contributes to political stability and social collaboration, which in turn create positive conditions for economic investment and urban growth. The success of community relations and social cohesion tends to be measured by community harmony and lack of strife rather than formal indicators. Important legal and policy measures have been taken to promote social cohesion and prevent discrimination.

The following guidelines for policy are therefore suggested by the conclusions of the project:

- **Social cohesion should be built on the existing strengths of the residential community resources. It is important to validate the existing sense of community, however fragile, while reinforcing networks and "capacity building". Such a sense of community takes time to develop. Social cohesion should be nurtured by the residents because they can see its value rather than cohesion being promoted as a necessity for public programmes or funding.**

- **External supports to social cohesion should be sensitive and co-operative rather than directive and prescriptive. Initiatives such as community education, which enables residents to build their community according to their own vision, should be supported.**

- **The root causes of disadvantage should be recognised as impeding social cohesion. Initiatives that promote social cohesion can lead to the solution of other problems through the participation of residents. It is a means to urban regeneration as well as a positive end in itself.**

Integrating the young: the role of social services, cultural and leisure activities and education

Main issues

Children, adolescents and young adults are an essential human resource for the future of societies. Comprehensive urban policies and programmes should of course be concerned with the whole population; but young people who live in metropolitan areas undoubtedly have special needs and problems. Although

113

children have certain legal rights, they are not a political constituency. Consequently, it has been commonplace for urban policy makers to overlook their requirements, or to rank them as a low priority: in fact, land-use planning regulations in some countries still commonly prescribe minimal requirements for car parking in urban neighbourhoods whereas places intended for the cultural and leisure activities of children and youth are not mandatory. Although the status of children and young adults varies between countries, too many young citizens suffer the social consequences of a lack of political will to recognise their problems and their unique place in society. These consequences include the growing incidence of alcohol and drug addiction, delinquency, vagrancy, homelessness and youth unemployment, as well as an increasing number of suicides.

Despite the gravity of these consequences, the legitimacy of young people's requirements and rights to housing, education, vocational training and employment, which characterise the transition from adolescence to adulthood and independent living, are not widely accepted. For example, in many countries young people are still excluded from targeted housing initiatives and income support subsidies. Grants to students for higher education and vocational training have in some cases been transformed into loans (*Cf.* Heddy, J., 1991). In the context of a multi-sectoral approach to urban regeneration, a reorientation of current policy formulation and implementation in relation to the young is required.

An appropriate response to the requirements of children and adolescents should stem from a comprehensive understanding of their lifestyle. Given the different requirements of children between birth and adulthood, it is important to understand their lives as developmental stages including physical growth, educational and emotional development, and social and psychological maturation. The age at which the transition from adolescence to adulthood occurs is determined by many factors, including cultural customs and class traditions, the family and personal biography. Consequently it is important to recognise that young people do not constitute a homogeneous social group. They can be differentiated by their ethnic group, class, education and gender. On the one hand, there are marked differences between the age at which young women and men leave the parental home. Women usually adopt independence earlier than men. On the other hand, in many Member countries of the OECD young people are leaving the parental home later than previous generations, owing to the delayed entry of adolescents and young adults into the labour market. This trend is linked either to those who choose to further their education in order to obtain higher qualifications, or to growing levels of unemployment. Consequently, there is a growing polarisation between one group of well-educated young people and those who leave school at an early age but remain unemployed. Both groups are financially dependent and share a demand for family support, as shown by data that confirm an increase in the age at which young people left home during the 1980s (*Cf.* EFILWC, 1989). Given the diversity of groups among children and young adults in contemporary societies, it is necessary to develop and monitor a socio-demographic profile of young people living in urban neighbourhoods.

It is also important at the outset to recognise the social context of the lifestyle and the requirements of children and youth. Negative societal trends in many western countries include the steady disintegration of extended and nuclear families; increases in domestic violence; the growth of crime, delinquency and vandalism in residential neighbourhoods; an increase in illiteracy and innumeracy coupled with a growing number of early school leavers and higher youth unemployment; and an increasing number of children and adolescents who are temporarily homeless. In 1986, the rate of unemployed young persons between 15 and 24 years of age, as a proportion of all unemployed persons, was 44.4 per cent in Spain, 33.4 per cent in Italy and 25.6 per cent in France. In 1990, the 15-24 years age group accounted for more than a third of all unemployed people in the Member states of the European Community (*Cf.* ECDGEMP, 1990).

In the United States, data for young males aged from 14 to 21 years in the 200 largest urban areas show that, while the overall percentage unemployed was about 25-33 per cent higher than the average for males of all ages, the percentage rate for young black males twice as high (*Cf.* Jencks and Peterson, 1991). Moreover, data show that homelessness disproportionately affects adolescents, single people, lone-parents and women with children. In recent years young people in particular have been increasingly affected, so that in some European countries the number of homeless people under the age of 30 has doubled (*Cf.* Daly, FEANTSA, 1993).

During the current period of multiple social and economic changes, the family has remained a key institution for the majority of children and young adults. Indeed, the political climate in many Member countries of the OECD has accentuated the role of the family and diminished the role of public services in providing support for those in poor or vulnerable social and economic circumstances. In this respect, fiscal austerity measures, plus the reorientation of government expenditure, have shifted tasks of caring for dependent young adults and the elderly onto the family. Despite this reorientation of policy, the meaning of the traditional family has been challenged by rapid changes in lifestyles, especially with respect to marriage, divorce, parenthood, family size, child-rearing, and the role of women in the paid-labour force. Consequently, an increasing number of children have a step-parent or step-siblings or are experiencing foster care and welfare services. Data show that these changes are not restricted to underprivileged groups; they concern the population as a whole.

Owing to these socio-demographic trends, the commonly shared rights and obligations of parents, and the expectations and rights of children have been challenged. Traditional role models and customs (such as the head-of-household being a secure bread winner for families) are no longer deemed to be relevant by many adolescents whose parents have been divorced, or unemployed for long periods. Hence, new positive models need to be presented to them. Furthermore, their participation in cultural and recreational activities need to be encouraged to help them overcome the negative images of alcohol and drug addiction, violence and random sexual behaviour transmitted by the mass media, and valued through peer group pressure. In contrast, children, adolescents and young adults should be encouraged to meet the challenge of their future social and professional livelihood. In searching for ways of enabling adolescents and young adults to achieve this objective, young people and policy makers need to debate questions, such as:

-- What policies and trends in the housing and labour markets disadvantage young people, such as sustaining dependence?

-- What policies and initiatives can best combat the dependency, disadvantage and marginalisation of young people?

-- What measures can enable groups of young people to develop innovative projects which correspond to their aspirations and life-style?

-- How can the direct involvement of young people in civic and political institutions be encouraged to ensure the representation of their interests?

There is a growing body of evidence about the nature of the interrelated problems which disadvantaged children, adolescents and young adults experience in cities. This evidence shows that during recent decades increasing numbers of young people have been excluded from the mainstream of society for a range of reasons, including the socio-demographic trends discussed above, educational disabilities, a lack of vocational training opportunities and inadequate access to cultural, health and leisure activities. It has also become clear that there are far-reaching social, economic and environmental consequences arising from the increasing numbers of disadvantaged children, adolescents and young adults. For example, in the Netherlands a government study estimated that up to 10 500 independent housing units, plus 13 000 supervised units are required to meet the needs of young people who currently can only rely on the welfare of hostels.

Moreover, in France, about 100 000 young people between 16 and 25 years of age have sought hostel accommodation each year during the last decade (*Cf.* EFILWC, *op. cit.*, 1989). In view of these circumstances specific policies for housing young people are necessary. Beyond traditional policies and programmes related to child health, education and vocational training, there is also an urgent need for personalised welfare which encourages children, adolescents and young adults to adopt a positive, structured view of their role in the community and a constructive image of themselves. The stake is important as it concerns the future of society as a whole.

Following the implementation and evaluation of innovative programmes and projects especially aimed at assisting those young persons in difficulty or at high risk, there is a growing recognition of the interdependence between positive investments in children, adolescents and young adults, and investments in other social and environmental programmes, especially remedial education and vocational training, health and counselling services, and cultural and recreational facilities for all age groups. Feedback from these new programmes and projects are serving as catalysts for the formulation and the implementation of integrative strategies aimed at creating opportunities for both personal and community development. These strategies are meant to reintegrate children, adolescents and young adults back into the mainstream of urban society by enabling these young people to play an active role. Successful projects in some countries recognise the diversity of requirements and problems and, therefore, seek multiple goals and outcomes.

Policy strategies and instruments

In Italy, the City of Turin launched an experimental Youth Project in 1977 following the request of various educational institutions, clubs and pressure groups. Between 1977 and 1980, a Youth Services Commission identified the aspirations and needs of youth and young adults in Turin. Then the Youth Project was revised, reformulated and enriched. In 1981, a programme for adolescents experiencing difficulty in adapting to society was launched. In 1983, a project for the prevention of drug dependency was instigated.

Between 1985 and 1990, the Youth Project addressed the general needs and problems of children, adolescents and young adults according to a classification by age. Three groups were defined by age: between 11 and 14; 15 and 18; and 19 and 29 years of age. During this period, the project was reinforced by the appointment of a Chief Officer for Youth. This position is considered to be interdepartmental. It is meant to serve as a co-ordinator for the local authority Departments of Cultural Services, Education, Employment, Social Services, Sports, Leisure and Tourism, as well as the local ward Centres in the city.

The Youth Project has implemented preventive measures to tackle delinquency, alcohol and drug dependency, and mental disorders since 1985. This approach is also being applied in the ongoing project for the period between 1990 and 1995. Furthermore, particular attention has been given to the current aspirations and needs of young people for new artistic and cultural services, information centres and leisure facilities.

The City of Turin's Youth Services Commission has been publicised and promoted by a series of scientific and public meetings, international exchanges and publications, including informative documentation addressed to young people living in the city. An Observatory on Youth was founded in 1987. Its objectives are to co-ordinate data and information for decision making about young people at both central and local levels; to serve as an informative reference point for all those in both the public and private sectors who work regularly with young people; and to enrich the experience of those who research and provide urban services to focus on young people (see Inset 24 for experience in Barcelona, Spain).

In Ireland, almost half the population is less than 25 years of age and more than 30 per cent of all young people live in Dublin. In 1988, the national rate of unemployment was 17.6 per cent, whereas youth unemployment was 24.1 per cent. Consequently, reforms of traditional educational and vocational training programmes have been implemented by the Irish Government according to goals stated in the Memorandum of the public vocational training authorities, plus a White Paper on Manpower Policy (1986) and the Programme for National Recovery (1987). Ongoing reforms have been implemented gradually: vocational training opportunities and combined training and employment programmes for unemployed young people and for long-term unemployed persons have been expanded. In 1987, the main authorities concerned with implementing vocational training programmes were amalgamated to form the National Employment Agency, which considers unemployment jointly in terms of job placement and career counselling; vocational preparation and training of young unemployed people between 15 and 25 years of age; supervision of apprenticeships and realisation of short- and long-term training measures in 18 Industrial Training Centres; and the further vocational training of employed persons. In 1987, about 65 000 young people participated in projects concerned with training and employment. For example, the Community Youth Training Programme (CYTP) offers unemployed young persons (less than 25 years old) basic vocational training and work experience within the framework of community projects that contribute to the improvement of living conditions by the preservation of historical buildings or the expansion of community organisations. During 1987, 120 projects of this kind were completed and 110 new projects were begun. The Limerick Youth Services, founded as a voluntary organisation, adopted this training programme with a notable innovation: between 25 and 35 per cent of all places are reserved for, and occupied by teenagers who have been accorded special probation rather than serving a prison sentence (*Cf.* ECDGEMP, 1990).

The Dublin Corporation has responded to the housing needs of disadvantaged young people by enabling them to reside in "difficult to let" properties that have remained vacant over long periods. In 1984, Focus Point, a new agency, was created to campaign in favour of homeless young people in Dublin, particularly young women. Apart from conducting and publicising studies on homelessness, Focus Point has also created a meeting place, an information centre, social welfare advice, an outreach team and facilities for creative leisure activities, all in one locality in Dublin, which is open 24 hours daily. It can also provide short-term emergency housing accommodation and child care services.

In Australia, a report titled "Our Homeless Children", published in 1989 by the Human Rights and Equal Opportunities Commission, estimated that 20 000 young persons between 12 and 14 years of age were homeless. Of these homeless, 16 000 young persons had temporary accommodation without security of tenure, whereas 4 000 had no shelter at all. The report noted that these circumstances were attributed to personal, medical, family or economic crises that were often associated with abuse or violence. The report also concluded that homelessness and unemployment are closely linked. In view of these circumstances the Australian Government established the Job Placement and Employment Training (JPET) Programme in 1992. This pilot initiative is intended to meet the needs of temporarily or long-term unemployed adolescents between 15 and 19 years of age.

The JPET Programme is based on a personalised case-work approach for the provision of vocational training and job placement which are linked to, and enhanced by low-cost accommodation and related services. This pilot programme is meant to establish newly tested and successful strategies for appropriate employment and training programmes, which existing government agencies and community organisations can integrate into their existing care and support services for disadvantaged young people.

Priority areas for implementing the JPET Programme were identified by the incidence of high rates of youth unemployment and homelessness, coupled with some employment opportunities in the local labour market, plus some extant supported accommodation and other services specifically for young people. Once these localities have been identified, the JPET projects in those areas are advised and managed by local councils, registered vocational training companies, general youth services and other community organisations, such as health clinics and local employment services.

The main outcome of the JPET Programme is employment for about 1 000 young homeless people. A comprehensive evaluation is being conducted to identify the achievements of different models and measures for providing support and special assistance which young homeless people need when entering the labour market (see also Inset 14). In addition, the Australian Government is formulating a Youth Housing Strategy which will identify ways of improving housing options and of reducing housing distress experienced by young people on low incomes.

In France, the Union Nationale des Foyers et Services pour Jeunes Travailleurs (UFJT) is a long-established group of 500 local associations which offers assistance for temporary housing accommodation, vocational training and job placement for young workers, trainees and unemployed adolescents and young adults. These associations comprise 40 training centres, 30 enterprise creation centres and temporary housing accommodation for 50 000 persons. The concept of a Foyer was formalised in France during the 1950s when charities and churches sought to meet the most fundamental needs of disadvantaged adolescents and young adults. During the 1960s this initiative was followed by Government Housing Support Programmes which primarily sought to provide hostel accommodation. Today, the main objective of Foyers is to integrate disadvantaged young people back into the mainstream of daily life by jointly providing assistance for housing, vocational training and employment in one locality that is meant to serve as a bridge between dependency and an autonomous livelihood.

In England, the Foyer Federation, was established in 1992 by the Grand Metropolitan Community Services Trust, Shelter and other institutions to serve as an information bank and clearing house for the standards and practice of Foyers. Supported by public and private sector partnerships, including the government, local authorities, housing associations, business and employers, Foyers are the foci of innovative initiatives in England which provide assistance to adolescents and young adults between 16 and 25 years of age, in order to break the link between unemployment and homelessness. Based on Foyers in France, yet different to them, the network of Foyers in England are intended to provide an integrated service of low-cost residential accommodation and vocational training, and for exploring employment opportunities. For example, although the French model is predominantly for short-term housing accommodation, it is anticipated that in the English context the length of residency is likely to average 12 months. Once young people are receiving an income from full-time employment they are expected to move and to establish their own independence. Five schemes have been successfully piloted in the urban neighbourhoods of Norwich, Nottingham, Romford, St. Helen's and Wimbledon. By the end of 1993 a network of 25 Foyers will be operating in Britain (see also Inset 9 and Inset 25 for Northern Ireland experience).

In Portugal, a Secretary of State for Young People was introduced by the national Government and since 1985 there has been a growing number of initiatives related to adolescents and young adults, especially their employment opportunities. For example, since 1986 the Minister of Labour and Social Affairs has introduced a scheme for improving the first-time employment prospects for young people. Consequently, firms which employ first-time entrants to the labour market do not have to pay the full contributions to the national social security and unemployment fund for a period of two years. Furthermore, financial support is accorded to young adults between 18 and 25 years of age who want to start their own business. Recipients must spend at least 36 hours per week working for their enterprise. This scheme is funded by the European Community Social Fund.

In the sphere of education, government initiatives have focused on providing facilities for young people during the long summer vacation. For example, the Open School scheme was developed for foreign adolescents between 14 and 20 years of age with the aim of increasing their knowledge of the Portuguese culture and, hence, improving their opportunities for social integration. Another initiative caters for more than 1 000 young people between 16 and 25 years of age who participate in architectural and environmental conservation projects.

In the United States, the Departments of Housing and Urban Development (HUD) and Health and Human Services (HHS) jointly convened a Youth Initiatives Summit, in February 1992. The purpose of this summit was to discuss measures that can channel the energies of youth living in public and Indian housing into constructive and productive activities and enterprises. The summit focused on six themes: education, health, families, job skills and employment opportunities, security, and youth recreation and sports. Grassroots success stories were discussed along with those initiatives of several Federal agencies addressed to young people (see Inset 26).

The European Organisation for the Integration and Housing of Young People (OEIL) co-ordinates the activities of non-governmental organisations, at both local and national levels, which aim to enable young people to participate actively in their own development. One initiative of this organisation is the PRIME Project which encourages access to housing and employment for young people in need.

One original approach applied in this project is, that disadvantaged young people are assisted in creating their own employment through local business networks that are part of a European network for Local Employment Initiatives (EURORILE).

Inset 26. Two Successful Initiatives for Young People in the United States

One success story is the **Youth Sports Program** sponsored by the Public Housing Youth Sports Program Grants. This programme is based on the principle that organised sports activities are an integral part of the educational and personal development of youth and may help them to stay in school and remain non-addicted to alcohol and drugs. This programme funds athletic, artistic, educational, cultural and leadership activities for high-risk youth living in public and Indian housing.

Another success story is the **Early Childhood Development Grants** that sponsor **Head Start** organisations serving public housing communities. Evaluations of pre-school Head Start projects show the positive impact on the educational development of low-income children between three and five years of age, coupled with reduced rates of delinquency and truancy. Given the success of Head Start, this programme should be extended to include more than a quarter of all pre-school age children who have access to it. Currently grants are provided to enable full-day child development services for young public housing residents whose parents or guardians seek, retain or train for employment or pursue further educational objectives.

The PRIME Project approach applies the concept of personal development, based on the active participation of young people who are considered as the source of innovation and the stimulus for the quality of project implementation. Hence the capacities of disadvantaged young people to take initiatives are valued, whereas traditional welfare approaches have normally considered them as individuals who need assistance to overcome a personal handicap. This reversal in attitude requires a profound change in the professional practice of those who work for the integration of young people in society. In particular, individualised attention and personal support are necessary, whereas an "expert" opinion and fund-raising have been commonplace in the past.

124

In principle, co-operation between national and local governments, as well as non-government associations and community groups, should be encouraged with the aim of formulating and applying co-ordinated policies and programmes for children, adolescents and young adults, especially those living in deprived urban neighbourhoods. Those programmes that go beyond economic and technological solutions to extant problems faced by families on low incomes are essential in meeting the requirements of young people.

A range of remedial and preventive policies can be implemented by utilising the experience gained from innovative approaches that have proven effective, such as those that have reduced illiteracy and innumeracy, improved vocational training, provided for cultural and recreational activities outside formal school hours, supported personal and household coping mechanisms, nurtured interpersonal bonds during adolescence, and provided a counselling service about education, health, legal, nutritional and vocational matters.

Successful programmes recognise the diversity of requirements of children, adolescents and young adults. Consequently, these programmes seek to define multiple goals and outcomes. Nonetheless, innovative projects usually include some kind of tailored approach that responds to the need for personalised attention, as well as a place to go that offers support and guidance for housing, remedial education, vocational training and job placement, counselling and peer group dialogue. A multi-purpose services unit in one location (preferably at the neighbourhood level) can best provide for both traditional sectoral welfare and non-traditional services.

In contrast to implementing predefined solutions by professionals, new programmes can directly involve children, adolescents and young adults in policy formulation and implementation using peer group dialogue, vocational training and job placement. The organisation and co-operation of government programmes, as well as non-government associations at the local community level, require long-term commitment and labour-intensive resources from both the public and private sectors. Investments in programmes for children and youth often need to be complemented by policies for family support and investments in urban infrastructure and housing.

The following guidelines for policy are therefore suggested by the conclusions of the project:

- **Policies should aim to be both remedial and preventive, covering a wide range of activities, including: illiteracy and innumeracy programmes, vocational training, cultural and recreational activities (including sport) and personal counselling.**

- **Young people should be involved directly in the formulation of policies and the design and management of programmes both to draw on their knowledge and experience and to maximise their involvement and commitment.**

- **Multi-purpose centres should be established in deprived neighbourhoods as a focus for a range of services, including: support and guidance in relation to housing problems, job placement and training, health clinics, counselling and after-school care.**

- **Voluntary and community resources should be encouraged to work in partnership with governmental agencies to provide personalised attention and co-ordinated programmes to meet the diverse needs of the young.**

Safer cities: a prerequisite for sustainable urban development

Main issues

Tragic events in numerous cities around the world, including Amsterdam, Bhopal, Chernobyl, Los Angeles, Mexico City and Seveso, illustrate the scope and extent of risks to human safety and well-being in contemporary cities and towns. These risks are related to the increasing complexity of urban and technological developments. Many residents in the above-mentioned cities have been confronted with the toll of well-publicised disasters. Yet, these kinds of events only account for a small portion of the omnipresent risks in everyday urban life. Although the threats of accidents, earthquakes, fire or flood have a long history in urban communities, in addition to these, there is a spectrum of urban pathologies that are related to safety and well-being in cities. These pathologies include diverse types of accidents; molestation, rape and sexual violence; homicides; burglaries, robberies and thefts; vandalism and damage to private property; juvenile delinquency; and social unrest, including group violence and urban riots. The difficulty in understanding the root causes of these urban pathologies has been compounded by the increasing volume and complexity of urban environments, the people accommodated therein and their activities, plus technological developments in communication and traffic circulation. For example, accidents in homes, workplaces and on roads are a leading cause of injury and death, especially to children, youth and the elderly. Indeed today accidents are ranked fifth among the leading causes of death by the World Health Organisation. In the United Kingdom, for example, accidental injuries and poisoning of all kinds are the single largest cause of death among young people aged between four and fourteen years. In England and Wales, 41.7 per cent of all deaths in that age group were attributed to accidental causes including road accidents, fires, falls and drowning (*Cf.* United Kingdom, 1984). Consequently, the economic, social and psychological costs of accidents are so great that policy makers should recognise that they constitute a major public health challenge. Unfortunately, policies intended to reduce or prevent urban pathologies usually follow publicised disasters, whereas they should be based on pre-emptive studies and counter measures. These preventive studies and counter measures can be grounded on comprehensive risk assessment and priority settings. From this perspective, any specific project for urban development can be formulated, not only in terms of return on invested capital, but also according to their social and political acceptability for diverse groups of people in the community.

Urban riots, group violence and social unrest in many Member countries of the OECD (including France, Germany, the United Kingdom and the United States) are the results of interrelated social, economic and environmental factors. Information and data confirm that the incidence of violence and riots has increased during the last three decades in several countries. In addition, offences involving illicit uses of drugs and "white collar" crimes including tax evasion and "the laundering" of money gained from the sale of illegal goods have increased, yet the latter remains a relatively neglected area for criminology despite increasing coverage by the media.

The recorded incidence of delinquency, crimes and vandalism has also increased in all Member countries of the OECD, except Japan, during the last three decades, and particularly in poorer urban areas including deprived housing estates. The results of an international study in 13 countries show that, in 1988, about a third of the population of Australia, Canada and the United States have been victimised at least once by a criminal act. In Canada, more than half of all women and about 60 per cent of the elderly do not feel safe in their own neighbourhoods at night (*Cf.* Van Dijk and Mayhew, 1993). Comparative figures for victimisation rates are shown in Table 4.3.

Table 4.3 Victimisation rate in 1988 in selected countries

Crimes	Eng[1]	Net	W.Ger	Swi	Bel	Fra	Spa	Nor	Fin	USA	Can	Aus	Jap
Car theft	1.8	0.3	0.4	0.0	0.8	2.3	1.3	1.1	0.4	2.1	0.8	2.3	0.2
Car vandalism	6.8	8.2	8.7	4.1	6.6	6.5	6.3	4.6	4.0	8.9	9.8	8.7	2.7
Burglary / entry	2.1	2.4	1.3	1.0	2.3	2.4	1.7	0.8	0.6	3.8	3.0	4.4	0.7
Robbery	0.7	0.9	0.8	0.5	1.0	0.4	2.8	0.5	0.8	1.9	1.1	0.9	0.0
Personal thefts	3.1	4.5	3.9	4.5	4.0	3.6	5.0	3.2	4.3	4.5	5.4	5.0	0.2
Sexual incidents	1.2	2.6	2.8	1.6	1.3	1.2	2.4	2.1	0.6	4.5	4.0	7.3	1.0
Assault / force	0.6	2.0	1.5	0.9	0.7	1.2	1.2	1.4	2.0	2.3	1.5	3.0	0.2
All crimes	19.4	26.8	21.9	15.6	17.7	19.4	24.6	16.5	15.9	28.8	28.1	27.8	9.3

1.   Figures given for England and Wales.

Source: Van Dijk, Mayhew and Killias. Experience of Crime Across the World, Deventer, 1990.

128

Although the growth of crimes and violence is reflected by statistics based on reported cases, these figures commonly underestimate their incidence, because they do not usually account for domestic violence and crimes located within homes. Consequently, sexual abuses against children and women of all ages can be underestimated. Understanding why persons adopt these and other criminal activities is a prerequisite to the formulation and the implementation of preventive and remedial policies.

Many crimes are rapid and surreptitious. The routine activities of victims ensures that, at least in cases of burglary, theft and damage to property, the probability of witnessing an offence is quite low. Nonetheless, there is a paradox about the impact of crime: although the experience of crime as a witness or a victim is relatively rare, studies show that anxiety and insecurity stemming from fear of crime is widespread and persistent, especially among the elderly who are not a high risk group (*Cf.* Maxfield, 1990). This significant socio-psychological problem can be considered in terms of the perception of environmental risks. Consequently, it cannot be assumed that crime has a uniformly negative impact on community and household life in cities. In fact, studies show that public housing estates with similar architectural, demographic and socio-economic characteristics can have very different rates of offence and offenders. Therefore, it cannot be assumed that the design and layout of the built environment is a root cause of crime or delinquency. Rather, it may be a potentially contributing factor in conjunction with many other economic, social, political and individual human factors. The cumulative experience and reaction of individuals to crime and violence, and their perceptions of risk in the neighbourhood, help to explain, at least in part, different rates of crime in residential areas that share many similar characteristics (*Cf.* Hope, 1986).

The Australian National Institute of Criminology has published a comprehensive review of what is known, at an international level, about the causes and incidence of, and remedies for crime and violence. Based on systematic research, those factors associated with the root causes of crime and violence, listed in descending order of their relative importance, include:

--   early childhood experiences in the family, such as erratic, uncaring parenting and violent behaviour;

--   the societal value attributed to cultures that sustain violence including aggressive behaviour of athletes in competitive sports;

--   the relative nature of economic inequalities between groups in societies;

-- cultural disintegration and stigmatisation, coupled with low prospects for social integration;

-- gender inequality;

-- abuse of alcohol, drugs and dangerous consumer products, such as firearms;

-- negative influences of the media;

-- personality and biological factors, coupled with peer group influence and education (*Cf.* Australia, National Committee on Violence, 1990).

Numerous studies have identified a high correlation between the geographical distribution of criminal offences and economic and social indicators of disadvantage. Furthermore, research confirms that there is a relatively small group of persons who are disproportionately involved in delinquency and juvenile crime and that the deviant or violent behaviour of parents is often repeated by their children. In England and Wales, the results of research funded by the Home Office indicate that amongst under 21-year-old male offenders, there is a group of about 17 per cent who are responsible for approximately 35 per cent of all convictions recorded for this age group (*Cf.* United Kingdom, 1989). Nonetheless, only about one third of all juvenile crime is brought to the attention of criminal justice agencies. In principle, criminal behaviour can be interpreted as developmental or sequential behaviour, deriving from personal decisions that may have antecedents stemming back to childhood.

Traditional measures for reducing delinquency, crime and violence have generally not proven effective. In principle, several studies by criminologists have shown that prison sentences have not rehabilitated offenders, nor acted as a dissuasive measure against recurrent illicit behaviour. Nonetheless, in many industrialised countries today, expenditure on prisons accounts for about 25 per cent of the total cost of law-enforcement and criminal justice. In the United States, current annual expenditure on policing, prisons and criminal justice is about US $70 billion, whereas it is Can. $7 billion in Canada and about £7 billion in England and Wales. Yet, the economic costs of delinquency and crime extend beyond these figures to include the repair of damaged property, the price of stolen goods and insurance premiums. In England and Wales, government research recently estimated that residential burglaries and car thefts resulted in at least £1 billion in unrecovered stolen goods (*Cf.* United Kingdom, 1993). Apart from the costs of damage to or loss of property, policing and criminal justice, crimes have many negative impacts on urban communities, including the insecurity of perceived high-risks, victimisation and fear.

Innovative approaches for reducing delinquency, crime and violence stem from an understanding of their root causes and underlying problems associated with illicit behaviour. Both situational crime prevention and problem-oriented policing have proven effective, without displacing deviant behaviour to other localities. Both these approaches accept that offenders have diverse sources and degrees of motivation. Their behaviour is the result of a set of decisions related to the identification of a target or a victim in the urban environment. The locality of a crime includes instrumental environmental cues about opportunities, risks and normative behavioural codes of conduct (*Cf.* Bennett and Wright, 1984).

Situational crime prevention has led to the formulation of a set of principles which include:

-- increasing the effort needed to commit crimes successfully by reducing cues and opportunities for them to occur; or by multiplying constraints on illicit behaviour;

-- increasing the likelihood of being detected or caught while enacting a crime by enhancing surveillance, formal screening and controlled accessibility;

-- reducing the rewards, especially those associated with burglaries and thefts, by removing targets and identifying property.

Policy strategies and instruments

Some inter-governmental institutions, including the United Nations, are formulating strategic policies to reduce urban violence and criminality. These policies derive from a resolution adopted at the 8th United Nations Congress on the Prevention of Crime and the Treatment of Offenders. Formulated in Montreal in 1989, this resolution is based on an Agenda for Safer Cities. The resolution states that preventive strategies should bring together those persons responsible for urban planning and development, family, health, housing, education, vocational training and employment, social services, leisure activities, policing and criminal justice (*Cf.* United Nations, 1990).

In 1991, about 1 600 mayors, city councillors, government representatives, police executives and social workers met in Paris to formulate and decide how to implement the Agenda for Safer Cities (*Cf.* European Forum, 1992). They recommended that those crime prevention strategies which had already proven effective should be implemented extensively, according to the following five principles:

-- governments should invest resources to implement urban policies that address the needs of alienated groups, such as young persons at risk;

-- governments should establish national crime prevention organisations to promote and undertake research and development, recommend preventive policies that have already proven effective and sponsor or implement programmes at the city scale;

-- municipalities should establish crime prevention units to mobilise those local officials responsible for policing in the community (*e.g.* in relation to housing, schools and community services);

-- national, regional and local governments, non-government associations and international agencies can encourage the public to participate in comprehensive crime prevention, and to understand the relationships between improving safety in cities and promoting sustainable urban development;

-- the foundation of an International Centre for Crime Prevention, which could be affiliated with the United Nations, should be supported by countries in order to realise the objective of the United Nations.

The Council of Europe is developing a European Urban Charter that will present the need for co-ordinated crime prevention as an integrated component of sustainable urban development. At a national, regional or state level, crime prevention institutions have been founded in Australia, Canada, England and Wales, France, the Netherlands, New Zealand, Sweden and the United States (see Inset 27). These initiatives have sometimes been coupled with new legislation and administrative support within extant Ministries or by the foundation of new ones.

The National Crime Prevention Council in the United States was founded to encourage citizens to take personal measures for reducing the incidence of crime which escalated during the 1980s. In that decade, although the number of prisoners increased from 325 000 to 650 000 (to reach the highest *per capita* rate of imprisonment in the industrialised world) it is noteworthy that expenditure for criminal justice increased four times as much as expenditure for education, and yet there was a steady increase in criminality each year (*Cf.* National Crime Prevention Council). Therefore, the National Crime Prevention Council has encouraged collaboration between more than 120 national and regional organisations that promote crime prevention. In one project, the City of San Antonio, Texas, founded the first official municipal crime prevention commission. The Texas Community Action Plans for Crime Prevention includes a co-ordinator in each city, who is meant to facilitate a process of assessing problems, examining those activities associated with the causes of and the remedies for crime and violence in order to formulate strategic counter-measures.

Inset 27. **Programme Evaluation in the United States**

In the **United States**, the privately funded **Eisenhower Foundation** was created in 1980 to implement and evaluate programmes, in inner-city areas, that are meant to reduce criminality and violence. During the 1980s the Foundation sponsored pilot programmes in ten communities that had social problems, including a high crime record. Funds were given to community based organisations which involved the residents in defining local problems and in developing counter-strategies. The evaluation of these programmes provided mixed results: positive outcomes were achieved in community involvement and reduced fear of crime, whereas there was no significant reduction in victimisation (Cf. Eisenhower Foundation, 1990). The evaluations of the Eisenhower Foundation have also indicated that pre-school, early intervention programmes like Head Start are one of the most effective long-term measures for preventing crime, drug abuse, truancy and welfare-dependency for high-risk children in deprived neighbourhoods. The Foundation has also identified and evaluated programmes which have successfully applied the same approach as Head Start to young people of junior and senior high school age. One programme is Job Corps, which provides intensive, supportive vocational training for high-risk youth, whereas Job Start is specifically intended for adolescents aged 17 or more, who left school early and lack vocational skills.

The Seattle Community Crime Prevention Council is based on the mobilisation of public interest by "neighbourhood watch" plus several additional management techniques. One innovative characteristic is that the programme in Seattle was initiated by the Mayor, rather than the police.

The Mayor established a special office to implement the programme according to successive steps, including analysis of the problem, priority setting, implementation and evaluation. In those neighbourhoods where this programme was implemented there was a sustained 50 per cent reduction in residential burglaries over a three-year period, whereas traditional neighbourhood watch programmes commonly resulted only in short-term reductions.

In the United Kingdom, a Safer Cities Programme was launched in 1988 (*Cf.* United Kingdom, 1991). This programme is meant to reduce criminality, confront fear of crime, and promote community development in target cities with high levels of crime and socio-economic problems. The project for each city is staffed by a local co-ordinator and collaborators whose salaries are paid by the United Kingdom Home Office.

In 1992, the United Kingdom government appointed a commission to examine what measures could be taken to confront rising levels of crime and violence. The recommendations of the Commission underlined the importance of active crime prevention. The Commission also emphasised that counties and municipalities should assume a more active role in co-ordinating those agencies involved in crime prevention, as well as the short- and long-term strategies that could be implemented. In 1993, the Home Office Minister announced the foundation of a new National Board for Crime Prevention which will bring together representatives from business and voluntary sectors, commerce and industry. The Minister also announced the decision to double the number of target cities in the Safer Cities Programme.

In the United Kingdom also, Crime Concern, a private trust, was founded in 1988 to enhance crime prevention and community safety (*Cf.* Crime Concern, 1992). This trust comprises representatives from the main political parties, the police and probation services, local government and the business and volunteer sectors. The goal of this partnership is to reduce juvenile crime by acting beyond the operation of criminal justice agencies, in order to remove incentives and reduce the disposition of young people to commit offences. Although Crime Concern acknowledges that a significant amount of preventive work has been, and is being done, it is rarely undertaken in a planned, systematic way. Furthermore, current programmes are rarely based on a solid data base, and there is a lack of co-ordination between agencies working at national and local levels. One priority of Crime Concern is to overcome these shortcomings.

In the Netherlands significant innovations in relation to crime prevention have been achieved by applying the principle that 10 per cent of all central government expenditure for preventive strategies will be devoted to the evaluation of programmes. Today, more than one hundred Dutch cities have crime prevention officers. The Netherlands approach differs from the United Kingdom approach in three major respects. The first is that a senior public servant, who is responsible for the prevention directorate, reports directly to the Deputy Minister of Justice, as do the directors of prisons and courts. Consequently, crime prevention policy is on the same influential level as criminal justice. The second difference is related to the Dutch commitment to evaluate preventive policies. The third concerns the greater amount of *per capita* funding for crime prevention in the Netherlands (see Inset 28).

Inset 28. A Municipal Anti-crime Project in the Netherlands

The Delft Anti-Crime Project is one example of an applied crime prevention programme administered by a municipality in the Netherlands. This project was implemented by the City of Delft in a poor residential estate which had a high level of criminality and a poor community image. A comprehensive project involving community development was applied. Plans for improving the estate, including the renovation of buildings, were developed by consultation between residents, estate management and municipal officials. Other measures included the provision of new recreation facilities for children and youths that were supervised by a social worker, the introduction of resident caretakers to improve the maintenance and the management of buildings, and new administrative measures for tenancy rolls to control the number of children residing on the estate. This project has been evaluated positively. The number of offences reported by 100 households declined from 70 to 30 over a period of three years. Following the success of this project, the Netherlands government has decided to contribute to the cost of introducing 150 resident caretakers in housing estates with social problems.

In France, a National Crime Prevention Council was established in 1983. This Council, chaired by the Prime Minister, includes members of parliament, officials of national ministries and local authorities, as well as representatives of local communities. Today there are more than 700 municipal crime prevention councils that work in partnership with national government. These municipal councils include regional directors of education, social services and housing, as well as the police and criminal justice. The French programmes of crime prevention focus on those socio-economic circumstances, such as youth unemployment, stigmatised residential areas and poverty that generate, at least partly, crime and violence in urban neighbourhoods. The City of Lille, for example, identified the links between a relatively high level of criminality and the localisation of youth unemployment, drug addiction and poverty. Consequently, a Mission Locale was established to provide counselling and vocational training for early school leavers. An alcohol-free cafe was opened at the request of representatives of the large African youth population in one deprived neighbourhood. This cafe provides a service for job training, while the schools in Lille have introduced instruction about drug abuse and vocational training.

Since this programme was instigated in Lille the crime rate has declined more significantly than in all the surrounding areas.

A Canadian example illustrates the scope for involving the community in anti-crime measures. It follows a Safe Neighbourhood Initiative which was launched in 1991 (see Inset 29).

Inset 29. A Safe Neighbourhood Initiative in Toronto, Canada

In Canada, the Metropolitan Toronto Housing Authority (MTHA) launched a Safe Neighbourhood Initiative (SNI) in March 1991 (Cf. Canada Mortgage and Housing Corporation, 1993). This initiative has two main goals:

- to evaluate security initiatives in eleven community neighbourhoods within the metropolitan area of Toronto;
- to assess whether the lessons learnt in those communities are relevant elsewhere in Canada, by arranging a series of workshops in St. John (New Brunswick) Halifax (Nova Scotia) Winnipeg (Manitoba) and Edmonton (Alberta).

A Strategic Security Framework (SSF) has been used to plan, develop, manage and evaluate those initiatives which are meant to constitute an on-going process leading to the improvement of safety and security in Toronto. Given that the Safety Neighbourhood Initiative is a community based and resident-centred programme involving a partnership between government and corporate commitment and local community resources, it explicitly builds on those positive initiatives which exist in some communities. Three key principles of the Strategic Security Framework are:

- the concentration on identifying and tackling the nature, impact, perpetrators, victims and timing of specific threats to security;
- the involvement of all sectors and resources of the community;
- the formulation of a set of priorities based on the effectiveness of outcomes in relation to three interrelated approaches, including direct security (*e.g.* policing), design strategies (*e.g.* landscaping and building design features) and community development.

Although there were some common security problems being experienced in the eleven Toronto-communities (particularly related to drug trafficking) there were also problems specific to each community. The strategies adopted to address the problems reflected the priorities and aspirations of the local residents.

The range and type of security initiatives undertaken in each community was determined by regular meetings and discussions between residents, MTHA staff, service providers and the police. The measures used for confronting security problems included:

-- the formation of community-based tenant and staff/tenant organisations to address security concerns, as well as other issues;

-- the hiring of community-development workers;

-- the staging of various social and recreational events;

-- increased security personnel, improved monitoring/surveillance and increased security staff hours; and

-- physical and technical measures to improve visibility and lighting within the community, as well as the appearance of the community.

A number of the measures introduced are on-going in nature, rather than one-time efforts. This is particularly the nature of community development initiatives, which are expected to produce long-term benefits in security as well as in other areas. Indeed, most of the communities in question have been revitalised by fostering community organisation, co-operation and mutual support.

An evaluation of the Safe Neighbourhood Initiative (SNI) has been completed using questionnaire surveys, workshops in the eleven communities involving local MTHA staff and residents, and workshops and interviews with MTHA central office staff. The key findings are:

-- certain SNI communities were experiencing very serious security problems and there have been tangible improvements in security conditions in these communities since SNI has been introduced;

-- some serious security threats persist in certain communities, so SNI measures must be continued and expanded;

-- the success of SNI shows the need to move beyond traditional security strategies to strategies which involve staff and resident resources from within all parts of social housing communities;

-- the SNI experiences confirm the need for a co-ordinated approach to security based on clear direction and commitments, a solid organisation, comprehensive strategies, adequate resources and strong support systems;

-- making communities safer and more secure requires support from all levels within a housing organisation;

-- security teams involving tenants and staff are essential, and local staff and residents should take responsibility for security problems and solutions;

-- security strategies must recognise differences between communities and be based on the security issues unique to a particular community;

-- initiatives should build on existing resource available in the community and be deployed to meet priorities identified in the community; and

-- administrative, technical, communication, financial and human resources management and information systems must play a role in community security.

Plans are now under way to extend the Safe Neighbourhood Initiative to other Metropolitan Toronto Housing Authority communities, as well as to use the model to address safety and security concerns in other public housing communities throughout Canada.

Policy analysis and guidelines

Successful initiatives to improve safety and reduce crime in cities recognise that known and agreed causes can be identified in order to formulate and implement preventive and remedial policies. Given that the causes of crime are multi-dimensional, multiple counter-measures and strategies are required. Alone, building design proposals and technical solutions are ineffective. Initiatives that concern both preventive and remedial measures can be combined and linked to government support and long-term commitment. National and municipal authorities can collaborate with non-government organisations to reallocate funds and invest resources in order to reduce crimes and improve safety in cities. The experience gained from successful pilot studies and on-going programmes can be disseminated within and between countries in a systematic way, and then only reapplied if and where deemed appropriate.

Those initiatives that are community based and involve residents have been effective. Partnerships between national and municipal authorities, the residents, local businesses, police and service agencies result in the most effective programmes. Given the significant psychological, social, economic and environmental consequences of crimes, preventive measures should be used as a means to ensure the long-term future of the community as a whole. Too frequently, however, the emphasis is given to traditional counter-measures (such as policing and law enforcement, or criminal justice leading to prison sentences for offenders) which have proven to be ineffective and costly. In contrast, preventive strategies can be based on comprehensive risk assessment and priority setting.

The following guidelines for policy are therefore suggested by the conclusions of the project:

- **Governments should encourage the establishment of partnerships between community organisations, private business, government agencies and the criminal justice authorities to formulate local strategies for crime prevention and safety.**

- **Measures to increase the safety of all members of the community should be an integral part of all strategies of urban regeneration and social renewal.**

- **Comprehensive risk assessments should be used to target preventive measures and to identify potentially deviant groups or individuals for whom appropriate integrative programmes can be devised.**

- **The environmental characteristics of neighbourhoods and the ways in which they are used, especially by vulnerable groups such as children, the elderly, women and racial minorities, need to be reviewed to identify measures that could reduce the opportunity for criminal action and assault.**

References

Housing, education, training and unemployment in the community

ARMSTRONG, R. (1993), "In Omaha, Nebraska, It's not Business as Usual" *Canadian Housing,* Vol. 9, No. 4, Winter.

BALLS, E. AND GREGG, P. (1993), *Work and Welfare,* The Commission on Social Justice, London.

DELEGATION INTERMINISTERIELLE A LA VILLE. *Accueil et insertion dans la ville par le logement*, Paris.

EUROPEAN FOUNDATION FOR THE IMPROVEMENT OF LIVING AND WORKING CONDITIONS (1989), *Accommodation and Social Cohesion in the Urban Environment -- The Implications for Young People*, Dublin.

EUROPEAN FOUNDATION FOR THE IMPROVEMENT OF LIVING AND WORKING CONDITIONS (1990), *EF News*, "Surviving the City", No. 25, Issue 5, Dublin.

EUROPEAN FOUNDATION FOR THE IMPROVEMENT OF LIVING AND WORKING CONDITIONS (1992), *Taking Action about Long Term Unemployment in Europe*, Dublin.

OECD-EUROPEAN FOUNDATION FOR THE IMPROVEMENT OF LIVING AND WORKING CONDITIONS (1993), Issue Paper: *Integrated Approaches to Accessing Employment* by Professor Alan McGregor, Conference on Partnerships for People in Cities.

OECD-EUROPEAN FOUNDATION FOR THE IMPROVEMENT OF LIVING AND WORKING CONDITIONS (1993), "The Minneapolis Employment Network" by M. Brinda.

OECD-ILE PROGRAMME (1989), *Self-employment Schemes for the Unemployed.* Notebook, No. 10, Paris.

OECD-ILE PROGRAMME (1990, 1991), *Innovation and Employment,* Issues: No. 4, No. 6, and No. 7; Paris.

OECD-ILE PROGRAMME (1992), *Whitfield Working for Jobs.* References.

Housing the homeless: towards social and economic integration

BINGHAM, R., GREEN R. & WHITE S. (Eds) (1987), *The Homeless in Contemporary Society.* Safe Publications, New York.

CATON, C.L.M. (Ed.) (1990), *Homeless in America.* Oxford University Press, New York.

DALY, M. (1992), *European Homelessness: the Rising Tide.* FEANTSA.

DALY, M. (1993), *Abandoned: Profile of Europe's Homeless People,* FEANTSA.

EVANS, A. & DUNCAN S. (1988), *Responding to Homelessness : Local Authority Policy and Practice,* Department of the Environment, HMSO, London.

LOVELAND, I. (1988), "Homelessness in the United States" *Urban Law and Policy,* No. 9, pp. 231-276.

MINISTERE DE L'EQUIPEMENT, DU LOGEMENT, DE L'AMENAGEMENT DU TERRITOIRE ET DES TRANSPORTS (1987), *La politique du logement des personnes âgées,* Paris.

OBERLANDER, P. & FALLICK, P., *Homelessness and the Homeless, Responses and Innovations.* The Centre for Human Settlements, University of British Columbia, Vancouver.

TUCKER, W. (1991), "How Housing Regulations Cause Homelessness". *The Public Interest,* No. 102, Winter.

The residential environment: ensuring a positive focus for health, prosperity and quality of life

ASHTON, J. (1991), "How to 'do' health". *Town and Country Planning*, December.

EVERSLEY, D. (1990), "Inequality at the Spatial Level -- A Task for Planners". *The Planner*, pp. 13-18, March.

HANCOCK, T. (1989), *Sustaining Health : Achieving Health for All in a Secure Environment*. Faculty of Environmental Studies, York University, North York.

OECD (1987), *Managing and Financing Urban Services*, Paris.

OECD (1990), *Environmental Policies for Cities in the 1990's*, Paris.

TENNYSON, R. & SHEPPARD, N. (1991), "The Process of Building-in Well-being". *Town and Country Planning*, décembre.

Involving and empowering residents

EUROPEAN FOUNDATION FOR THE IMPROVEMENT OF LIVING AND WORKING CONDITIONS (1992a), *Strengthening the Role of Local Community Action: Strategies, Dilemmas and Problems*, EFILWC Conference "Citizen Action: Involving People at Local Level", Dublin.

EUROPEAN FOUNDATION FOR THE IMPROVEMENT OF LIVING AND WORKING CONDITIONS (1992b), *Out of the Shadows, Local Community Action and the European Community*, Dublin.

INNOVATIVE INSTITUTIONS (1990), *The Power to Change Lies Within Families*, International Seminar for Innovative Institutions, October 10-19, The Hague, Netherlands.

JOINT OECD/SCOTTISH OFFICE (1992), *Reports of Session Rapporteurs and of the Chairman of the Conference*, Seminar on "Integrated Housing Strategies: Creating Opportunities for People and their Community", 7-8 October, Edinburgh, Scotland.

US DEPARTMENT OF HOUSING AND URBAN DEVELOPMENT (1988), *Partners in Self-Sufficiency* (Guidebook), Washington, D.C.

Improving social cohesion in neighbourhoods

BAROU, J. (1990), *Immigrant Housing: Comparative European Approach.* Meeting of Experts on the Impact of Housing and Town Planning on Community Relations, Council of Europe, Strasbourg, 22 June.

COUNCIL OF EUROPE (1989), *Community Relations and Solidarity in European Society.* Strasbourg: Council of Europe.

MACEWEN, M. (1990), *Planning for Ethnic Minority Housing in Britain.* Meeting of Experts on the Impact of Housing and Town Planning on Community Relations, Council of Europe, Strasbourg, 22 June.

OECD (1992), Keynote Presentation, Dublin Conference. *Improving the Social Mix and Promoting Social Cohesion in Neighbourhoods.* Prepared by Mr. McConnell, C., Paris.

OECD (1993*a*), Presentation, Dublin Conference. *The Finglas Enlivenment Project -- A Community Planning Approach.* Prepared by Haughton, J. and Larkin. D.

OECD (1993*b*), Presentation, Dublin Conference. *Promoting Social Cohesion and Integration in New Housing Estates.* Prepared by Mr. Patrick Cogan.

OECD AND COMMUNITY DEVELOPMENT FOUNDATION (1993), The Challenge of Urban Regeneration. Report of a joint OECD/CDF Conference, Birmingham.

SALINS, P. D. (1993), "Cities, Suburbs and the Urban Crisis" *The Public Interest*, No. 113, Fall.

Integrating the young: the role of social services, cultural and leisureactivities and education

DALY, M. (1993), *European Homelessness -- The Rising Tide,* Brussels, European Federation of National Organisations Working with the Homeless (FEANTSA).

ECDGEMP (European Commission, Directorate General for Employment, Industrial Relations and Social Affairs) (1990), *Building the Future,* Brussels.

EFILWC (The European Foundation for the Improvement of Living and Working Conditions) (1989), *Accommodation and Social Cohesion in the Urban Environment -- The Implications for Young People,* Dublin.

HEDDY, J. (1991), *Housing for Young People: A Survey of the Situation in Selected EC Countries,* Paris.

JENCKS, C. and PETERSON, P. (1991), *The Urban Underclass,* Washington D.C., Brookings.

Safer cities: a prerequisite for sustainable urban development

AUSTRALIA, National Committee on Violence (1990), *Violence: Directions for Australia.* National Institute of Criminology, Canberra.

BENNETT, T. and WRIGHT, R. (1984), *Burglars on Burglary,* Gower Press, London.

CANADA MORTGAGE AND HOUSING CORPORATION (1993), *Reclaiming Urban Neighbourhoods: Assessing New Strategic Approaches to Security in 11 Canadian Social Housing Communities,* Ottawa.

CRIME CONCERN (1992), *Family, School and Community: Towards a Social Crime Prevention Agenda,* Swindon, Royaume-Uni.

EISENHOWER FOUNDATION (1990), *Youth Investment and Community Reconstruction: Street Lessons on Drugs and Crime for the Nineties,* 10th Anniversary Policy Report, Washington, D.C.

EUROPEAN FORUM FOR URBAN SAFETY (1992), *Safety in the City: The Prevention of Crime, Recidivism and Drug Abuse,* Paris.

HOPE, T. (1986), "Crime, Community and Environment" *Journal of Environmental Psychology,* Vol.6, No. 1, pp. 65-78.

MAXFIELD, M. (1990), *Fear of Crime in England and Wales,* Home Office Research Study No. 78. London: HMSO.

UNITED KINGDOM (1984), *Mortality Statistics -- Childhood 1984.* London: HMSO.

UNITED KINGDOM, Home Office (1989), *Home Office Statistical Bulletin 32/89,* London.

UNITED KINGDOM, Home Office (1991), *Safer Communities: The Local Delivery of Crime Prevention through the Partnership Approach,* London.

UNITED KINGDOM, Home Office (1993), *Digest 2: Information on the Criminal Justice System in England and Wales,* London.

UNITED NATIONS, General Assembly (1990), *Prevention of Urban Crime,* Report of the 8th UN Congress on the prevention of crime and Treatment of Offenders. A/CONF.144/28, New York.

US NATIONAL CRIME PREVENTION COUNCIL (1992), *Planning to Stop Crime in Our Cities,* Washington, D.C.

VAN DIJK, J. and MAYHEW, P. (1993), *Criminal Victimisation in the Industrialised World.* Ministry of Justice, The Hague.

Chapter 5

Housing Affordability: Key Issues and Policies
by Mr. Kenneth Gibb

An unfavourable policy context

Modern cities are undergoing a process of economic restructuring and fundamental societal change which is having a critical impact on housing and housing policy. The need for shelter and for improvements to the existing housing stock has not diminished. But the array of needs has become more complex. For political and financial reasons some traditional solutions to the shortage of affordable housing, notably the construction of new social housing and increased utilisation of privately rented housing stock, appear no longer to be viable options, at least in some Member countries.

Global economic restructuring and spatially unbalanced de-industrialisation in many OECD cities have combined with changes in lifestyle patterns to alter the structure of housing demand. The effect has been to increase the share of single and two person households, a trend reinforced by large scale immigration, increased separation, and the ageing of the population. At the same time housing demand has also been affected by the increased economic vulnerability of many households. This is due not only to the unemployment effects of the global recession, but also to the permanent reduction in lower skilled jobs throughout OECD countries and the increased risk of job loss for many established white collar workers. These heightened risks have raised questions about the continuing viability of the traditional debt-financed route to asset accumulation through home ownership.   Yet, just when newly-formed households appear to be re-assessing the merits of tenure choices, the long term effects of housing policy in many Member countries have been to reduce the non-owning options for many households at the margins of renting and owning.

OECD Member countries can be divided into two main groups: those, like the United States and Australia, which have relied on a buoyant private rental

147

sector to satisfy a large share of housing demand; and those, like France, the United Kingdom and the Netherlands, in which publicly-funded social rental housing has been the main supply of affordable dwellings for low-to-moderate income households. (Germany is notable for combining the two sets of characteristics, due to the relatively small proportion of owner-occupiers).

In much of Europe, during the period up to the mid-seventies, shortages of affordable housing were tackled through the provision of new social housing, in an attempt to compensate for the increased use of poor quality inner city private rental housing. However, by the middle of the decade in question, the numerical imbalance between the number of dwellings and the number of households had all but disappeared. Economic growth, the demand for higher housing standards, disillusionment with past social housing failures and public spending restrictions combined to create the conditions for a new approach to housing policy. The basic tenets of this approach were:

-- an increased role for the private housing market and support for an expansion of home ownership (reinforced by financial deregulation);
-- a shift in housing assistance towards means-testing and demand-side subsidy;
-- a reduction in the level of social housing investment and its re-direction into the improvement and modernisation of the existing stock rather than new buildings.

However, within many cities, the longer term consequences of these policies for the processes of urban social integration have subsequently become apparent. The interaction between the new approach and the underlying trends -- growing long term unemployment and low income elderly populations, increasing numbers of one parent low income families, increased in-migration and at least in some European countries a long term decline in private rented housing -- has speeded up the process of social exclusion in low income neighbourhoods (*Cf.* Harloe, 1993). In the process a number of critical elements have become clear. Firstly, there is a contradiction between policies aimed at encouraging higher income households to leave social renting and at the targeting of assistance to the most "needy", on the one hand, and the growing concern or impetus for action in the neighbourhoods where the most disadvantaged reside, on the other hand. Secondly, this process has been worsened by the growing use of means-tested allowances, subsidies which offset the use of higher rents. And finally, this has made the management and ownership of social housing in disadvantaged neighbourhoods increasingly difficult. Expected to house an increasing proportion of low income and disadvantaged households, the residual social housing sector is left with the client group most associated with arrears of rent, neighbour disputes, security issues and inter-agency demands for services, such as social work.

Although these developments stem from the significant changes that have been occurring in the housing market and in housing policy in many European countries, they have strong echoes also in those countries where the publicly-funded social housing sector has always been small and has been seen primarily as a stock of "housing of last resort". All three factors serve to increase the financial cost of operating social housing with little concomitant increase in funding. An additional factor, it has been argued, is the diminishing effectiveness of the social housing lobby in making its case for additional funding (*Cf.* Harloe, 1993). This is attributed to the declining middle class client base of social housing who were at one time an effective voice for the social housing movement. A direct consequence of a more residualised social housing sector is therefore less political impact, although there is some evidence in the United Kingdom of increased support among home owners for more social housing provision as a form of social insurance to protect households against the consequences of income loss, due to unemployment or inadequate provision for old age (*Cf.* MacLennan and Gibb, 1993). However, it is also important to stress the variety of experience across the OECD.

The meaning of affordability

Affordability refers to a number of problems in the housing market. At the most basic level it refers to an over-burdening of housing costs relative to income either for the average household or, more usually, for some sub-set, for example low-to-moderate income households or those entering the housing market for the first time. But affordability problems are often associated with wider housing market issues, such as inadequate access or the unsuitability of the available accommodation, reflected in, for example, severe disrepair and over-crowding.

From a policy perspective, many of the most acute problems arise at the point where policy-makers have to define what affordable housing means in order to operationalise and define targets. Inset 30 summarises the problems that the United Kingdom faced when it tried to operationalise a target affordability ratio for rent-setting in the voluntary housing association sector. The answer is that there is no single, correct ratio that is universally acceptable. The issue is bound to be contentious, positions simply reflecting the interests of different groups. As a consequence, many have come to feel that affordability ratios used as targets to determine price and subsidy policy create more problems than they solve. No consensus exists except that there is no one critical ratio of affordability.

Inset 30. Affordable Rents in the United Kingdom

As part of the United Kingdom government's policy to expand housing association investment through an element of private finance, the 1988 Housing Act proposed that the previous system of administered "fair rents" should be replaced by rents set at the associations' discretion. These were to be guided by a principle of affordability: that rents should be set taking into account the income of a low-income in-employment household (*i.e.* a household not in receipt of housing benefit or social security payments). The question that confronted voluntary housing associations was what should that proportion be and what could be deemed unaffordable and yet still balance their rental revenue with their spending.

Housing associations, faced with this dilemma, carried out surveys to assess their own tenants' affordability ratios. At the same time they were also bombarded with advice from different quarters about what an acceptable ratio would be. Figures for a reasonable rent-to-income ratio were as diverse as 10 per cent (reflecting the position of local authority tenants), 20 per cent suggested by the National Federation of Housing Associations and 35 per cent (the notional figure from the Housing Corporation, the Non-Departmental Public Body (NDPB) that funds most housing association activity). An alternative suggestion was that they should look at the incomes and expenditures of households with average earnings or, perhaps, tenants on average earnings.

Nonetheless many countries continue to use explicit targets in the design of affordable housing policy. In the United States, rent-to-income ratios have been used to qualify builders for supply subsidies and similar policy instruments have appeared in Europe. Table 5.1 describes rent-to-income and house price-to-income ratios for several cities recently collected by the World Bank for their Housing Indicators Programme (further data of this type is reported in Annex 1 on affordability). These figures show that the experience of the median household varies considerably from country to country and city to city. The unanswered question is whether or not, for policy purposes, affordability ratios for particular projects or allowances should reflect the median experience or some other market benchmark.

Table 5.1 **Median rents, house prices and incomes, 1990, selected cities**

City	Rent ($ pa)	Rent (% of annual income)	House price ($)	Price (multiple of annual income)
Amsterdam	2 523	17	69 935	4.8
Athens	2 009	14	54 070	3.8
Helsinki	5 130	14	132 500	3.7
Hong Kong	5 938	39	112 022	7.4
London	2 145	11	135 774	7.2
Madrid	2 404	10	84 844	3.7
Melbourne	3 700	14	100 960	3.9
Munich	5 339	15	343 333	9.6
Oslo	2 363	7	187 500	5.5
Paris	6 392	20	136 452	4.2
Seoul	5 720	29	179 500	9.3
Singapore	3 211	32	35 862	3.6
Stockholm	4 510	11	187 780	4.6
Tel Aviv	3 770	23	83 880	5.0
Tokyo	3 863	10	441 719	11.6
Toronto	5 734	13	186 855	4.2
Washington	7 992	16	194 150	3.9
Vienna	2 817	13	105 926	4.7

Source: The Swedish Housing Market in International Comparison, edited by Eva Hedman, Boverket, 1993. Table 4.2, Data from World Bank Housing Indicators Programme.

Inevitably there are strong implicit assumptions involved in the use of these affordability ratios and in the very concept of affordable housing. These point to more fundamental questions concerning the interpretation of expenditure-income ratios. For example:

-- is a high affordability ratio a housing market or a poverty problem?
-- is a high affordability ratio a permanent or a transitory problem?
-- is a low ratio always a sign of success in affordability terms?
-- is a high ratio usually a sign of excessive housing market speculation?
-- do average ratios sufficiently take account of different household structures and circumstances?

151

Policy makers concerned with the issue of housing affordability need to satisfy themselves that they know the answer to such questions if they are going to design successful policies for market intervention.

The basis for intervention to improve housing affordability

The arguments in favour of market provision of housing are well known. Using markets to allocate housing resources implies operating under a system of voluntary exchange for the mutual benefit of the parties concerned. Moreover, housing markets use and store a great deal of information and this allows property to be allocated to its best or most highly-valued use, reflecting the opportunity costs. Markets also allow individuals maximum freedom of choice in their consumption and investment decisions, rather than being allocated housing on a quasi-compulsory basis.

Administrative allocation processes tend to encourage black markets. Government intervention moreover is costly and there is little evidence that governments can allocate resources as efficiently as markets. Nonetheless in every OECD nation, governments intervene widely in the housing market, through subsidy, legal restrictions on property rights and other forms of regulation, direct provision and a host of other activities that directly and indirectly affect the working of the housing market. One justification for this is the scope for market failure in housing. The major potential market failures arise from:

-- monopoly among housing and construction suppliers;
-- severe supply unresponsiveness;
-- externalities;
-- informational failures and discrimination;
-- the effects of discriminatory lending practices;
-- the need for co-ordinated decision-taking;
-- over-regulation.

The major reason for intervention does not, however, relate to efficiency-based market failures, but rather reflects equity considerations. A high density urban system is particularly likely to produce unacceptable outcomes: for example excessive rents and overcrowding. Government policy is not in these circumstances motivated primarily by economic considerations but instead seeks to redress an outcome originating from vertical and/or horizontal forms of inequity. Not surprisingly, many see the solution to these problems lying outside the housing sphere and in the domain of the general distribution of income.

Governments (at all levels) intervene to re-direct the housing market toward outcomes that will both make the market work better and help achieve wider social objectives (such as increased levels of home ownership). However, because urban housing markets are complex, interactive systems, the effects of market failure, and *a fortiori* of policies designed to efficiency or equity goals, are felt throughout the system. Policy makers need to realise therefore that their policy responses will have knock-on effects throughout the housing market. For example, this is seen clearly when an increase in subsidy to market renting reduces the supply of new housing for owner occupation; or where a social housing project in an inner city area increases private property values. The housing market is made up of spatially-contiguous neighbourhoods which have more or less connections between them in terms of economic, leisure and transport attributes. This pattern of linkages determines how the effects of actions or policies in one area are likely to affect other areas or groups. To the extent that housing shortages and unaffordability are a key element in the physical and social decline of parts of cities, redressing the affordability gap can play an important role in the revitalisation of run-down areas in OECD cities.

Affordability issues and policy responses

In this section the recent experience of affordability policies and programmes in Member countries is discussed, looking in turn at the demand-side, the supply-side, housing finance, the regulatory environment and methods of evaluation. Table 5.2 summarises some of the main types of problems found in urban housing systems, classified according to the origin of the problem.

Demand factors

For many households, the lack of a steady income, continuing poverty or inadequate savings are the critical factors that underlie housing unaffordability. Many programmes focus on working age households; but poverty is an especially severe problem also for elderly households, including those who are outright owners but face serious problems of disrepair. Where affordability is

153

Table 5.2 **Problems of affordability**

Demand side	Supply side	Finance	Regulatory environment
Low income/uncertain income	High construction costs	Credit rationing	Rent controls
Little wealth/savings	Residential land shortages	Mortgage inflexibility	Zoning/land us e systems
High/accelerating housing and land costs	Zoning/planning restrictions	Deposit: loan ratios	
In-migration	High infrastructure costs	Indebtedness	
Rapid urban expansion	Alternative subsidised investments	Discrimination	
Discrimination	Gentrification and conversion	Tax treatment of housing	
High transactions costs		Constraints on public spending on housing	
		Failures in the social security/taxation system (such as personal housing subsidies)	

essentially an income problem, social security and tax measures may be required to alleviate them. For first time buyers low income and inadequate savings also reduces the amount of credit they can raise.

Table 5.3 (and Annex 1 on affordability) shows the rapid increase in house prices in the capital cities of London, Paris and Tokyo (metropolitan region) during the late 1980s. Increases of this magnitude quickly erode the savings of low and moderate income households and as a consequence price-to-income ratios rise alarmingly, putting house purchase out of many households' reach. The explosion in Tokyo land prices, described in Table 5.4, illustrates the problem in more detail.   The increase in land prices in 1988 was quite unparalleled and the effect of rising land prices was reflected in the doubling of the house price to income ratio between 1986 and 1990. At the same time rents have risen, outstripping inflation, with the positive differential between Tokyo and Japan as a whole maintained in the decade to 1990.   The experience of Japan is perhaps an extreme case; but it illustrates the consequences of rapid economic growth combined with an over-concentration of industrial and commercial activity and widespread speculation in the urban land market (which was ultimately tied to the fortunes of general stocks and shares on the Nikkei index).   This has done much to undermine Japan's efforts to improve the affordability of housing (see OECD report on Urban Land Markets, 1990).

Table 5.3 **Annual house price increases, selected cities, 1987-89 percentage change**

Year	Greater London	Paris	Tokyo
1987	20	7	26
1988	18	30	31
1989	5	11	12

Source: OECD Issue Paper (1991): *Economic Growth, Concentration of Service Industries and Provision of Affordable Housing in Big Cities.*

Real housing demand is a function of demographics as well as prices and incomes. Table 5.5 summarises demographic trends in the European Union from 1960 to 1988, prior to the democratisation of Eastern Europe. While population growth rate has fallen markedly, the net formation rate of households, which ultimately constitutes the raw material of housing demand, has continued to grow. In addition to marriages (in slow decline since 1960) and single people forming households, there is also the increasingly important factor of household fission. Table 5.5 shows clearly that divorce has grown significantly, alongside the growing incidence of elderly, increasingly female, single person households. In general average household sizes have fallen continuously and this has serious implications for dwelling mix and house type in OECD cities. (Table 5.6 shows the growing proportion of single person households in Europe).

155

Table 5.4 Posted land price index 1980-90 (1980 = 100)
Tokyo metropolitan region

Year	Land index	Price to income ratio	Rents (000 Yen) Japan	Rents (000 Yen) Tokyo
1980	100.0		47.8	64.2
1981	114.1			
1982	122.5		54.1	73.6
1983	127.6			
1984	130.4		59.3	85.4
1985	132.6			
1986	136.6	4.2	62.2	80.0
1987	165.9	5.4		
1988	279.8	7.0	68.0	94.0
1989	280.9	7.4		
1990	299.4	8.0	71.1	102.7

Source: OECD Issue Paper (1991): *Innovative Financing Strategies for Affordable Owner Occupied and Rented Housing.*

Table 5.5 Population growth, marriages and divorces per 1 000 persons, European Union, 1960-88

Year	Population growth	Marriages	Divorces
1960	8.2	7.8	0.4
1965	8.2	7.8	0.5
1970	7.8	7.7	0.7
1975	4.2	7.2	1.1
1980	4.5	6.3	1.3
1985	2.5	5.7	1.6
1986	2.7	5.7	1.6
1987	3.0	5.9	1.6
1988	3.5	5.9	1.6

Source: Kleinman, M. (1992), *Policy Responses to Changing Housing Markets: Towards a European Housing Policy.* London School of Economics/Welfare State Programme WSP/73.

Table 5.6 **Single person households as a percentage of all households**

Country	1950	1960	1970	1980
Austria	18	20	26	28
Belgium	16	17	19	23
Denmark		20	21	29
France	19	20	20	25
Greece	9	10	11	15
Ireland		13	14	17
Iceland	18	13		
Italy	10	11	13	18
Luxembourg		12	16	21
Netherlands		12	17	22
Norway		14	21	28
Portugal	8	11	10	13
Sweden	21	20	25	33
Spain			8	10
Turkey	7	3	3	7
United Kingdom	11	13	18	22
West Germany	19	21	25	31

Source: The Swedish Housing Market in International Comparison, edited by Eva Hedman, Boverket, 1993.

In Europe a particularly important demographic contribution in recent years, however, has come from immigration. As a consequence housing policies are having to be reassessed, since there is no longer a situation of relative balance between demand and supply (and hence an overriding concern with quality rather than quantity). Once again in many European countries there is a need to tackle shortages and excess demand for housing among immigrant groups. Up until the mid-seventies, the natural instrument would have been new social housing. Since then, new social housing provision has gone into sharp decline; yet it is evident that neither home ownership nor the dwindling stock of cheap private rented housing can cope with this problem or with the general decline of many social housing neighbourhoods.

Alongside large-scale immigration there is a growing problem of discrimination in housing markets. This affects especially renter households because discrimination is most acute when there is the combination of low

income with some other potentially discriminatory factor such as race. Higher income groups can exercise choice in a way that poor households cannot. Owner occupiers, if they face some form of discrimination, tend to do so at the point of mortgage lending, where it is somewhat easier to control and eliminate. Discrimination may also exhibit itself in the planning system where exclusionary zoning prevents the building of mixed developments which include affordable housing units which would be likely to go to minority groups.

Policy responses: access to home ownership and policy for low income renter households

Objectives: Most countries in the OECD support the widening of home ownership for socio-economic reasons, and, in particular, seek to encourage younger households into owner occupation. Table 5.7 illustrates the recent tenure distribution in European Union countries, showing that Germany and the Netherlands are the exceptions to the trend to owner occupation. In the past access to home ownership has been aimed at the middle classes. However, policies since the late 1980s show evidence of a move to extend home ownership to lower and moderate income families, as well as the better-off tenants, through a variety of innovative schemes. (Table 5.8 indicates the differential importance of social and private rented housing in Europe).

The attitude of the United States is characteristic of a generally emerging view:

"Home ownership has long been recognised as a desirable social policy, as a means of promoting stability, social responsibility and civic involvement" *The President's National Urban Policy Report* 1991, p. 11.

One reason for widening home ownership to relatively disadvantaged groups is the belief that, by diverting households into owner occupation, resources can be focused on the most pressing problems of low income renter households. Furthermore, the undoubted preference for ownership can be more effectively met. But owner occupation is not necessarily a cheap option in terms of public resources. Tax revenues foregone through concessions to owner occupation are a significant proportion of government budgets across the OECD but particularly so in the United States and the United Kingdom. Direct tax expenditures typically take the form of mortgage interest deductions (sometimes targeted to first time buyers) as well as remission of property taxes and taxes on imputed income and capital gains. The mix varies between different countries, just as there are widely diverging taxation principles relating to transaction taxes and value added (or sales) tax. Nonetheless, policies that promote home ownership by reducing the direct and indirect costs of home ownership do make an important contribution to tackling problems of affordability.

Assistance for home owners: Member countries have developed a variety of measures to improve affordability by helping the prospective owner occupier. The potential owner faces a formidable array of costs when choosing to purchase a house. There are significant down-payments to be made, transactions taxes, removal costs, legal and real estate agency fees, plus the considerable monetary and non-pecuniary costs of searching for a home. These can in fact constitute an important barrier to obtaining affordable housing and are, in many countries, one major focus for policies aimed at increasing home ownership.

Demand side programmes to assist potential purchasers have existed for a long period of time. The most enduring and significant is, of course, the tax deductibility of mortgage interest payments, specifically aimed at easing front end loading problems for purchasers. In some countries such as Australia, however, there is no provision for offsetting mortgage interest against tax since they are thought to be regressive.

Table 5.7 **Housing tenure in the European Union**

Country	Owner-occ.	Private rent	Social rent	Year
Spain	88.3	10.6	1.2	1989
Ireland	74.4	10.1	12.4	1981
Greece	70.0	26.5		1981
United Kingdom	67.0	7.0	26.0	1989
Italy	64.0	23.5	5.3	1990
Belgium	62.0	30.0	6.0	1986
Luxembourg	59.2	35.1		1981
Portugal	55.9	35.5	4.4	1981
Denmark	55.5	22.1	21.2	1988
France	54.2	19.7	17.2	1988
Netherlands	43.7	13.0	42.9	1988
Germany	40.0	43.0	17.0	1989

Source: Kleinman, M. (1992), Table 7, p. 12.

Table 5.8 **Rented housing in the European Union**

Country	Social units	Social units % of total stock	Social units per 1 000 inhabs.	Private rented as % of total stock
Netherlands	1 989 000	43.0	136.5	11.0
United Kingdom	5 966 000	26.4	104.5	7.0
West Germany	7 755 000	25.6	99.2	45.0
Denmark	488 793	21.2	95.5	13.0
France	3 661 578	17.1	66.6	20.0
Ireland	124 741	15.0	33.9	8.0
Belgium	253 278	17.0	25.7	36.0
Italy	1 200 000	15.2	20.9	19.0
Portugal	118 000	14.4	11.6	36.0
Spain	104 630	10.9	2.7	
Luxembourg	1 000		2.7	
Greece	0	0	0	27.0
EU	**21 662 020**	**14.9**	**63.5**	

Source: CECODHAS.

Another common feature is savings plans for first time buyers to help fund down-payment and provide a link to scarce mortgage loanable funds. In Germany, for example, such vehicles have been an important aspect of the owner occupied sector for many years. Similar policies have been developed in France and elsewhere. In Australia, the First Home Owner Scheme, introduced in 1983 was basically an income-tested grant scheme which attracted considerable demand from potential owner occupiers, when interest rates were high. It has now been phased out.

In Canada a number of policies were used in the 1970s and 1980s to assist demand side affordability objectives. The Assisted Home Ownership Programme assisted first time borrowers with moderate incomes by providing subsidies in the early years of the mortgage. This was achieved by lowering down-payments (to a minimum of 5 per cent), interest rate reductions and additional loans and grants subject to eligibility. This federal scheme was followed by a number of similar state-backed schemes (Ontario, Prince Edward Island, etc.). A further federal scheme was the Registered Home Ownership Savings Plan, which offered a savings plan with tax deductible savings for a maximum of ten years which could be used for down-payment purposes.

In the United States, as a result of 1988 electoral pledges, savings plans linked to mortgage down-payments were targeted at moderate and middle income households. Assistance on down-payments is limited to $10 000 and the maximum price is 110 per cent of the average purchase price in the local market area. HUD contends that this policy will make home ownership more accessible for only a modest reduction in tax receipts ($220 million over three years).

In France, savings banks offer special subsidised (tax-free) savings and housing accounts. Since at least the 1960s, there have been housing-savings schemes (Le Compte d'épargne logement and Le Plan d'épargne logement) which operate with minimum deposit periods and then yield loans proportionate to the total amount saved. In 1977, a preferential loan programme was introduced (Prêts aides à l'accession à la propriété or PAP) which subsidises home ownership loans. These preferential loans are similar in value to market rates and eligible households qualify for varied subsidised interest rates depending on location, household and dwelling type and income.

The use of contractual savings plans has had a traditional central place (now diminishing) in the German mortgage finance system. At the same time mortgage subsidies exist for those who qualify, depending on household income, household type and mortgage specifications. Until 1990 there was also a ten year tax concession on the land component of property taxation for new owner occupiers.

In Norway long term housing policy is based on the principle of owner-occupancy by which young people are assisted as first time home-buyers. The State Housing Bank provides loans to municipalities so that they can provide financial assistance as a supplement to mortgage loans. Municipalities have, however, been hesitant in providing this assistance due to associated risk.

In the United Kingdom various policies have been pursued to increase access to home ownership. The most well known is the granting of large subsidies based on length of tenancy to public housing tenants to enable them to buy their house. (This typically results in a subsidy of 40 to 50 per cent of capital costs but can go as high as 60 to 70 per cent). This "Right to Buy" has been enjoyed by more than 1.3 million tenants in the period 1980 to 1991. Recent policy has been explicitly aimed at lower income tenants by deep subsidies on the proportion of the capital value of a property that current gross rents could finance as a mortgage (Rent to Mortgage). This, like many other shared ownership and low cost home ownership schemes, is recognised to be a narrow niche product, without the mass appeal of the "Right to Buy".

Nevertheless, these policies indicate the government's continuing intention to widen home ownership (see Inset 31 for experience in Finland).

Inset 31. First Time Buyers in Finland

The government operates a system to help young people aged 18-30 buy their first home. This requires the prospective buyer to enter into a savings agreement with a bank under which they are required to save 20 per cent of the probable cost of a home. It is also a stipulation that this cost does not exceed a level specified by the government.

When the target has been reached the state provides, during the first six years, an interest subsidy for a bank loan. Subsidy under this scheme is not means-tested. The buyer may also obtain a state loan with low interest, but may not have at the same time the interest subsidy for a bank loan and a low interest state loan. There are no age-limits for the state loan but the interest subsidy is means-tested.

Source: Doling, J. (1990), Housing Finance in Finland, in MacLennan, D. and Williams, R. (ed) *Affordable Housing in Europe.* Joseph Rowntree Foundation: York.

Assistance for low income tenants: In Table 5.9 the relative positions of poor owners and renters in the United States in 1989 are contrasted. There is a not unexpected difference between owners and renters: 38 per cent of renters have a rental burden of at least 30 per cent of income while this is true of only 7 per cent of owners. This table shows very clearly that the key indicator of inadequate housing, defined in terms of quality or in terms of cost, remains low income. The two arms of policy to help low income households have been, from the demand side, housing allowances, and from the supply side, financial support to landlords. Both sets of policies reflect the desire to enable the housing market to work and are in effect an acknowledgment of the distortions created by general price subsidies and the failure of taxation policies accurately to target those in need of affordable housing.

The typical housing allowance discriminates between different household types and circumstances, depending on age, income, wealth and number of dependents. It is now widely recognised that allowances are preferable to rent controls, provided they minimise some of the more unfortunate side-effects of income-based subsidies.

Table 5.9 **Housing problems in the United States, 1989**

Tenure	Income as a percentage of local median family income				
	Very low (0-50 %)	Low (51-80 %)	Middle (81-120 %)	Upper (121 % +)	% of all rent/owner
Renters' rental burden:					
>50 %	41	2	0	0	17
30-50 %	29	33	11	1	21
Inadequate housing	17	11	8	7	12
Crowding	8	5	3	2	5
% assisted	26	7	3	2	13
% no problems	12	48	76	88	48
Owners' cost burden:					
>50 %	19	2	0	0	3
30-50 %	16	7	3	1	4
Inadequate housing	14	9	5	4	6
Crowding	3	3	2	1	2
% no problems	54	82	90	95	87

Source: Nelson, K. and Khaddiri, J. (1992), "To Whom Should Limited Housing Resources be Directed?", Housing Policy Debate, Vol. 3 pp. 1-57.

First, it has to be recognised that such allowances are heavily dependent in expenditure terms on wider economic cycles and income-distributional policies. Public money may be reaching those defined to be the most worthy but that does not mean it will be cheap: in the United Kingdom, for example, reductions in current subsidy to the public rental housing stock has been effectively off-set by increasing volumes of housing benefit expenditure.

Second, these allowances are subject to problems of high marginal tax rates or "poverty traps" where the marginal increase in net income is wholly or substantially offset by increases in taxation or reductions in benefits. Means-tested benefits suffer from stigma and low take-up, although these problems can be minimised through sensitive administrative procedures.

Finally, it is to be remembered that housing allowances have market effects by stimulating the demand for rented housing. This means that households who are ineligible for allowances may face higher rents than would be the case in their absence. At the same time, allowance schemes, such as that in the United Kingdom (housing benefit), which are designed in such a way that marginal increases in rents are fully reimbursed in subsidy, provide no incentive for households to economise in housing consumption, which cannot be a rational feature in the design of any sort of allowance scheme.

Housing allowances were originally introduced in many cases to offset the impact of the decontrol of private renting (for example, France in 1948, Germany in 1965, the Netherlands in 1975, and Australia in 1981). Inset 32 describes the housing allowance programme developed in Denmark. However, while there is a perceptible trend towards allowances in assisting low income households, not all OECD Member countries have moved in this direction (*Cf.* Kemp, 1990). In 1990 Italy, Switzerland, Belgium and Austria were reported to have no general system of housing allowances. In Ireland, local authorities employ differential rent-setting practices such that rents are related to household income of the occupant. Even in the United States, the origin of the market case for housing allowances, the allowances are strictly cash-limited, superseding eligibility by right, and restricting their impact to around 15 per cent of eligible renters (Kemp, *op. cit.* p. 22-23). The subsidy to private tenants in the United States has the interesting incentive mechanism that, where eligible households can economise and take acceptable housing at a level less than the mandated standard, then the household keeps the difference.

Supply factors

The aim the policies discussed above is to increase the effective housing demand of lower income groups; but none will generate further affordable housing unless the market failures on the supply side are tackled. For low income households, affordable rented housing policy has been developed in a number of ways that encourage the provision, funding and pricing of rented housing, private and social. These have involved a variety of measures to subsidise loans, to grant concessionary tax status for rental investments, to provide subsidised land for affordable housing developments and to offer outright grants for preferred rental developments. In many cases this has also meant the reduction or removal of rent controls.

Inset 32. **Housing Allowances in Denmark**

The allowances (for normal housing) are set for each household individually in relation to the actual rent, household income, number of children, size of the dwelling and a few other factors. Only households whose incomes are below certain maximums are entitled to receive the allowances. The payment by the household itself is at present, for average pensioners' households, who do not live in extremely large dwellings, set to 15 per cent of household income, while for non-pensioners it is set to approximately 25 per cent of the household income.

In practice, a so-called margin of tenant's own payment is calculated on the basis of actual rent, income, number of children, etc. If the actual rent exceeds this margin, allowances are given to the difference between margin and rent. Allowance to pensioners covers the whole difference while for non-pensioners it covers only 75 per cent of the difference.

If household income increases, the amount of subsidy is lowered; if the number of children in the household increases, however, more subsidies are granted. For both schemes the subsidies are paid to the households by local government but central government refunds 75 per cent of the outlay to pensioners and 40 per cent of the outlay to non-pensioners.

Subsidies are primarily granted to households with relatively high housing expenditures and with only modest incomes. Allowances predominantly in practice are given to tenant households in new housing. In the most expensive dwellings the allowances cover up to 50 per cent of the rent for the most disadvantaged groups.

Housing allowances have only to a small extent been subject to budgetary cuts in recent years. Emphasis has been put on maintaining a decent relationship between housing costs and incomes but changing some of the mechanisms that automatically trigger public spending if rents are increased has been considered.

Source: (1989), Distributional Aspects of Housing and Taxation Policies, Ministry of Housing and Building, Denmark.

Policies to restrict rent increases have a long history in policy-making in OECD countries. They display substantial variety across countries, though there is a clear cyclical pattern. In the high inflationary period of the mid 1970s to early 1980s, the re-imposition of rent restrictions in many countries acted as an insurance policy against macroeconomic turbulence, and even as a form of income stabilisation policy. However, counter-cyclical measures of this kind tend to reinforce the problems faced by landlords in trying to make adequate and reasonable rental returns. Disintermediation was common during this period. The sector remains in need of structural reforms that will help to reduce the shortages and gluts that periodically happen in urban housing systems. In most countries a significant contributing factor is the imbalance in the tax treatment of the tenures which typically favours owner occupation as an investment. Taxation reforms can assist the rental market to overcome the distortions which in some countries have prevented it contributing to the supply of affordable housing for low income households.

In Canada the matching of need to provision is supported by a system to identify core housing need which is then targeted by individual programmes. This model is related to the direction of federal housing assistance rather than solely tax-based incentives (see Inset 33).

In many countries, rent allowance programmes are linked to construction subsidies, on the basis that subsidised construction loans are given only where affordable or low income housing is included in the development. For instance, in the United States, subsidised builders, under some such schemes, have to provide a certain percentage of units which will yield rents below a government-imposed ceiling, although this will only be for a limited time (usually 20 years) before it can be rented out at market rents (*Cf.* Gyourko, 1990). The United States has also made extensive use of tax expenditures through, for example, the accelerated depreciation of properties, although it became clear during the 1980s that favourable tax provisions could be abused: they contributed more to lowering the effective tax rates for high income earners than to providing a stable, long term supply of affordable housing. Nonetheless the practice of negative gearing (which permits losses to be offset against other taxable income) is used to encourage higher post-tax returns in private renting in the United States and Australia. Significant tax expenditures were also offered in the United Kingdom through the Business Expansion Scheme, which allowed accelerated tax write-offs for individual investors. In this case, however, the working life for the subsidy was only five years, after which time the selling of shares in BES companies attracted no capital gains tax. The scheme has now been replaced.

Inset 33. Core Housing Need in Canada

In 1990, 1.16 million or 12 per cent of total Canadian households were in core housing need (*i.e.* lived in crowded, inadequate or unaffordable housing and could not obtain suitable housing in their market area without paying 30 per cent or more of household income for shelter). More households fell below the norm affordability criterion than were living in unsuitable or inadequate housing. Approximately 70 per cent of all households in need were renters.

A number of federal social housing programmes address the problems of those in core housing need. The Non-Profit Housing Programme provides subsidy assistance to non-profit organisations to develop and operate rental housing, on a rent-geared-to-income basis, for households in core need. In 1992, this programme accounted for 26 per cent of federal social housing programme activity. In an attempt to improve the targeting of the programme, greater emphasis has been placed on ensuring that projects are smaller and integrated into their neighbourhoods, and local concerns about the development of projects are addressed.

The Rent Supplement Programme provides subsidy assistance, on a rent-geared-to-income basis for households in core need that rent housing in the private market, Non-Profit Housing and in Federal Co-operative Housing projects. In 1992, this programme accounted for 7 per cent of new federal social housing commitments. Greater emphasis is now being placed on the utilisation of this programme to serve households in need, based on the recognition that most people in need are adequately housed, but experience affordability problems. As well, in some circumstances, the programme is more cost-effective to government than funding new construction, and it provides benefits in terms of social integration by mixing assisted and unassisted households within private market rental accommodation.

The Residential Rehabilitation Assistance Programme provides loans and subsidies to low income households in both urban and rural areas to repair and improve their properties. A component of the programme also provides loans and subsidies to home owners and landlords to make modifications to homes to accommodate persons with disabilities. In 1992, this represented 67 per cent of federal social housing activity.

The experience of these tax-based incentives to rental housing production and management in a variety of countries highlights the difficulty of ensuring a long-run commitment to the supply of rental units, as opposed to a short-to-medium term focus on tax shelter and the realisation of capital gains (see Inset 34 for experience in France).

Ultimately, however, more fundamental action to stimulate housing supply may be called for, since, as the World Bank has noted, the supply of the housing market is:

"highly idiosyncratic between countries ...[It is] strongly influenced by public sector action in the provision of infrastructure, the regulation of the housing sector and, to a limited degree, the direct production of housing by public agencies... Nothing influences the efficiency and responsiveness of housing supply more than the legal and regulatory framework within which housing suppliers operate" (World Bank, 1991, p. *iii)*.

Inset 34. The Need for Housing Construction in France

In 1989 the annual increase of households in France was 240 000. That figure is expected to be 210 000 annually from 1990 to 1995. Crude surpluses arise as vacant housing in some areas cannot meet the demand elsewhere and existing older housing has to be rehabilitated.

The need for new construction was estimated as 325 000 per year for 1987/89, 340 000 per year for 1990/92 and 300 000 per year for 1993/95. However, the overall number of completions is less important than an analysis of need according to the *bassin d'habitats* -- areas of housing demand -- to ensure that the supply is carefully attuned to the demand. The decentralisation of town and country planning is expected to help local supply meet local demand, leaving the national authorities to monitor local and regional balances.

In the social housing sector, it is estimated that 60 000 new social rented units are needed each year, and that 150 000 existing dwellings should be modernised each year.

Source: Schaefer, J. (1990), Housing Finance and Subsidy Systems in France, in MacLennan, D. and Williams, R. (ed) *Affordable Housing in Europe*. Joseph Rowntree Foundation: York.

In modern developed economies, a considerable constraint on interventionary policies aimed at the supply of affordable housing is the continuing volatility of house and land prices, market transactions and vacancies (see Table 5.10). In most economies, moreover, there has been a secular increase in house prices, after inflation and adjustments for quality.

Table 5.10 **Estimated percentage of population changing usual residence in one year: circa 1981**

Ireland	6.1
Belgium	7.3
Austria	7.6
Netherlands	7.7
France	9.4
Japan	9.5
Sweden	9.5
United Kingdom	9.6
Israel	11.3
Switzerland	13.7
Australia	17.0
United States	17.5
Canada	18.0
New Zealand	19.4

Source: Fannie Mae (1991), *"International Housing Markets: What we know; what we need to know",* p. 21. *Objectives.*

Table 5.11 shows house price inflation rates for cities in the United States in the period 1960-86. In real terms, house prices doubled in San Francisco but barely rose at all in Atlanta or Chicago. Dallas enjoyed extreme swings in fortunes over the period, indicating how erroneous it can be to take too much from national figures. In the United Kingdom, there have been three major house price cycles in the period since 1969, although the depression in the housing market that commenced in 1990 is the first time that house prices have sustained widespread falls in nominal as well as real terms (see Inset 35).

The supply of serviced land is critical. Many OECD cities use master plans to ensure an orderly flow of housing land. However, much of this land is found only on the periphery of cities, and with low mobility an increasing problem, this tends to create isolated communities, cut off from "normal" city life and opportunities. In the countries where low housing densities predominate, such as Australia and the United States, increasing attention is being paid to measures designed to increase the density of development within existing built-up areas and to consolidate urban form.

169

Table 5.11 **Long term house price change, United States cities, 1970-86**

	1970-75	1975-81	1981-86	1960-86
In nominal terms				
Atlanta	41	56	35	196
Chicago	46	71	20	200
Dallas	39	125	31	309
San Francisco	54	187	29	407
In real terms				
Atlanta	1	-8	13	5
Chicago	5	1	0	7
Dallas	0	33	9	45
San Francisco	11	70	8	103

Source: Holmans, A. (1990), House Prices: Changes Through Time at National and Sub-National Level, Government Economic Service Working Paper No. 110, London, Table E.7.

In regions of rapid economic expansion, high and rising land prices create numerous problems. This has been seen clearly in the United Kingdom, Japan, Canada and Australia. When land is an important speculative asset, the incentives for active housing development are reduced and this can lead to fragmentation of land holdings, making co-ordinated and consolidated housing development impractical. Land use planning is an arena of conflict between many interest groups, since land has many external effects. As a consequence land use planning has to account for residential, business, recreational, amenity and environmental concerns, often bringing government and interested parties into conflict. In this context resolving the housing supply problem requires a consensus about land use planning generally, which, in many if not all OECD countries, remains an elusive goal.

The cost of new housing depends on the cost of raw materials and building components, which typically rise when demand is high. Housing construction moreover remains labour-intensive and dominated by skilled labour. Wage costs are often more volatile than general prices. Given the extremely cyclical nature of the construction industry, a significant proportion of entire working cohorts of skilled craftsman and builders can be laid off in times of recession, many ultimately lost to the industry for good. In the long run, the cyclical nature of the house construction business has served to greatly increase labour costs.

A way to protect affordable housing is to take a segment of land out of the market through special provisions to encourage low cost housing. This is the policy pursued in Finland through the HITAS experiment (see Inset 36). In Scotland, the government, though its housing agency, Scottish Homes, has developed a system of GRO-grants (Grants for Renting and Owning) which subsidise private development and building costs on approved schemes. To date most of the several million pounds devoted to this programme has been spent on private owner occupied housing built on large public housing estates at affordable prices. By so doing, owner occupation is encouraged in previously uniform areas, injecting housing, tenure and income mix into them.

These supply subsidies have the potential to direct investment into otherwise unprofitable but socially worthwhile programmes which in turn improve housing market performance.

Inset 36. Housing Price and Quality Control, Helsinki, Finland

In the municipality of Helsinki there is a particular type of subsidy for owner-occupiers called HITAS (housing price and quality control). For many years the municipality had offered land at below market prices to those wishing to build their own homes, as part of a deliberate strategy to make housing more affordable to a wide range of households. One drawback of this policy, however, was that when the house was sold the subsidy was capitalised, so that it helped only the first owner. Subsequent policy changes led to the adoption of the HITAS system in 1979.

As before, the intention is to make low cost housing available to a wide range of income groups and, in a context of rapidly increasing prices, to achieve this through market rather than public provision. The system works through the provision of municipal land which is leased at prices below the market level to reduce the cost of any housing built on it. The main difference from the earlier system is that the municipality retains control over the resale price. The owner of a HITAS-financed dwelling can legally ask for the original price plus an inflationary increase tied to the national construction index or house price index or a combination of these two indexes. In this way, the initial subsidy is passed on to subsequent owners. Although the owner may sell to anyone, the municipality itself may purchase on behalf of a third party.

Source: Doling, J. (1990), "Housing Finance in Finland", *Urban Studies*, Vol. 27, No. 6, pp. 965-6.

Policy responses to stabilise housing markets

Instruments: In Germany, tax policy, in particular, that for mortgage interest deductions, has been used to act counter-cyclically on the housing market. Rent controls in various forms have also been introduced ostensibly to deal with short run volatility in the form of housing shortages in rental housing markets. There is considerable evidence, across the OECD, that price volatility is often the result of unresponsive supply systems, particularly due to characteristics of the land market and the land use planning systems in operation in individual countries. The most severe land shortages have been reported in Japan, especially in the Tokyo metropolitan area: but similar stories recur across other OECD cities. Innovative policies to stabilise real property markets must be tailored to local circumstances but they share general principles.

Land costs have risen above general prices in most OECD countries in recent years. It can be argued that this leads to a more efficient use of land resources. However, for the housing market, rising and volatile land prices can produce serious consequences. Land costs typically contribute 20 to 40 per cent of new construction costs, and this is transmitted into second hand housing costs, adding to affordability problems. The outcomes are increased commuting, suppressed mobility and tenure choice, congestion, over-crowding, and the continual threatening of green spaces around cities.

What are the innovations that can be used to address these problems? The OECD report *Urban Land Markets: Policies for the 1990s* suggested seven policy guidelines:

- *land price controls*, as used in Japan in the 1980s to attack the symptoms of land market pressure;
- *decentralisation* and related methods to diffuse urban demand for land uses through the use of active relocation policies and the development of alternative growth poles;
- *land readjustment schemes*, to which could be added the use of tax concessions and grants in special zones such as United Kingdom enterprise zones which reclaim derelict or under-used industrial land for new supply purposes;
- *public sector land banking* circumvents speculative land-holding, allows land release to be used to tackle local cyclical pressures and the receipts from sales can be used to minimise the need for planning gain and other disincentives to private developers. This policy is restricted by the extent to which land ownership structures do actually constrain development;
- *pre-emption rights* allows the municipality to pre-empt any sale (France) and thereby influence the price of land;
- *land information systems* (such as in Denmark) are the backbone of policy and allow for the efficient development of land taxation, which can become the major tool in the State's attempt to influence land markets;
- *promotion of land for residential use* has been encouraged in countries such as Spain and Sweden which have developed programmes to promote the more efficient and intensive use of under-used or vacant land for affordable residential developments for specific income groups (*Cf.* OECD, 1990, p. 64).

Japan provides a good example of the use of decentralisation policy to reduce the pressure on over-heated housing markets (see Inset 37).

Inset 37. Metropolitan Decentralisation Policy in Japan

Because of the new demand for offices and surplus funds in the real estate market, land prices, especially the prices in the Tokyo business sector, rose remarkably in the latter half of the 1980s. In 1988, the price of commercial building land rose more than 60 per cent compared with the previous year. The rise in real estate prices also led to increases in the price of residential building land. This has to be set beside the lack of high quality housing stock. During the 1980s building boom, land shortages led to high density, small, for rent properties being constructed, which are generally unsuitable for typical families.

Moreover the volatility of the market, especially in the Tokyo metropolitan area, has been highlighted by the more recent falls in price that have accompanied the downturn in the Japanese economy and the falling stock market.

Policy makers in Japan have accepted that to supply a large quantity of affordable housing within the outskirts of Tokyo, where the commuting time is short, is the best way to solve the housing problem. This can be achieved by changing land use through the redevelopment of vacant and derelict land, the removal of dense areas of privately rented wooden housing to be replaced by more appropriate housing, and by relocating public sector offices outside Tokyo and finding ways to encourage the private sector to do likewise.

It is also recognised, however, that finding a viable long-term and comprehensive solution will require both the resolution of current planning debates and reform of the existing basis of the land use planning system, as well as the resolution of the conflict between the use of subsidy mechanisms to support housing, on the one hand, and the desire to protect the long term development of the private sector in Japan, on the other hand.

Housing systems of OECD countries have, through the 1980's and early 1990's, undergone a period of change unprecedented in the post-war era. Following the Depression and World War Two, governments intervened to provide housing at a time when the private sector was unable to meet demand. But interventionist policies in the form of subsidies for housing suppliers and home owners, public-sector housing, credit controls, publicly financed infrastructures, rental market regulations, land-use controls and other regulatory mechanisms remained in force long after the immediate post-war demand was over. With the opening of domestic economies to international trade and finance in the 1990's, however, governments have sought to give greater scope to market forces and institutions in the housing sector. Housing markets have become more volatile and unpredictable, with consequences for macroeconomic conditions and urban patterns that have been difficult to predict.

In July 1993, a meeting entitled "Housing and National Economies", organised jointly by the Joseph Rowntree Foundation and the OECD, discussed the recent boom and bust cycles of housing markets. The meeting concluded that the property sector showed two complementary aspects of the relationship between housing and macroeconomic conditions. Property values were closely influenced by business cycles, interest rates and fiscal policy. Housing price movements were, however, also a factor in economic growth and decline, intensifying trends in other aspects of the economy. It was determined that a well-functioning housing system is critical to the role that cities play in national and international economies.

The importance of housing is not an economic factor alone. Housing is critical to social well-being, affecting access to employment and public services. The nature of housing can determine a freedom of movement for all groups throughout a city as well as the shape of the city itself. The private sector alone cannot provide all the constituents of viable communities, nor can it produce enough housing for the spectrum of social and income groups. Community planning for social, environmental and economic objectives is needed to guide regenerative investments as well as new construction. The major question which arises is how the state can facilitate the operation of the housing system in the market economy on the one hand, while looking after the long-term social, environmental and economic consequences on the other? It was concluded at the meeting that in a period when the character of the next recovery is unclear, governments should take steps to enhance and strengthen the housing system by:

- providing a macroeconomic environment with low long-term inflation;
- encouraging the expansion of the rental housing sector through changes in the tax code and in land-use standards;
- discouraging highly geared mortgages, those with debt equal to 80 per cent or more of the purchase price;
- improving the management of social rental housing, encouraging not-for-profit providers in this sector, giving recipients of housing assistance greater choice and mobility;

- changing land-use planning and regulatory frameworks so that:
  - *i)* they move more quickly; and
  - *ii)* a greater variety of housing and tenure types can be accommodated in a given area, with better co-ordination with public and commercial services;
- giving greater consideration to the existing housing stock so that cycles of obsolescence, decay and renewal will be less severe and destructive;
- promoting consumer awareness of risk and financial instruments that stabilise risk;
- undertaking studies of the changing economic functions of cities so that the spatial needs of businesses and residences can be anticipated with due recognition of their economic and environmental consequences.

Housing finance and access to home ownership

Access to home ownership requires access to considerable funds relative to average earnings for first time buyers. Housing demand can only be made effective if there is an efficient housing finance system to filter or transmit surplus savings or deposits to those who wish to borrow for house purchase. For several decades, regulations in the housing finance system have been seen as important inhibitors for low and moderate income households gaining access to owner occupation.

For example, in some retail savings systems of housing finance (for instance in the United Kingdom), the dependence of lending on inflows from the savings market led to queuing and mortgage rationing. In systems characterised by savings contracts, young potential first home buyers and those without the ability to muster sufficient savings (particularly non-nuclear families) can be excluded from home ownership. By contrast in the United States and Canada, public mortgage insurance has enabled national governments to ensure that citizens have access to finance.

Since the early 1980s, housing finance in most OECD Member countries has become increasingly more integrated with the general finance system: housing finance organisations and practices have been significantly deregulated. Previously it had been the case that housing finance bodies specialised within their own national markets through what was often referred to as a privileged circuit of finance. In the 1980s, these privileges have generally been removed, either by opening up the system to competition from the wider banking sector or centralised lenders, or by allowing other bodies to take over the ownership of the specialised lending institutions.

Though there is some debate as to whether financial deregulation has itself led to higher house prices, it certainly has been associated with considerably higher levels of housing demand and increased housing opportunities for younger households. More consensus exists that the increased fungibility of housing wealth (through additional lending to non-movers) has had important macroeconomic effects on consumption, savings, inflation and even current account balance of payments (see Tables 5.12 and 5.13). It also true that a more efficient and deregulated system of housing finance may have brought forward and intensified the present recession and housing market slump.

Table 5.12 **Financial deregulation in OECD countries: some indicators**

	Average new house multiple of GDP per person	Mean real house price increase	Personal savings ratio		Mortgage debt: GDP	
	1981	1980-89	1982	1989	1983	1989
United Kingdom	6.4	5.9	11.6	5.0	32.1	58.3
Japan		4.2	13.7	14.4	18.7	25.1
United States	6.3	2.0	9.3	7.4	33.5	45.2
Germany	10.2	-0.6	13.8	13.6	22.2	21.9
France	7.6		19.5	11.4	19.2	21.0

Source: OECD Issue Paper (1991), Recent Developments in Financing Home Ownership in the OECD Countries.

Policy responses: improving the housing finance system

Objectives: The finance system is the filter which makes demand programmes effective by easing the access problems of potential purchasers and thereby contributing to affordability goals. To that extent policies that reduce the cost of finance, that make finance more available and that increase competition between lenders, all contribute directly to the increased accessibility objectives of the previous section. At the same time, however, more appropriate controls and greater efficiency can also directly increase affordability and widen the range of choice for all mortgage product consumers. This may lead to greater competition for the disadvantaged from more affluent households.

Table 5.13 **Housing consumption as a percentage of GDP**

Country	1980	1985	1990
Belgium	10.5	12.2	10.2
Denmark	13.0	13.7	14.3
France	10.2	11.9	11.6
Greece	8.1	8.9	8.3
Ireland	6.2	7.5	6.0
Italy	8.1	9.7	9.1
Luxembourg	12.2	12.3	11.8
Netherlands	9.0	11.5	10.8
Portugal	12.0	6.3	8.1
Spain	8.2	10.8	8.2
United Kingdom	11.4	12.4	13.1
West Germany	10.6	12.3	11.5
EU Average		**11.6**	**10.8**
Australia		14.1	12.4
Austria	9.3	11.1	10.4
Canada	11.1	13.1	13.1
Finland	9.7	9.8	9.3
Iceland			9.3
Japan	9.7	11.0	11.2
Norway	7.0	8.4	9.5
New Zealand		9.3	14.0
Switzerland			10.4
Sweden	12.7	13.6	12.4
Turkey		9.4	16.2
United States		13.0	13.0
OECD Average			**11.8**

Source: The Swedish Housing Market in International Comparison, edited by Eva Hedman, Boverket, 1993, Table 5.3.

178

These policy objectives have been set in the context of the more wide-ranging changes in financial systems that affected most OECD countries in the 1980s. The process of financial deregulation has been widespread, affecting countries as various as the United States, Canada, Finland, Denmark and Australia, as well as Southern Europe and the United Kingdom. For example, the institution of stricter capital adequacy ratios for financial institutions generally, which particularly favoured home lending, encouraged these institutions to increase their portfolio of housing debt. The wider use of wholesale funds and greater competition among lenders has increased house purchasers' and investors' choice and has reduced the effective level of credit rationing (institutional requirements permitting). In many places, the greater ability to borrow and this general loosening up of credit is thought to have been a major contributor to housing market and macroeconomic volatility. There has also been increasing concern about the prudential status of lenders, particularly as a result of the Savings and Loans collapse in the United States and similar events in other countries, including Australia. The regulatory authorities in these countries have taken steps to improve capital adequacy ratios and as a consequence the recent trend of deregulation may, to some extent, yet be reversed, with consequences for the supply of loanable funds for affordable housing (see Inset 38).

Instruments: The main aims of measures to reform housing finance have been to increase the flow of funds to housing, to improve consumers' choice, to lower the effective cost of capital and to remove the distortions that resulted from over-regulation. Securitisation is a good example of these initiatives.

In the United States, the need for wholesale finance to increase the supply of loanable mortgage funds has for a long time been met by splitting the servicing and origination functions of a mortgage from the risk-bearing and funding processes. This creates a tradeable financial asset, which in turn stimulates a secondary market, allowing the financial institutions to expand their mortgage supply and, it has been argued, to cut down on their transactions costs through large mortgage issues. While this system remains well developed only in the United States, embryonic secondary markets exist in France, Australia and the United Kingdom. Other countries, such as Spain, Italy and Greece, also see securitisation and secondary markets as a potential way to increase finance for owner occupation.

In Northern Europe, a wholesale market has always been used for housingfinance but in a way that caps credit expansion. Mortgage bonds operate in highly regulated systems in Germany, the Netherlands and Denmark. The bonds remain on company balance sheets and this restricts the ability of the institution to grow.

A good system of housing finance should provide flexibility for borrowers in the face of housing market and labour market volatility, and in the face of price inflation. All countries have some form of mortgage insurance for the lender and these schemes have moved to the private sector in recent years despite worries that the insurance industry would have difficulty levying premia in this area. At the same time borrowers have increased access to private unemployment schemes that will finance mortgage repayments during periods of unemployment. In many countries mortgage interest payments are covered by the social security or housing allowance systems. Mortgagors with some equity can also easily restructure their repayment profile to lessen their current outgoings.

Inflation has been a key affordability constraint because it front loads repayments so that mortgage costs as a proportion of income are much higher in real and nominal terms in the early years of a mortgage. A variety of policies have been used to reduce this cost burden, through the use of subsidies and the restructuring of mortgage costs across the lifetime of the mortgage. Some forms of this rescheduling involve changing the mortgage instrument. In the United States, for example, the federal mortgage refinance agency introduced graduated repayments, by which part of the interest in the early years was simply capitalised into the outstanding mortgage. This arrangement was confined to low income households and involved both guarantees and implicit subsidies. In Finland, an index-linked form of mortgage instrument based on real interest rates has been introduced. These schemes have to be backed by governments simply because the market is not prepared to provide sufficient matching funds without some level of protection against advance repayment or default (see Inset 39). Indexation, involving considerable government intervention, is quite commonly applied in Iceland, applying to all housing finance, and similar protection is found in Denmark and, to a lesser extent, in Sweden.

In Spain, the national government operates a system of compulsory investment ratios which provide direct finance to desired projects, including loans for housing (32 per cent of all official credits went to the state mortgage bank). Interest rate ceilings on deposits kept the cost of finance down until their abolition in 1987. However, since 1977, this protected housing system has been in decline, so that by 1990 only 20 per cent of loans came in this form. In Greece, the liberalisation of the housing finance system led to sharp increases in the cost of credit, so that in 1988 a new system of subsidies was introduced, funded directly by central government. This reduces interest payments for first time buyers subject to the income level of the household. In France, the PAP subsidised loans to low income households are being phased out and are declining in numerical importance.

Regulatory issues

The planning process directly influences the allocation of urban resources and access to services. The regulatory system, be it through zoning, standards or by-laws, is designed to impose order on urban growth, to mediate between

182

competing interests, to assure health and safety, to protect the interests of local residents in terms of the maintenance of property values and, in some contexts, to protect the local tax base which ultimately funds a proportion of the cost of services (see Inset 40).

Inset 40. Regulations and Housing Affordability

Although building standards and planning regulations have contributed to a steady improvement in housing quality in OECD countries, recent studies have questioned whether the current regulatory frameworks permit the development of the kind of housing people need, want or can afford. A certain level of regulation is necessary to ensure adequate housing standards. However, some regulations, by stipulating large minimum lot and house size, single-family detached housing, the use of expensive building materials and so on, restrict development to expensive housing. Such excessive regulations also limit redevelopment and intensification activities, such as the addition of accessory apartments. This kind of development practice tends to exclude those who cannot afford, or do not demand, large houses.

Residential development standards often exceed public health and safety requirements, or are outdated and overly complex. Such over-regulation affects the affordability of housing by restricting the supply of land available for housing (low-income and affordable housing in particular), and by raising costs of construction and rehabilitation by employing high standards for buildings and infrastructure. Not only do excessively high standards of building and land-use regulations add to the cost of new and rehabilitated housing, they also tend to increase operating costs for home owners, tenants, and ratepayers. Components of housing developments that tend to be over-specified or over-sized in zoning and subdivision by-laws and in building codes include lot sizes, setbacks, minimum lot sizes, street widths, parking requirements, water and sewer lines, and construction materials and techniques.

The price and availability of land have major repercussions for housing markets. Zoning regulations governing density and permitted uses have a major influence on land costs; this affects not only the cost of new housing, but that of existing properties as well. Regulations should favour development that optimises land use, especially underutilised, developed land. As noted, definitions of optimal land use are required.

Some issues that need to be addressed are: which building standards and planning regulations present barriers to the provision of low-income and affordable housing, and under which circumstances? How can regulations be redefined to improve housing affordability without jeopardising the ability to meet other planning objectives, such as protecting the environment or the existing housing stock? How can governments identify which standards are appropriate, and when?

Along with policies such as rent controls, these systems of control and regulation have come to be seen, especially though not uniquely in the United States, to be a fundamental barrier to the achievement of affordable housing and the attainment of a more efficient urban housing supply system. In the United States, in 1991 the Bush administration explicitly targeted regulatory barriers as a major hindrance to affordable housing.

Removing barriers to affordable housing

Measures to increase low-income demand for housing, to increase home ownership, and to target affordability programmes are all likely to fail in the long run, if there is insufficient capacity in the supply system to produce and redevelop land for residential use in sufficient variety. Landlords and developers can be subsidised through grants or taxes, measures can be taken to reduce the amplitude of construction industry cycles, the public sector can build directly but in the end there has to be land available for residential building, there have to be building codes which allow rehabilitation and construction work to be economical, and planning systems have to be flexible, realistic and fair.

Barriers to the efficient workings of the housing market cause numerous problems. In the United States, for example, because of the side-effects of regulation, key community employees are forced to live many kilometres from the community they serve. By commuting they harm the environment. Low income and minority households have a hard time finding suitable housing. The elderly cannot find appropriate housing; and young couples find it difficult to find affordable housing in their own community. As a result of regulations that exclude some housing types and small lot sizes or that require developers to build to the highest standard and to incorporate community facilities, house prices can be as much as 35 per cent higher than in the absence of such practices. These requirements effectively prevent multi-family and other affordable housing developments. Building codes are geared toward new construction, making rehabilitation impractical. Different tiers of government have different policy agendas and objectives, and the consequence of this is often that affordable housing developments remain unbuilt. An example of this is the recurring conflict in the United States between environmental protection of species and wetlands and residential development. Similar problems arise in Canada and Australia.

Inset 41. Regulatory Barriers to Affordable Housing in the United States

The local nature of building regulation causes problems that are unique to the housing construction industry. Families most in need of affordable housing often do not reside in the communities where it might be provided, and have little influence on the ordinances controlling the supply of housing. Local regulations are determined by, and attempt to serve the interest of, residents and taxpayers who already live in the community and whose priorities often include open space, "managed growth", enhancement of property values, or maintenance of a particular lifestyle.

Barriers to affordable housing can take many forms at many points in the housing production process. Many barriers are of long-standing, but in recent years new types -- such as growth controls and impact fees -- have been created that are more pernicious than the traditional ones and appear to serve less of a public purpose. The new barriers have raised costs substantially in many jurisdictions and resulted in considerable disparities in the cost of similar houses in different areas of the country.

Processing delays: Approvals and permits have always been part of the building regulatory process but in recent years the process has taken longer and longer. ... These delays can impose heavy costs that ultimately push the price of the housing beyond the reach of moderate and middle-income families.

Environmental regulations: These objectives are certainly legitimate goals of public policy. Unfortunately, they are sometimes used as an excuse to protect the lifestyle of existing residents in a community or to exclude affordable housing.

Subdivision requirements and impact fees: Many communities have imposed increasingly onerous requirements for builders to construct or pay for public facilities. ... In addition, communities have established excessive "gold-plated" standards for infrastructure. These requirements add to total development costs, decrease the density of development, and reduce affordability. Such exactions give a free ride to existing residents, as the cost of amenities benefiting the entire community is transferred to the new generation of home buyers in the form of higher house prices.

Zoning: Zoning and related land use controls are the most powerful instruments that localities wield to regulate the environment. In many communities, the cost of land for new housing now exceeds 50 per cent of total development costs.

Building codes: Building codes have been used in the past to delay the introduction of new, cost-saving technology, but this problem is not as severe as it used to be. Some significant regulatory barriers remain. Many communities do not systematically update their codes when the model codes are revised, while in other communities the model codes are amended or modified to reflect local interests. In addition, problems continue to arise when building codes aimed at new construction are applied to housing rehabilitation. In some communities, local code provisions leave no choice but total reconstruction, when less costly forms of rehabilitation would suffice.

Source: The President's National Urban Policy Report, 1991.

185

Another difficulty is the NIMBY ("Not in My Back Yard") sentiment of many groups and individuals. This enables neighbourhood residents to exert great influence over the electoral and land development processes to the exclusion of non-residents, prospective residents, or, for that matter, all outsiders.

Instruments: The Bush administration in the United States committed itself to finding ways to reduce and remove regulatory barriers to affordable housing (see Inset 41). The United States Housing and Urban Development Department views its role as essentially an enabling one, encouraging state and local governments to remove legal and administrative impediments. In 1989 therefore the United States government set up a major commission to look into the regulatory barriers to affordable housing. The Commission made a number of recommendations concerning the role of federal government, the role of local government and the role of local and private sector participants. These included the following:

-- *Assistance conditional upon barrier-removal strategies*: This and several of the federal policy recommendations were based on providing incentives to local and state tiers of government to reduce barriers.
-- *Housing impact analysis*: Using the federal government as example, the Commission recommended that each federal agency rule change that might have some bearing on the provision and cost of affordable housing should be the subject of an in-depth housing impact analysis, examining its impact on housing and land costs, supply and demand.
-- *Active federal intervention*: This could take the form of legal initiatives, consensus-building about the need for reform and action to encourage the development of model building-codes.
-- *Recognising that states face different situations and any proposals have to be flexible, the Commission recommended that government recognise affordable housing as a legitimate state goal*: The report focused on a number of positive measures, including: the creation of procedures for reconciling local regulations with state goals, the elimination of redundant regulations and the resolution of development disputes; the development of state-wide standards in support of affordable housing; the progression towards the elimination of discrimination against certain types of affordable housing options; and the provision of financial incentives by state governments for affordable housing and local regulatory reform.

In response to these recommendations the United States government came up with a number of proposals. One proposal was the creation of Housing Opportunity Zones, which would be located in areas within a city or county that have significant amounts of vacant land or vacant buildings with potential for rehabilitation for eventual housing production. Federal government would provide incentives in the form of speeded-up planning and grant mechanisms to those communities that most successfully removed regulatory barriers to affordable housing: *e.g.* restrictive zoning, obsolete building codes, complex planning permission and high permit fees.

Policy analysis and guidelines

Access to home ownership

Policies aimed at easing access to owner occupation are common throughout OECD Member countries, relatively successful and increasingly targeted to moderate and lower income households, reflecting the low life cycle savings accumulated by young families, couples and single people. However, recent experience in countries, such as Australia and the United Kingdom, highlights the dangers involved in attempting to extend home ownership to vulnerable groups, so long as interest rates and house prices remain volatile and the employment situation for many remains uncertain.

Assistance for low income renter households

In the short term, some form of subsidy, that minimises interference with the normal workings of the market (*e.g.* rent allowances) is preferable. In the longer term, more housing, including social housing, needs to be produced to meet the demand and the need for affordable rented accommodation. Supply subsidies and tax incentives both have a role to play but especially in a context of public spending constraints, it is important in the longer run that market renting (and social renting) operate in an environment which allows suppliers to make an adequate return for providing a given level of housing quality. Demand-side and supply-side initiatives should work in tandem.

Policies to stabilise markets

Market volatility tends to reflect deeper problems or market failures, notably rigidities in the supply system in the face of unstable housing demand. Microeconomic reform, particularly in the fields of taxation, land supply and land use planning, remains the instrument most likely to improve market stability. Failure to act can have significant public expenditure implications. For just as economic recession naturally pushes budgets into deficit, so the decline in affordable owner occupation and growing mortgage default increase social security expenditure and the need for alternative, often subsidised housing provision.

Housing and mortgage finance

Most OECD governments have encouraged the deregulation of their housing finance systems. As a result, there are more funds available for mortgages through the growth of wholesale and secondary markets. There is a greater variety of mortgage products, including index-linked loans which directly aid affordability by reducing problems of front-end loading. Down-payment conditions have eased in many countries. And consumers are able increasingly to shop at one-stop financial centres when buying a house, thereby greatly reducing transactions costs.

However, following the recent downturn in economic activity and the housing market, innovations in the housing finance sector over the next few years are likely to be consumer-oriented, reflecting greater competition between financial institutions, greater flexibility among mortgage products and lower profit margins than in the 1980s. This may lead to problems in later years.

Moreover it has to be recognised that easier access to finance for the majority of house purchasers may create additional problems for the more disadvantaged if the supply of new or existing housing is not sufficiently responsive.

Lowering regulatory barriers

The supply of adequate affordable housing in urban areas can be encouraged by reducing regulatory barriers, by creating incentives for simpler and more sensible planning and building controls, through inclusionary zoning and through the more sensitive use of impact fees and other forms of planning impost. However, there is an irreducible constraint in democratic societies, namely, that the incumbent majority wants to protect its property values and, implicitly, wants to protect its property from perceived threat.

In many areas therefore more affordable housing will only be built if there is an incentive-compatible mechanism that benefits existing residents while producing affordable housing, for instance, through the diffusion of neighbourhood benefits from new developments. To achieve this, there will have to be serious and continuing consensus-building about the future patterns of land use, about the need for affordable housing, and about its place within the wider questions of the environment, sustainable development, rising property values and mixed land uses. Finally, the supply of affordable housing would be assisted if building codes and many other regulations were standardised. All housing consumers would benefit from the reduction in land, transactions and housing costs associated with wasteful and counter-productive regulations.

The basic problem of transforming a zero-sum or fixed cake into a non-zero sum or larger cake is the same in any planning system where vested interests and different tiers of government meet. The responsiveness of supply to demand pressure is weak in many countries because the conflicts and regulations within the planning system can be exploited by speculators, existing residents and landowners to prevent more affordable forms of housing development. Consensus-building, incentive-compatible policy mechanisms, and the radical simplifying of regulations to uniform standards are essential to tackle the supply problem for affordable housing. One cannot guarantee a swift success with such policies but they would mark a considerable improvement.

The following guidelines for policy are therefore suggested by the conclusions of the project:

- **The issue of housing affordability needs to be set in a multi-sectoral context. Affordability is not simply about housing finance, housing subsidies or construction costs. It relates also to** employment security, macroeconomic policy, land use planning, ecological sustainability, financial competition and a range of other factors.

- Measures to improve housing affordability must be based on a sound understanding of the workings of the local housing market and of the relationship between national, macroeconomic influences -- such as taxation and interest rate policy -- and local market factors -- such as the structure of neighbourhoods, accessibility patterns, the changing location of employment and the responsiveness of local housing supply.

- Policies designed to improve affordability should take into account possible "second round" effects and should assess carefully the risks involved, especially where vulnerable groups -- such as those with unstable incomes or single parent families -- are the targeted clients for affordability initiatives.

- Governments at all levels should recognise the need to involve private sector housing agencies -- landlords, developers, house-builders as well as private employers -- in partnership to address the problems of affordability in the local context. There is a clear need to build a political consensus around viable long-term strategies for affordable housing.

- Broadly-based subsidies, and implicit subsidies from below-cost public infrastructure provision, should be replaced by more selective and carefully targeted programmes to assist those groups most vulnerable to problems of housing affordability. Tax subsidies to owner-occupiers should be reviewed.

- Rental housing provision, both private and public, should be based on market prices and a realistic return on capital, to ensure a buoyant long-term supply of accommodation at minimum public expenditure cost. Barriers to efficient, low-cost private supply should be eliminated.

- However, in the desire to make housing more "affordable", governments should not lose sight of the long run environmental costs of different forms of housing provision and should aim to establish a broadly-based consensus concerning the need to make housing in future compatible with the requirements of an ecologically sustainable urban form.

References

DOLING, J. (1990*a)*, Housing Finance in Finland in MacLennan, D. and Williams, R. (ed), Affordable Housing in Europe. Joseph Rowntree Foundation, York, United Kingdom.

DOLING, J. (1990*b)*, "Housing Finance in Finland", *Urban Studies*, Vol. 27, No. 6.

EUROPEAN LIAISON COMMITTEE OF SOCIAL HOUSING (CECODHAS) (1993), *A Roof Over the Head of Every European: 5 Years of Involvement and Action.*

FANNIE MAE (1991), International Housing Markets: What we know; what we need to know.

GYORKO, J. (1990), "Controlling and Assisting Privately Rented Housing", *Urban Studies*, Vol. 27.

HARLOE, M. (1993), Social Housing in Europe, University of Essex.

HEDMAN, A. (1993), The Swedish Housing Market in International Comparison, Boverket.

HOLMANS, A. (1990), "House Prices: Changes Through Time at National and Sub-national Level". *Government Economic Service*, Working Paper No. 110, London.

KEMP, P. (1990), Income Related Assistance with Housing Costs: A Cross National Comparison. Joseph Rowntree Foundation, York, United Kingdom.

KLEINMAN, M. (1992), Policy Responses to Changing Housing Markets : Towards a European Housing Policy. London School of Economics/ Welfare State Programme WSP/73.

MACLENNAN, D. and GIBB, K. (1989), "Housing Finance and Subsidies in Britain after a Decade of Thatcherism". *Urban Studies*, Vol. 27.

MACLENNAN, D. and GIBB, K. (1993), Nesting, Investing or Just Resting. Joseph Rowntree Foundation, York, United Kingdom.

MINISTRY OF HOUSING AND BUILDING (1989), Distributional Aspects of Housing and Taxation Policies, Denmark.

NELSON, K. and KHADDIRI, J. (1992), "To Whom Should Limited Housing Resources be Directed?" *Housing Policy Debate*, Vol. 3.

OECD (1990), Urban Land Markets: Policies for the 1990s, Paris.

ONTARIO MINISTRY OF HOUSING (1989), *International Home Ownership Policy and Programme Review*.

RENAUD, B. (1990), *Housing Reform in Socialist Countries*, World Bank Discussion Paper.

SCHAEFER, J. (1990), Housing Finance and Subsidy Systems in France, in MacLennan, D. and Williams, R. (ed.), Affordable Housing in Europe. Joseph Rowntree Foundation, York, United Kingdom.

US DEPARTMENT OF HOUSING AND URBAN DEVELOPMENT (HUD) (1991a), *The President's National Urban Policy Report*, Washington D.C.

US DEPARTMENT OF HOUSING AND URBAN DEVELOPMENT (HUD) (1991b), *Not in my Back Yard -- Removing Barriers to Affordable Housing*, Washington D.C.

WORLD BANK (1991), *The Housing Indicators Programme*, Washington D.C.

Chapter 6

The Collection and Use of Data

The need for data

Policy makers in most OECD Member countries have had great difficulty in measuring, describing and explaining constancy, change and disparities in housing, social and environmental conditions in cities. Part of the difficulty has been the lack of systematic data collection. A dynamic data set is required, covering a wide range of sectors across several administrative levels and geographical scales. The limitations of traditional approaches and systems for data collection are widely recognised and a number of reforms have been proposed. These would be designed:

-- to overcome the sectoral division of data;
-- to develop a correspondence or compatibility between statistics referring to different geographical scales;
-- to establish consistent time frames in order to account systematically for constancy and change over time;
-- to develop methods for multi-dimensional accounts of social, economic and environmental characteristics; and
-- to promote "user friendly" systems that can be utilised in different fields.

In principle, there is a broad consensus that three basic types of information ought to be obtained prior to analysing the social, economic and environmental characteristics of cities. These include: *a)* quantitative and qualitative data at the scales of the region, city and neighbourhood; *b)* dynamic or time-series data designed to diagnose and monitor conditions at these scales over an extended time period; and *c)* surveys of the local populations' current expectations and living conditions.

In practice, it is not an easy task to obtain these kinds of information. However, this challenge has been met in some countries, often in the broader context of national programmes related to problems in urban areas.

Experience in France

In France, for example, the following types of data have been assembled as part of a policy programme for social development in cities:

-- reference data on the local population, in order to develop a population profile including demographic, ethnic and health characteristics; an account of the housing stock and of poverty, employment, education, crime, health, citizenship, economic activity and community and public services;

-- data of a quantitative and qualitative kind about urban decay at regional and societal levels including economic and social imbalances and social unrest;

-- data about urban decay within cities including the social stigmatisation of specific neighbourhoods, house types and the development of urban enclaves.

The authors of this programme recognise that there are problems in obtaining these kinds of data at these different geographical scales, particularly the co-ordination of statistics from authorities and institutions working at different administrative levels. In view of these difficulties it is commendable that comprehensive programmes for data collection and monitoring change have been initiated by the Interministerial Committee for Cities (CIV) in France. Although the basic unit of statistical analysis is the urban neighbourhood, an important component of this programme also concerns the formulation and application of policies at the level of the city as a whole (see Inset 42).

The scale of the neighbourhood has been adopted because it corresponds to the level at which low-cost housing associations -- HLM organisations -- are operational. Furthermore, it has been noted that this is the scale that enables dialogue with citizens. The HLM movement consists of about 1 000 organisations and 12 000 administrators who are in direct contact with local government, as well as with the daily circumstances of citizens. The scale of the city is the level for property policy based on factors such as past, present and future housing markets.

Under the auspices of the Interministerial Committee for Cities (CIV) a programme of data collection and analysis at the city and neighbourhood levels has been instituted in France. This comprises the following four types of exercise.

Initial diagnosis

Urban audits (for communes)

- examining the city's main policy areas (urban planning, housing, the economic and social situation, etc.);
- making rapid use of existing studies and reports;
- identifying the main challenges;
- proposing a comprehensive plan;
- stating strategies.

"Satisfaction survey" (for the commune)

- surveying residents to find out what they expect from the city;
- identifying neighbourhoods and issues in need of stronger, more innovative policy;
- inviting municipal services to participate in the design of improved service quality.

Operational phase

Communal real estate plan (for the commune)

- inventory/evaluation of all communal property (buildings, land, public facilities, etc.);
- broad-based diagnosis, obtaining the views of players (municipal services) and partners, and assessing user satisfaction;
- real estate planning;
- action plan and time frame.

Inter-organisational real estate plan (for HLM organisations working in the same commune or housing area)

- pooling information and analyses on the local situation (housing market, urban and social problems, etc.) compiled by housing officers;
- streamlining real estate policy in the various organisations;
- drawing up a joint project contract between local authorities and central government (scheduling, upgrading neighbourhoods, new schemes, etc.).

To date, two types of programmes have been instigated at both the city and neighbourhood levels:

-- **City Housing Agreements**, to address issues related to urban development and housing at city level;
-- **City Contracts** for large cities with particular problems (13 cities are involved);
-- **Social Development of Neighbourhoods** for neighbourhoods with social, cultural and urban handicaps (up to 300 neighbourhoods are involved);
-- **Neighbourhood Agreements** for sectors of a city that fail to function correctly from either a social or urban viewpoint (200 neighbourhoods are eligible).

For these programmes, HLM organisations are the primary operators. They are commissioned to innovate, apply specialist know-how and work with city authorities and central government to formulate and implement policies. Owing to the large number of HLM Organisations the above-mentioned programmes have been applied in many localities.

The programmes instigated by the Interministerial Committee for Cities in France show that an integrative, multi-sectoral approach can be applied both for the collection of data and policy formulation. Since 1981 the stated policy of central government has been to help combat problems in urban neighbourhoods by adopting a partnership with institutions and actors at different levels and over an extended, ongoing period. This commendable approach has led to the co-ordination and standardisation of procedures for collecting data. In concrete terms, a Neighbourhood Tracking System for the Rhône-Alpes Region has been developed, on the initiative of the Secretariat-General for Regional Affairs, by the Planning Department of the Lyon Urban Community in liaison with other Planning Departments in the region (see Figure 1).

Another example of data collection and analysis in France has been carried out by the Social Studies Division of the Institut national de la statistique et des études économiques (INSEE). Demographic, economic and social data have been collected and interpreted in order to identify whether disparities exist between neighbourhoods in a city and between cities; and then to formulate a typology of all neighbourhoods in large cities in France, except the Paris region. The typology that has been elaborated is founded on household size,

Figure 1. **Neighbourhood tracking system**

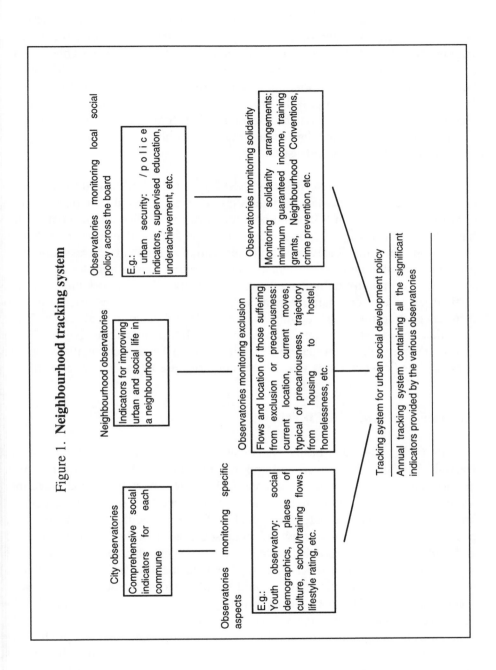

and composition, as well as the socio-professional category of the reference person for each household. The use of data interprets forms of tenure, nationality, type of district and the economy of the city as variables. This approach has enabled the authors to identify the similarities and differences between the social and economic characteristics of urban neighbourhoods. However, while this approach provides a "fine grain" analysis of these characteristics, it remains synchronic rather than longitudinal, and it does not include data relating to the environmental conditions of housing nor an evaluation of state of the infrastructure.

In another comparative study by INSEE however, data related to the social, economic and environmental characteristics of 33 boroughs in London have been compared with those of 335 neighbourhoods in Paris. The characteristics that have been studied include: population trends; population densities; distribution of socio-professional categories, salaries and employment; gross domestic product; commercial property rents; housing tenure; mortality rates and causes of deaths; crime and delinquency and road safety. The authors underline the difficulties of any comparative approach across national boundaries owing to differences in terminology, administrative levels and geographical scales. They note that statistical data are not always available at different levels. These inconsistencies and incompatibilities will have to be overcome if systematic comparisons between cities in different countries are to be developed further.

Experience in other OECD countries

In Finland an area-based statistical description of living conditions in Helsinki has been formulated and applied since the 1950s. The city has been divided into seven major statistical areas. These areas have been subdivided into 33 districts and 117 subdistricts. These subdistricts have been further divided into local areas and the latter into blocks. Data on population structure have been used for a longitudinal study of social segregation in the city between 1955 and 1985. This study established that socio-economic differences between the populations of the subdistricts had declined during this period. In order to recommend how available funds should be allocated to the seven major social service districts of Helsinki, a descriptive system of living conditions and well-being was elaborated and applied using 32 indicators, including income level, education, housing standards and health. A multi-variate analysis of the data was completed to identify those indicators that best reflect the differences between districts while identifying the relative need for social service resources.

In Scotland, areas of urban deprivation have been identified using data from successive population censuses. The analysis of the decennial Census used the statistical technique of principal components analysis to combine 12 indicators of social, economic and housing characteristics into a single deprivation score. This technique was used to rank the 15 000 census districts in Scotland on the basis of this score. Those urban districts categorised among the worst 10 per cent of all districts qualified for support under the Government's Urban Programme. This list of deprived districts has also been used in the selection of initiative areas including the four "New Life for Urban Scotland" partnerships.

Apart from this use of data at a national level in Scotland, there have been important contributions at the district or local level. For example, the Strathclyde Regional Council has compiled three compendiums of data concerning the demographic, economic, social and health characteristics of the population of the area served by the Regional Council (*Cf.* Strathclyde Regional Council, 1992) (see Inset 43).

The Strathclyde Regional Council has also published three in-depth studies of poverty in Strathclyde (*Cf.* Strathclyde Regional Council, 1988-92). These studies present data from a variety of sources that identify the nature and extent of poverty in the Region during the 1980s. In general, the three groups most vulnerable to poverty are households with lone-parents, single young people, or very elderly people. The increase in poverty during the last decade is largely due to the rise in lone-parent households and the increase in unemployment, the decline in full employment or the increasing number of jobs which are part-time. Collectively, the combined use of these sources of data shows that increases in poverty in the Strathclyde Region have been greater in areas of multiple social and economic deprivation which are concentrated more in urban than in rural areas. These sources also enable comparisons between demographic, social and economic characteristics of the total population of Scotland, as well as the United Kingdom as a whole.

This use in Scotland of past and present data together with projections for the next seven year period is one illustration of how a dynamic multi-sectoral data base can be developed at diverse geographical scales to identify the strengths and weaknesses of particular areas. The information can then be used at different political levels to formulate, implement and evaluate policies at these geographical scales. Despite these positive aspects of the data base, however, it is noteworthy that there is no comprehensive source of information about housing and urban conditions in the region, especially about changes through improvement and demolition. The results of a recent national house condition survey are expected to fill this gap.

Inset 43. Data Collection in the Strathclyde Region, Scotland

The **Strathclyde Regional Council** has compiled three compendiums of data concerning the demographic, economic, social and health characteristics of the population of the area served by the Regional Council.

The Strathclyde Region is subdivided into 6 subregions and 19 districts which are compared systematically. The data in each compendium are presented in 12 sections:

- past, present and projected populations by age from 1981 to 1997;
- past, present and projected household size, structure and composition for the same period;
- housing stock by tenure, prices and rents, capital expenditure, waiting lists, house lettings and homelessness;
- employment by vocational sectors;
- unemployment by age, gender, length of time employed and vocational sectors;
- income including benefits and wages;
- poverty including income support, housing and supplementary benefits, family income supplements and debts;
- crimes and offences including racial incidents;
- education including enrolments, attainment levels and destinations of school leavers;
- social work including young children, adolescents and the elderly receiving assistance or institutional care;
- multiple deprivation in urban and rural areas;
- health in terms of accidents, life expectancy, infant mortality, birth and death rates.

In the Netherlands, since 1989, some municipal authorities including the City of Rotterdam, have adopted what they term "programmes of social renewal" which have subsequently been endorsed by the national government. These programmes have been based largely on statistical evidence about the number and distribution of ethnic minorities, the number of unemployed by sector, the state of repair of housing and the use of health and care services. This is one example of how local and national governments have adopted data led and data supported policies. Reference can also be made to the identification of the housing and living conditions of minority groups in Switzerland, as well as the regulation of land and housing markets in several Member countries of the OECD (*Cf.* OECD, 1992). In this area, authorities in Denmark, Japan and the United Kingdom have sought to understand how their land markets operate by developing a dynamic and long-term data base that can lead to the identification of patterns and trends (see Inset 44 for experience in Australia).

Inset 44. An Analysis of Urban Health Data in Australia

In Australia, the Commonwealth Department of Human Services and Health has recently published "A Social Health Atlas of Australia" (Cf. Glover and Woollacott, 1992). This two volume publication of maps, charts and tables presents a multi-dimensional account of the health, social and economic well-being of the nation by local government areas. This approach links data related to mortality and morbidity (*e.g.* accidents, cancer, heart disease, asthma, suicide, etc.) to the socio-economic status of the population and their lifestyle (*e.g.* smoking, alcohol consumption, obesity, etc.). Hence, for each city of more than 10 000 citizens a set of maps and charts show, for example, where single-parent households live, where there are low-income households, where unskilled workers are located, where adolescents leave school early to seek employment, where rates of infant mortality are relatively low and high, and so on.

This multi-dimensional and inter-sectoral approach provides overlays of socio-economic maps and health maps, not only in terms of geographical location but also with respect to specific social groups; for example, women of the lowest socio-economic group have more than average serious chronic illnesses and they are more likely to be overweight, smokers and single parents, who receive income support from the government. This approach makes possible the identification of inequalities not only defined in terms of a population profile but also according to local government districts in particular cities.

The data used in this two volume publication were supplied by the Australian Bureau of Statistics, other federal and state government departments and several non-government organisations. The basic unit for comparison is the statistical local area.

The use of data for policy formulation, impact assessment and evaluation

In Australia, a National Housing Strategy was established by the Commonwealth Government in 1990 to review housing and urban policies. The final report of this venture published in 1992 is the first comprehensive statement of policies in these fields since 1945 (*Cf.* Australia, Department of Health, Housing and Community Services, 1992). This report synthesises the effects of demographic change, the state of environmental issues, the need to improve housing equity and micro-economic reforms in the construction industry. From this perspective, the report emphasized the importance of housing policies being integrated with others including policies on taxation and urban development. The basic policy goals are that citizens will have a greater choice of housing types, sizes and localities that are affordable. This will enable high rates of owner occupation within existing housing markets. Furthermore, viable forms of public and community housing and assistance to those who pay more than one fifth of their income on rent are basic policy goals. These goals are to be achieved by means of a new National Urban Development Programme, a Building Better Cities Program and the introduction of an expanded Community Housing Programme and a new Social Housing Subsidy Programme under the Commonwealth/State Housing Agreement. A comprehensive survey of the way Australians are housed is planned for 1994-95 by the Australian Bureau of Statistics. This survey will seek information about housing conditions, costs and amenities; the characteristics of households including their residential biography; and access to services. Data from this survey will allow analysis of housing issues, such as accessibility to and availability of affordable housing; the adequacy and suitability of the current housing stock; and the ease of access to services by households.

The Australian Government has also established a National Housing and Urban Research Institute for data collection and economic, planning and housing research. Moreover, the extant Institute of Health and Welfare has had its charter extended to cover data collection, including Commonwealth-State welfare programme data, extending to the non-government welfare sector in the future. This includes the collection of data about housing assistance.

In France, action plans for urban social development are implemented once underprivileged urban areas and priority neighbourhoods have been identified by the Neighbourhood Tracking System and other complementary uses of data presented in the preceding section. The Neighbourhood Tracking System is the principal tool for obtaining information to help formulate and evaluate policies. Trends in specific neighbourhoods are explicitly related to developments and conditions at other administrative levels and geographical scales, notably the characteristics of, and trends in, the city and the region as a whole. This instrument enables impacts of decentralisation, for example, to be considered simultaneously with developments in specific neighbourhoods. The approach is designed to encourage dialogue between partners in the urban regeneration process, especially between local and regional authorities and HLM organisations. In this respect current urban policies and programmes have been enacted by contracts signed by national, regional and local authorities. The broad aim is to improve the quality of life of the residents of neighbourhoods designated for priority action, following the analysis of multi-dimensional data by INSEE described above (*Cf.* INSEE, 1992). In all, three million citizens, most of whom reside in low-cost housing estates in the suburbs of the largest cities, are implicated by this programme. These neighbourhoods are characterised by a relatively young, foreign population with a relatively high rate of unemployment. Nonetheless, the analysis of data shows that generalisations of this kind should not overlook some significant local and regional differences.

The neighbourhoods have been designated by the three tiers of authority following analysis of the national census returns by INSEE. This analysis has led to the formulation of two categories of priority neighbourhoods. The first category consists of those neighbourhoods located in an agglomeration or city which is suffering from long-term economic decline. This is the case of 30 per cent of all neighbourhoods located in the region of Nord-Pas-de-Calais; of 25 per cent of those in the region of Provence-Alpes-Côte d'Azur; and of 7 per cent of those in the region of Lorraine; whereas at a national level there are 23 per cent of neighbourhoods in this category. Each of the neighbourhoods in this category has an unemployment rate which is about the same as that of the surrounding municipality or agglomeration, whereas it is about twice as high as the national average.

The second category of priority neighbourhoods is composed of localities of exclusion. In these neighbourhoods the unemployment rate of about 15.8 per cent is more than double the rate of 7.2 per cent for the region or agglomeration as a whole. Generally, these neighbourhoods are usually located in regions with relatively low levels of unemployment. This is the case for nearly all the priority neighbourhoods located in the region of Alsace. The effects of exclusion can be reinforced by the modernisation of the urban or regional economy, especially if this process assumes that urban neighbourhoods are like nodes that are independent of economic activities, and the qualifications of the locally unemployed. From this perspective no transition from an undesirable to a more desirable situation is considered by policy makers.

Collectively, over 60 per cent of the priority neighbourhoods are localised in agglomerations with more than 100 000 residents, whereas 25 per cent are in cities with less than 50 000 residents and 10 per cent are in towns with less than 10 000 residents. Bearing this distribution in mind it is not surprising that the largest cities have instigated the most policies and programmes to promote social development. At a national level the Ile-de-France is the agglomeration with the greatest concentration of contracts between authorities, as well as the highest concentration of residents implicated by them. In fact it includes 96 priority neighbourhoods, three of which are in the centre of Paris, and 52 on the outskirts at an average distance of 18 kilometres from the centre. The Nord-Pas-de-Calais region has the largest number of residents living in priority neighbourhoods, followed by Provence-Alpes-Côte d'Azur, then Corsica and the Lorraine region.

Beyond the localisation of priority neighbourhoods, another of their characteristics is their spatial demarcation and detachment from the urban agglomeration as a whole. This often occurs following the construction of rail and road thoroughfares which are not meant to serve the residents of these neighbourhoods. In fact, transportation and infrastructure are limited, as only 40 per cent of all priority neighbourhoods are served by a railway station.

In general, the priority neighbourhoods have a rate of unemployment about double that of the national average. Moreover, the unemployment levels of both young and female residents is relatively high, and those who have no employment remain unemployed for a longer period. Again there are significant regional variations that should be borne in mind.

The housing in priority neighbourhoods is often, yet not always, provided by HLM organisations. The residential buildings are dominated by high towers or long slab blocks. According to the 1990 census returns, 55 per cent of households living in the 499 neighbourhoods which have been analysed in detail are renters of an HLM housing unit (whereas at a national level 15 per cent of all households rent these kinds of housing, and 20 per cent of households in urban areas rent them). Moreover, one third of all housing units in these neighbourhoods are in residential buildings with 20 or more flats, and about two-thirds are in residential buildings with 10 or more flats. Furthermore, two-thirds of all housing in these neighbourhoods was built between 1949 and 1971, whereas only one third of all occupied housing in France was constructed during this period. In contrast, only 4 per cent of all residential buildings in these neighbourhoods was constructed after 1982, whereas 13 per cent of the housing stock in France has been built since that year.

Given that all housing units in the priority neighbourhoods were not provided by HLM organisations, it is noteworthy that old workers' housing and substandard private rental units, including both detached and semi-detached housing units, are commonly below normal standards of comfort in the regions of Lorraine and Nord-Pas-de-Calais. Some regions such as Provence-Alpes-Côte d'Azur include several neighbourhoods with abandoned substandard buildings.

The housing areas in priority neighbourhoods are also characterised by relatively large households. In 1990, 7.5 per cent of households in these neighbourhoods included 6 or more persons, compared with only 3.1 per cent in the urban agglomerations of which they are a part. Furthermore, the local population comprises 18.3 per cent of foreigners, compared with 6.3 per cent for France as a whole, and 9 per cent for the urban agglomerations. The effect of ethnic concentration is accentuated by the fact that 81 per cent of foreigners living in priority neighbourhoods did not emigrate to France from a European country. Nonetheless, it is noteworthy that a quarter of all priority neighbourhoods have less foreign residents than the urban agglomerations in which they are located and 40 neighbourhoods have less foreign residents than the national average. Hence, the in-depth analysis of data shows that generalisations cannot be made at either local or regional levels. Between 1989 and 1993 procedures for the social development of priority neighbourhoods were enacted with 363 communes. Concurrently, 407 conventions have been signed by communal, regional and national authorities. In all, 546 neighbourhoods are implicated by this joint programme.

The work of the Institut national de la statistique et des études économiques (INSEE) in France shows that in-depth studies of data can identify the multi-dimensional nature of deprivation in urban areas. Furthermore, when this use of data is reapplied at repeated intervals it is possible to show improvements or decline in the economic, social and environmental conditions of urban areas. In sum, the approach elaborated and applied by INSEE provides a useful instrument for both researchers and decision makers.

In Canada, a Core Housing Needs Model has been elaborated to establish whether housing conditions fall below norms calculated with respect to adequacy, suitability and affordability. The main objective of this model is to establish an explicit relationship between information about housing needs and an equitable housing policy, as shown in Figure 2. The model enables administrators to identify those deprived areas and underprivileged groups which do not have access to market housing that is affordable, in adequate condition, and of suitable size. This information enables the federal government to establish the number, types and locations of households in need, in order to decide whether to regulate the design and delivery of new housing, and to evaluate existing social housing policies. In 1990, 1.16 million or 12 per cent of all Canadian households were confronted by core housing need (see Inset 33).

Figure 2. **Core housing need measurement in Canada**

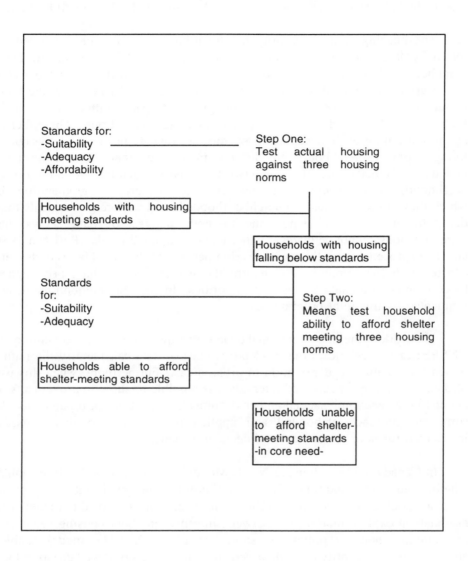

Standards for:
-Suitability ——————————— Step One:
-Adequacy   Test actual housing
-Affordability   against three housing
                                         norms

Households with housing
meeting standards ——————————

                                    Households with housing
                                    falling below standards

Standards
for: ———————————
-Suitability   Step Two:
-Adequacy   Means test household
                                         ability to afford shelter
                                         meeting three housing
                                         norms

Households able to afford
shelter-meeting standards ——————————

                                    Households unable
                                    to afford shelter-
                                    meeting standards
                                    -in core need-

It is notable that all data for the measurement of core housing needs are not available from the national census returns. In addition the long time-lag between the collection and availability of census data means that information is never current. For these reasons comprehensive housing questions are periodically sponsored on Canada's Labour Force Survey (LFS) to provide a complete and timely source of housing needs information. Statistics Canada, Canada's national statistical agency, administers the survey with extensive input by Canada Mortgage and Housing Corporation in collaboration with provincial housing representatives (see Inset 45).

Inset 45. **The Canadian Housing Information Centre**

The Canada Mortgage and Housing Corporation (CMHC) includes the Canadian Housing Information Centre, which acts as a central information source for practitioners in the housing field throughout Canada. The Centre not only includes information on housing and urban policies in Canada, but also from countries around the world.

The Canada Mortgage and Housing Corporation (CMHC) has been active in the collection, analysis and distribution of data about housing market conditions, trends and forecasts. Moreover, the Statistical Services Division of CMHC provides explicit links between the housing sector and other sectors. This Division co-ordinates several CMHC Surveys about housing starts and completions, market absorption rates, and rental market vacancies and rents. Although the evaluation of social housing policy in Canada (which includes a third of the total housing stock) is based largely on cost-effective programming and management, it is also appraised in relation to programmes concerning health, education, income support, taxation and community based services. Given these multi-dimensional criteria, the Canada Mortgage and Housing Corporation collaborates with several federal government departments and authorities as well as locally based institutions and associations. This collaboration between administration at different levels is similar to the partnership approach applied in France, the Netherlands and the United Kingdom.

These surveys have overcome the above-mentioned limitations, and illustrate the pertinence of collaboration between diverse national agencies for systematic data collection. They explicitly relate demographic, social and economic characteristics to household living conditions. However, they tend to devalue the quality of urban neighbourhoods and the environmental conditions of the region. Finally, it is important to note that the homeless and those accommodated in institutionalised housing are not included in these surveys. Hence, although these subjects are addressed elsewhere, a more integrative approach could be used to measure core housing needs.

The use of indicators

Indicators can provide an alternative to more extensive programmes of data collection and analysis. A well chosen indicator can assist in:

-- measuring and interpreting past improvements or decline in these conditions;
-- predicting probable changes from similar processes in the immediate future;
-- monitoring conditions prior to and following policy implementation;
-- proposing improvements.

The choice of indicators depends on definitions (which are context dependent); measurement techniques (which are envisaged in terms of level of detail, accuracy and compatibility); and the purpose of the indicator (which should be related to the objectives and priorities of those who use them). As a result there are likely to be divergent views between authorities, institutions and groups who use indicators of environmental, social and economic conditions in urban areas. A clear distinction should be made between those indices of environmental, social and economic conditions that can be measured objectively, and those which depend on a subjective evaluation of what is "acceptable". Such judgements are bound to vary between cultures, from group to group within the same society, between individuals and over the course of time.

A number of international organisations and some national authorities in Member countries of the OECD have elaborated and applied sets of indicators to measure, monitor and compare environmental, economic and social conditions. The OECD, for example, has organised working groups specifically devoted to urban environmental indicators and has published the results of case studies conducted in Indianapolis, London, Rouen, Stockholm, Vienna and Zurich (*Cf.* OECD, 1978). More recently, housing needs indicators have been elaborated and applied in some Member countries of the OECD including Canada, the United Kingdom and the United States. Currently, a Housing Indicators Programme is being conducted jointly by the World Bank and the United Nations Centre for Human Settlements (Habitat) (*Cf.* World Bank, 1992). This programme is one component of the response to the "Global Shelter

Strategy for the Year 2000" adopted by the General Assembly of the United Nations in 1988. This charter recognised the significant contribution of the private formal and informal sectors to housing, and it requested a shift in the role of government from that of "provider" to "enabler" of housing.

The general aim of the Housing Indicators Programme, launched in October 1992, is to develop conceptual, analytical and institutional frameworks for managing the housing sector using a holistic perspective. The specific goals of this programme include four objectives:

-- to elaborate a framework for monitoring the performance of the housing sector;
-- to create a set of practical tools which measure performance by using quantitative, policy-sensitive indicators, and to test them in several countries;
-- to provide new empirical information about the high stake of housing policy for all societies, especially their economies;
-- to initiate new institutional frameworks, that will be more appropriate for formulating and implementing new housing policies based on research findings, and to improve the management of the housing sector.

The responsible officers of this programme acknowledge the large variety of housing conditions within countries. Consequently, they state that it does not appear sensible or meaningful for data related to housing indicators to be collected at national levels (*Cf.* Angel *et al.*, 1992).

The United Nations Housing Indicators Programme has formulated, tested and applied a set of key housing indicators starting with one urban area or city in each of the 52 participating countries. The applications are being extended to other cities, followed by the urban agglomerations as a whole and then rural areas. The criteria for the selection of indicators are that:

-- they should refer to the main constituents of the housing sector;
-- they should be relatively few to enable repeated and systematic data collection every two years at a reasonable cost;
-- they should be policy sensitive and relatively easy to interpret by policy makers.

The selected indicators are shown in Inset 46.

In the United Kingdom, the Department of the Environment has adopted data-supported policies to tackle the economic, social and environmental problems of urban areas. Drawing on Census and other data, an Index of Deprivation has been formulated, combining indicators on unemployment, overcrowding, housing amenities and population groups at risk of disadvantage. This produced a deprivation "score" for 110 000 areas at the neighbourhood level, *i.e.* areas with about 150 households or 500 persons. These areas are capable of being aggregated and used for ranking local authorities in terms of their relative urban problems and also for defining the spatial targeting of policy instruments. This Index of Deprivation has been used, in combination with updated unemployment statistics, to designate those local authorities which should receive urban aid and to target other policy instruments.

The monitoring of individual programmes against performance criteria is undertaken routinely and evaluation has been made a requirement of all government policies and programmes. Programmes are measured against their stated objectives and value for money criteria in terms of efficiency, economy and effectiveness. In addition, factors are considered such as deadweight (the extent to which projects within a programme would have gone ahead irrespective of government assistance), displacement (where increased employment resulting from assisted projects is achieved at the expense of unassisted competitors) and leverage (the ratio of public to private sector investment). The purpose of all evaluative work is to feed back into policy and programme development to improve cost-effectiveness.

Within the United Kingdom, the Estate Action Programmes, Housing Renewal Areas and the programmes of ten Urban Development Corporations in England are all designed to reduce, or overcome, housing deprivation and decline, while improving educational and recreational facilities, and reducing crime and delinquency in inner city areas. For this purpose, a General Needs Indicator (GNI) and a Housing Needs Indicator (HNI) have been elaborated and applied as composite measures of socio-economic and housing problems of residents in different geographical areas. While these two indicators are similar in composition, the GNI applies to local housing authorities, whereas the HNI applies to housing associations. These indicators enable housing resources to be allocated on an equitable basis according to data and information that is compared at the level of Housing Corporation Regions for particular groups (*e.g.* the disabled, the elderly and the homeless).

The calculation of need is based on a three-step process:

-- a needs assessment based on nine weighted indicators;
-- a cost compensation using a multiplier to the GNI and HNI scores of authorities in order to account for regional differences in the cost of new building or renovation works;
-- an allowance for Urban Programme Area Enhancement based on the number of deprived Enumeration Districts that identify multiple deprivation.

211

The composition of the General Needs Indicator and the Housing Needs Indicator for 1992-93 is shown in Table 6.1.

Table 6.1 **General Needs Indicator (GNI) and Housing Needs Indicator (HNI) for England, 1992-93 indicator shares**

General Needs Indicator (GNI) Indicator	1992-93 Indicator shares % Share
New provision and general group	**45**
Homelessness	20
Temporary accommodation	5
Overcrowding	4
Full household dwelling balance	3
Marginal household dwelling balance	4
Elderly needs	3
Disabled needs	3
Access to owner occupation	3
Local authority renovation group	**50**
Local authority stock condition	50
Private sector renovation group	**5**
Private sector stock condition	3
Defective dwellings	2

Housing Needs Indicator (HNI) Indicator	1992-93 Indicator shares % Share
New provision and general group	**73**
Homelessness	14
Temporary accommodation	4
Access to owner occupation	4
Overcrowding	17
Marginal household dwelling balance	8
Full household dwelling balance	8
Elderly needs	14
Disabled needs	4
Private sector renovation group	**27**
Private sector stock condition	27

A growing number of cities in Member countries of the OECD have made a commitment to the World Health Organisation's Healthy Cities Project (*Cf.* Ashton, 1992). This project has established a network of cities that share a common goal, to promote and experiment new ways of promoting health and improving the quality of living conditions in cities. The project endeavours to encourage political commitment to this goal, to share ideas and experiences between cities, to innovate action plans and to encourage institutional change. Health is considered, together with environmental conditions, as a social and political responsibility, as well as a matter of household and individual choice (see Inset 47).

Inset 47. Healthy Cities Indicators in Europe and Canada

In Europe and Canada, a set of health and social and environmental indicators for the monitoring of health planning and for assessing the progress of this project is being formulated and evaluated under the World Health Organisation's Healthy Cities Project. These are based largely on experience in Barcelona, Milano, Nancy and Montreal (Quebec).

These indicators include:

- health indicators (mortality and morbidity rates);
- health service indicators (availability, accessibility, etc.);
- environmental indicators (air and water quality, nuisances, population and room densities, green space, recreation facilities and public transport...);
- socio-economic indicators (including household data, homelessness, unemployment, poverty, substandard housing, crime and delinquency).

All these indicators are intended:

- to encompass both objective and subjective criteria;
- to incorporate both quantitative measures and qualitative statements;
- to reflect concern both for the population as a whole and for specific target groups; and
- to focus on epidemiology, as well as health promotion.

This project is implemented by multi-city action plans that are intended to encourage innovative policies. In some regions, such as those around the Baltic Sea, a network of cities are actively collaborating to enact a plan. The objectives and priorities of each city vary according to local conditions and problems, such as the incidence of air and water pollution, or the efficiency of solid waste management (*Cf.* World Health Organisation, 1992).

The Healthy Cities Project is significant: because it has elaborated an integrative approach; and because it not only seeks to identify and treat the social, economic and environmental symptoms of urban problems, but also aims to formulate, implement and evaluate preventive policies and programmes.

Impact analysis

A small yet growing number of governments acknowledge that impact assessment of project plans is necessary for effective policy formulation prior to project implementation. These assessments can help resolve multi-dimensional problems and complex urban issues by facilitating the application of inter-sectoral approaches. In order to achieve long-lasting and sustainable outcomes, it is necessary to establish a balance between complementary actions which are mutually supportive and which minimise negative impacts. New methods are necessary in order to assess the impacts of any policy or set of plans in urban areas. Such methods should:

-- assess both the intended and the unintended outcomes of a proposed policy, project or plan for a specific locality so that the proposal can be discussed among all parties involved, including local residents;
-- account for emerging problems resulting from external factors and unintended side effects during the implementation of a policy, plan or project;
-- provide a basis for the sharing of tasks and costs between the parties involved in the project;
-- contribute to an improved short-term and long-term understanding of the inter-relations between policies, plans and projects which are effective in dealing with urban problems;
-- provide a bench-mark document for the evaluation of policies and plans, once the projects stemming from them have been implemented.

Impact assessments including economic, environmental, health and social criteria need to be integrated into policy formulation for project definition and then evaluation after implementation. Each type of assessment requires its own specific kind of data and time span: economic impact assessments deal with monetary values and usually target effects in the near-future; environmental impact assessments deal with ecological and biological variables over several decades; health and social impact assessments are concerned with a variety of human impacts that may occur within the time span of one or more generations. The objective of these impact assessments is to maximise the positive outcomes and minimise the negative consequences of specific projects.

Policy analysis and guidelines

Although there have been encouraging and significant advances in the collection and uses of data in many Member countries of the OECD, in too many cases the overall situation remains unco-ordinated and piecemeal. Relatively few governments, authorities and institutions have collaborated to develop a dynamic, multi-dimensional data base for use as an archive of information for the analysis of living environments in cities. There is a pressing need for the development of Co-ordinated Information Systems.

Co-ordinated information management for urban affairs stems from recognition of the fact that the collection and updating of data is an important resource for urban policy administration, especially decision making and monitoring. No single-focus information system can equal the potential of a Co-ordinated Information System to support an inter-sectoral and an inter-organisational approach. A recent report of an OECD Working Group on Urban Affairs, however, found that only a few countries have formulated explicitly a common strategy for the definition and application of Co-ordinated Information Systems.

Much collected data are not only delimited according to traditional administrative and sectoral approaches, but may be even further defined to meet precise project-oriented objectives. In contrast, the aim of an information management policy based on the Co-ordinated Information Systems (CIS) approach should be to enable diverse groups of users to co-ordinate and integrate different types of data and information for multi-sectoral uses. From this perspective an overall information management policy should examine:

-- how to formulate and apply a holistic conceptual framework for networking diverse types of data and information within and across sectors;
-- how to elaborate and apply appropriate tools to deal with information flows between the public and private sectors as well as among authorities, institutions and firms in the same sector;

-- how to promote and co-ordinate the interest and input of authorities, institutions and firms to rationalise the basic units of recorded data and information.

In principle, the formulation and application of Co-ordinated Information Systems should overcome the piecemeal approach commonly applied for data collection by providing a co-ordinated network of information across different sectors and between parties in the same sector. However, it is necessary to recognise that there are many difficulties involved in sharing and transferring data and information:

-- diverse, sometimes incompatible languages, formats and systems of hardware and software:
-- the lack of protocols for standardisation that adequately reflect the personal, organisational and institutional requirements of both current and potential users;
-- the need for new collaborative ties between parties in the public and private sectors, and between those in the same sector;
-- the need also for new policy initiatives to harmonise concepts, definitions and indicators; ..
-- problems concerning access to data, confidentiality or privacy and the circulation of information which prevent collaboration and co-ordination between users.

There remain many difficulties associated with the definition and application of data-led and data-supported policies to counteract urban problems. In many respects this is not surprising, since these problems are often specific to their context. For example, in Turkey, the focus of attention has been on ways and means to integrate squatter settlements, that account for about quarter of the housing stock. Concurrently, in Italy, attention has concentrated on policies to counteract immigration in order to ease the burden it provokes on inner city areas. At the same time, in Spain, housing affordability has been a priority and policies to regulate both supply and demand, using specific fiscal measures and legislation, have been implemented. These diverse policies and programmes point to the need for different types of data, relating to different geographical scales, if they are to be evaluated systematically.

But despite the significant differences between countries, several countries, for example Belgium, Finland, Sweden, France and the United Kingdom, have shown that the careful analysis of data can form the basis for an area-based approach to the improvement of housing and living conditions in urban and suburban areas. The role of data remains critical to the definition, evaluation and monitoring of area-based programmes and policies for urban regeneration.

The following guidelines for policy are therefore suggested by the conclusions of the project:

- **The need for adequate and up-to-date area-based data to form a basis for the formulation of policies to address the social, environmental and economic problems of disadvantaged neighbourhoods should be clearly acknowledged.**
- **Governments should review the data needs for urban regeneration to identify priority categories, with particular reference to:**

    i) **appropriate geographical scales;**
    ii) **availability of time series;**
    iii) **co-ordination between economic, social and environmental data.**

- **Traditional "hard" data on urban conditions -- such as data relating to housing, employment and transportation -- should be supplemented both by periodic qualitative assessments of local social, environmental and housing conditions in disadvantaged neighbourhoods and by continuous monitoring of community attitudes and aspirations.**
- **A Co-ordinated Information Management system for urban and housing policy should be instituted, based on the integration of previously distinct data collection exercises.**
- **Data needs and data collection responsibilities should be assessed in the context of a partnership between public and private agencies, with a view to meeting the diverse needs of groups of users.**
- **A set of basic indicators should be constructed, in association with community groups, private business interests and voluntary organisations, both to provide a continuing source of information about urban and housing conditions as a basis for building a wider political consensus about the need for action and as a basis for the allocation of scarce resources.**
- **Standard procedures and protocols should be established to enable all agencies and groups of data users to relate new and existing data sources to the issues under consideration.**

References

ANGEL, S., MAYO, S. and STEPHEN, W. Jr. (1992), *The Housing Indicators Programme: A Report on Progress and Plans for the Future*, Paper presented at the International Conference on Housing Indicators in Europe, at Delft, 2 & 3 November.

ASHTON, J. (ed.) (1992), *Healthy Cities*, Milton Keynes, United Kingdom; Open University Press.

AUSTRALIA, Department of Health, *Housing and Community Services (1992), Housing-Choices for a Changing Nation*, Canberra.

FRANCE, INSEE (1992), *Les quartiers prioritaires de la politique de la ville*, INSEE Première, No. 234, December.

GLOVER, J. and WOOLLACOTT, T. (1992), *A Social Health Atlas of Australia*, Canberra.

OECD (1978), *Urban Environmental Indicators*, Paris.

OECD (1992), *Urban Land Markets: Policies for the 1990's*, Paris.

STRATHCLYDE REGIONAL COUNCIL (1988-1992), *Poverty in Strathclyde: A Statistical Analysis*, (Reports Nos. 1, 2 and 3), Glasgow.

STRATHCLYDE REGIONAL COUNCIL (1992), *Strathclyde Social Trends*, No. 3, Glasgow.

WORLD BANK (1992), *The Housing Indicators Programme Extensive Survey, Preliminary Results*, Washington D.C., June.

WORLD HEALTH ORGANISATION (1992), *The Multi-city Action Plan on Baltic Cities and Indicators*, Regional Office for Europe, Copenhagen.

Chapter 7

Examples of the Multi-sectoral Approach:
National Strategies and Local Initiatives

The search for an effective but sustainable programme for urban renewal has led many Member countries to develop multi-sectoral programmes. Though they were meeting a common challenge, each country followed an individual path, particularly suited to its urban problems and its institutional arrangements, for the development of such multi-sectoral programmes.

Member countries were invited to present case studies that would illustrate their multi-sectoral approach, providing details regarding objectives, scale of operation, sources of funding, partners and implementation methods. In this chapter, a number of these case studies are summarised, for the purposes of identifying promising avenues for policy development, good practice and successful implementation strategies. Where available, the results of any evaluations have been included. Following the case studies, the multi-sectoral approaches are compared to highlight key points that would be beneficial to OECD countries.

Implementing multi-sectoral policies through partnerships

The reliance on multi-sectoral policies calls for new methods of policy development and implementation. It requires a process which involves citizens in determining their destiny while it engages stake-holders, mobilises political will and harnesses private sector investment to achieve strategic and equitable outcomes. Because of the involvement of partners it is possible to integrate international trends, national objectives, city aspirations and citizens welfare in the objectives of partnered action. Such partnerships, created to deal with urban problems, are involved in problem definition, priority setting, programme design, customisation and implementation.

Depending on the nature of the objectives, a variety of partners can be invited to make their contributions. Partnerships should be built on shared interests, reciprocal support and mutual benefit with each partner contributing according to their respective resources, strengths and areas of expertise. Reciprocity is built on valuing the resources of the partners, whether it is the sweat equity of residents, entrepreneurship of retailers or the altruism of volunteers. In synergistic action, the varying requirements of each partner, such as the need for public accountability of governments, profit for private sector organisations and personal gratification for volunteers, must be recognised.

There is a great deal of variation and experimentation in the models of joint action among the Member countries. The partnerships models in use among the OECD countries vary with respect to polarity and intensity on five scales, which are described below.

-- Composition: Membership in the partnership can vary in range and number. A good mix of partners is essential for legitimacy and synergy. A diverse composition enables compensating for weaknesses and reinforcing strengths of individual members. Some partnerships are local in nature, based on vested interests, stake holders and groups impacted. Others have a wider membership, where local interests are augmented with outside participants, such as other levels of government, potential investors and business. Local membership promotes buy-in and empowerment while wider membership optimises the use of internal and external resources, skills and ideas. The group size of the members in partnerships may impose certain conditions on operation. Large bodies may be unwieldy for decision making while smaller groups may not be able to leverage action by unrepresented groups or organisations.

-- Structure: Structures can vary from established national structures to *ad hoc* specific area networks. Established structured frameworks for joint action, such as the structure in France, may link governments at various levels with the neighbourhood to be regenerated. Such structures lend credibility to the partnership, reducing jurisdictional impediments and improving the flow of funding. In other cases, some joint action organisations are incorporated as non-profit corporations. Sometimes, a general blue print for partnership is provided by national governments as a condition for funding. In such cases, strategic economic, social and infrastructure investments are possible on a national scale.

Ad hoc specific area networks may arise at the grass roots level, galvanised by shared loss or common cause. They are close to informal networks and driven by mutual help philosophies. Because of their nature, they are able to utilise non-traditional and innovative means for urban generation. Some cities have been able to work with such organisations in low income areas where much was achieved through self help.

--   Time: Some joint action organisations are temporary structures functioning for a specified time or until a goal is reached. Time limited organisations facilitate the introduction of public funds at the beginning and the withdrawal of public interventions at the end. Other organisations are more enduring structures, building stable alliances which could be mobilised in a variety of situations. Such long term organisations have longer horizons and are, therefore, able to seek sustained investments and long term commitments from a variety of sources. For example, loans may be negotiated from banks and private-public joint investments may be made.

--   Scope: The mandates of joint action groups vary widely in scope with regard to spatial or policy factors. Some partnerships are clearly linked to declining areas of cities or housing estates, enabling the concentration of effort and funnelling resources to reverse the process of decline. Others work for city-wide solutions and sustainable results by developing differentiated responses for various neighbourhoods. The mix of partners may also be affected by the mix of policy objectives. When policy objectives are linked such as job creation and housing, selected actors may be invited to the partnership.

--   Operation: The roles played by the partnership and its members can differ significantly. Within the partnership, differences in power may be evened out by democratic processes or they may be maintained by assigned roles based on potential contributions. The partnership may work as a consultative or advisory body or it may have decision making powers, particularly with respect to budget and priorities.

There are no ideal solutions because the choice of approach must depend not only on the results desired, but also on the availability of partners, the gravity and nature of the urban problems, the existing organisational and institutional structures and the national ethos. For example, some countries favour a spirit of citizen activism while others prefer to pursue a philosophy of nationally supervised renewal.

Partnerships have an especially important role in a number of the examples of multi-sectoral approach programmes quoted below.

Selected examples of the multi-sectoral approach

Canada

Montreal's course of development over the past two decades illustrates the challenges facing many core cities in large metropolitan areas. The main trends in Montreal's development are typical of the impacts of urban sprawl that have been experienced by many large North American cities.

The City of Montreal has adopted three integrated policies in the areas of urban planning, housing and economic development. These policies enable the City to capitalize on its assets and further its economic and social development. Each of the three policies propose, among other objectives, to maintain an active and dynamic population, to improve the quality of the urban environment and to ensure affordable housing for all.

The housing policy is intended to be balanced, coherent and comprehensive. It has enabled Montreal to succeed in integrating social housing within the urban fabric, thus avoiding the creation of ghettos. Furthermore, the policy has enabled Montreal to maintain its existing housing stock in good repair and has encouraged the development of new housing, particularly in the downtown area. The following are two examples of the policy in action.

Renovation assistance programme

Montreal has devoted considerable effort to the renovation of existing housing over the past two decades. The main focus of the Renovation assistance programme has been on upgrading housing conditions, as opposed to preserving architectural values. Since 1988, the programme has focused mainly on low-rent buildings and has set conditions to limit the impact of renovation costs on tenant rents. Up to 50 per cent of the costs of renovation may be covered by the programme, depending on the size of the dwelling and the rent level. In order to obtain assistance, the building owner must provide an agreement, signed by the majority of tenants, which sets out the type of renovation work to be completed, any moving arrangements that may be involved, compensation to tenants for temporary accommodation and proposed post-renovation rent levels.

The economic impact of the municipal renovation assistance activity has been impressive. Between 1969 and 1993, Montreal invested C$169.2 million in renovating 28 578 conventional housing units and 4 382 rooming house units, and in demolishing 26 483 out-buildings (coal sheds). Over the same period, the federal and provincial governments provided contributions of C$113.6 million and C$43.6 million, respectively, for housing renovations in Montreal. In 1992, housing grants are estimated to have generated over C$65 million in renovation work and nearly 3 000 jobs.

The renovation programme also makes it possible for the SHDM, a paramunicipal housing organisation, to acquire and then renovate rental properties, facilitating the transfer of these properties to residents in the form of housing co-operatives. The City of Montreal is one of only a few municipalities in Canada to be involved in such direct action in the development of social housing (in other municipalities this type of activity is usually done exclusively through federal and provincial programmes). Between 1988 and 1992, the City acquired 3 176 units in this way.

Support for private residential development and housing in the downtown core

Over the past decade Montreal has succeeded in slowing the flow of young households from the City to the suburbs. This has been largely accomplished through encouraging home ownership and fostering the construction of new housing that is better-suited to the needs of young households, yet compatible with the densely built-up environment of the city. The development of new housing in the downtown area of Montreal has been actively encouraged.

A relatively large number of vacant lots and tracts of land remain to be developed in the downtown area. For the most part these areas are already serviced by infrastructure. As a result, the development of these lands can raise funds for the municipality without requiring any major capital investment, unlike the case in outlying residential areas. It is estimated that approximately 10 000 new housing units could potentially be brought on stream in the downtown area.

A number of initiatives have been implemented simultaneously to encourage the development of housing in Montreal's downtown core. These include:

- changes to existing land-use by-laws to facilitate residential development;
- the sale of land to the private sector through a competitive process (proposal calls) which stresses architectural qualities;
- financial incentives (up to C$10 000) for people who buy homes in the downtown core; and,
- a major marketing campaign aimed at potential buyers which extols the virtues of an urban lifestyle as a viable alternative to the suburbs.

Five major housing projects, offering 2 500 condominium units are already under construction or will be in the near future. Private investment in this housing represents nearly one half of one billion dollars. This is considered to be a major accomplishment given the traditional preference of most Montreal homebuyers for single detached homes.

The two programmes described above are both based on the principle of City leadership but are carried out through partnerships with other actors and in collaboration with Montreal residents.

Ireland

The Dublin Inner City Partnership focuses on combating long term unemployment. The Irish Programme for Economic and Social Progress (PESP) began in 1991 when government, trade unions, employers, construction and farming organisations identified the need for an area-based response to chronic unemployment. The programme in Dublin was area-based and community led. The Dublin Inner City Partnership set up a board, consisting of partners noted above but also equal representation from the community sector. With knowledge of the local situation, community groups were to provide leadership, innovative ideas, new methods of delivery of services and refocusing the use of existing resources. Their programme for action assigned tasks to organisations in the partnership and consisted of six elements.

-- Job provision: To ensure the availability of worthwhile employment opportunities, job placement offices were located locally, initiatives for self employment were launched and job creation through Inner City Enterprise was negotiated.

--   Income distribution: If legitimate wage income was not possible, sustainable income and quality of life must be maintained. Therefore, means to supplement unemployment compensation with legitimate income generating activities were sought.
--   Community development: Various funding programmes were tapped to run community resource Centres and capacity building activities in the inner city.
--   Urban regeneration: Urban regeneration was planned so that there was minimum disruption and possibilities for employment during and after regeneration. A Code of Practice was prepared for developers which included local employment clauses.
--   Education and training: Community based skill training was made available for the long term unemployed. Vocational training and adult and community education were introduced to increase marketable skills among residents.
--   European Commission funding: The formation of the partnership, provided a mechanism for a more direct method of obtaining and dispensing European Commission funding to the community.

Work is continuing on this two year pilot project.

Switzerland

Chance Oerlikon 2011 is still in the planning stage but it will be implemented through public-private partnerships. The Oerlikon industrial area in the north of Zurich, Switzerland, declined as a result of major changes in industrial and economic conditions. The Zurich city government initiated a plan to redevelop the area for more profitable uses while improving urban quality. A partnership was built between the city, land owners and the Swiss Railroad (SBB). The industrial area will be transformed by a new urban concept including housing, parks and green spaces, pedestrian and bicycle paths, commercial spaces, public institutions and industry. Based on this plan, the public transportation links are going to be modified to serve the community while minimising pollution.

France

In France, the social renewal of cities has been established as a national priority. A total of FF 730 million was spent in 1989. Initially, CNV, a national council for towns and urban social development, responsible for urban policy, was chaired by the prime minister. CIV, the Interministerial committee on towns and social development consisting of ministers, then also chaired by the prime minister, set priorities, allocated state funds and launched actions. DIV, the interministerial commission on towns and urban social development co-ordinates and implements the programme. This structure simplifies the administrative machinery by assisting the orderly flow of public resources and co-ordinating effort by government departments to areas of priority. The projects are developed by local governments according to need and a long term agreement (3-5 years) is signed. There are two types of programmes: the territorial programmes and social solidarity programmes. Under the territorial programmes, initiatives are designed to deal with problems in an urban district, neighbourhood or sectors affected by industrial decline. Under national solidarity programmes, initiatives are designed to meet the needs of population groups threatened by exclusion. Groups such as elderly persons, nomads, the underprivileged, youth in marginal situations and delinquents may be assisted independently of territorial contracts but are often combined with territorial contracts.

The example of Marseille is explained here to illustrate how actions are undertaken. The contract with the city, signed in 1990, has two parts: Marseille solidaire and Marseille métropole. Under Marseille solidaire, social development is promoted through a coherent multi-sectoral programme projected to cost FF 274 million. The funds are accessed from a number of national programmes as well as national agencies such as the Caisse des dépôts et consignations. The five priorities are housing, quality of life, urbanisation, education and social action (health promotion, insertion into the economy and culture). Eleven declining sectors of the city were selected. Housing in these areas were renovated and the city is improving the infrastructure and exterior spaces. When housing units in large blocks were renovated, actions were taken to introduce much needed services into the neighbourhood. Neighbourhood centres, local theatre groups, youth clubs and city newspapers have been launched. Voluntary organisations are responsible for these activities, involving a wide range of residents. Training and job placement organisations have been created jointly by private and public organisations. Many small enterprises, such as garages for car repair and maintenance of sports fields, have been started. The second part, Marseille métropole has developed an urban pact, with a budget of FF 40 million. It aims to improve the economic base of the city, to attract new industries and to create opportunities for scientific and cultural organisations.

More than 300 neighbourhoods are being revitalised under conventions de développement social and about 200 neighbourhoods are being helped by territorial agreements. The national HLM organisation plays a major role. Among the actions taken are renovation of neighbourhood buildings, neighbourhood improvement, improvement of suburban neighbourhoods (Banlieue 89) and improvement of heritage buildings. In addition, projects have improved transportation networks, security and urban services. Efforts have been made to improve neighbourhoods for families (Nouvelle famille -- nouvel habitat) and to attract commerce and investment. Among the programmes with social goals are crime prevention and increased urban security, insertion of disadvantaged households into the urban mainstream, aiding elderly households and providing legal assistance to urban residents. Special programmes focus on the problems of youth, drawing them by positive activities of training, and jobs while providing them help to discard negative activities such as drugs and petty crime.

The process is a mix of grass roots and national will. The programme is developed through locally conducted diagnosis of the problem including a survey of residents. Technical and building surveys are also conducted. The city government then prepares the final plan and negotiates the contract to receive public funding. Partnerships may be formed with non-profit organisations to carry out the programme.

Japan

The provision of affordable housing within the city has been an enormous challenge for Tokyo. The landmark project, River City 21, is an innovative new community, housing a mix of moderate and low income households, right in the heart of the city. How was this accomplished? A small island lies in the middle of the Sumida River, just a couple of kilometres away from the Ginza. Under the Okawabata Redevelopment Plan, a new community of 7 500 people was designed for a 17 hectare site on the island, which was occupied by abandoned factories and warehouses. The community includes 2 500 units of housing, commercial and cultural space, primary and junior high schools, parks and recreational space with access to the water front, a multi-lane access bridge and a subway station. The project is a joint undertaking by the Tokyo Metropolitan Government Bureau of Housing, Tokyo Metropolitan Supply Corporation, Housing and Urban Development Corporation and a private corporation, Mitsui Real Estate Development Corporation. The partners jointly own the land. Good road access is available but traffic and parking (600 cars) is limited. The Tokyo

Metropolitan Government Bureau of Housing has built 280 units of public housing for low income households. The units are designed to accommodate a wide variety of households. The Tokyo Metropolitan Housing Supply Corporation and the Housing Urban Development Corporation have built 425 and 625 units respectively for moderate income households. The Mitsui company has developed 1 170 larger luxury apartments, which are leased by companies for their employees. Government subsidies to construction varied from 30 per cent of the costs for low income housing to 1.7 per cent of the costs of private development. Development is relatively dense, with approximately 30 hectares of floor area on about 6.4 hectares of land. The high and moderate rise buildings provide area for green spaces that include play areas for children, a golf driving range, wading pools, waterfront paths, jogging trails, etc. Roofs of schools and commercial buildings are used for swimming pools and recreational space. The profile of occupants shows that a mix of residents has been achieved. Almost a quarter of the residents either lived with relatives or in company housing before moving to the site. While 45 per cent of the households had a bread winner in a management or professional position, over a quarter of the households received a housing allowance. Roughly a third of the households had two earners and the average age of the main bread winner was 42 years. The average household size is 2.48 persons and over a quarter of the households had children. Efforts are in place to integrate the new community with the older resident community on the island.

The Netherlands

The process of "social renewal" was pioneered by the City of Rotterdam when it launched the programme "The New Rotterdam" in 1986. The objective of social renewal was to offer better prospects to all city residents, even those who generally benefit little from urban and economic renewal, by encouraging participation in all aspects of community life. To achieve it, new relationships were established between the people of Rotterdam, their municipal government, social institutions and industry. In 1990, the city signed an agreement with the national government to manage state funded social renewal projects locally.

The concept links economic recovery with the resolution of social problems through multi-sectoral action. It specifically works to include those that were marginalised by economic revival and those that suffered social exclusion as a result. The municipality accepted the responsibility for the city as a community and as a place to work and live. The municipality also recognised the citizen's responsibility for his or her own future.

This concept of social renewal was adopted at the national level and introduced in a majority of Dutch municipalities through agreements for social renewal "to improve the position of people who are socially disadvantaged or who are in danger of becoming so". In 1991, alderman from the 200 municipalities undertaking social renewal addressed a letter to the national government to remove obstacles such as regulations and limited funds and to more fully support the process.

This case study describes the experience of the city of Rotterdam. Three guidelines were established for the process of social renewal:

-- reassessing the policy on social disadvantage: the aim was to make full use of resident potential and to engage personal responsibility;
-- re-evaluating services to reduce dependence and social divisions: the four criteria used were client orientation, activation, prevention and co-operation;
-- re-ordering responsibilities: decentralisation to the appropriate levels, partnerships with private and non-profit organisations and initiatives from the public were key elements.

In 1991, the municipal government issued a policy document for Social Renewal in Rotterdam, for the years 1991-94. The document analysed the problems, set concrete targets to be attained, described tasks to be done and established criteria for success. The municipality frankly stated that it was neither willing or able to do it alone but offered to facilitate a process in co-operation with non-government bodies. Social Renewal Project Offices were created, which were responsible for creating the right conditions for partnerships working for social renewal. The office is responsible for programming, political support, co-ordination and monitoring results. Model projects and action areas were created and the priorities of residents and local organisations were identified. "Social investments" were solicited from developers, investors and companies and a "social return" was anticipated.

Five priorities were targeted for action. First, disadvantaged ethnic minorities were to be integrated through education and employment. The Integration of Newcomers Project will work with migrant organisations to introduce them to the Rotterdam community and to facilitate entry into the labour market. Second, the education level of Rotterdam residents was to be improved. A "Fund for Combating Educational Disadvantage" was set up to improve the standard of education in schools and to encourage graduation. The "Rotterdam Compact" aimed at potential drop-outs offered a combination of work experience and schooling. Third, labour market programmes of training and job placement were relied upon to increase participation, particularly among the long term unemployed. The "Work Centre" co-located the social service department, the employment office, the job pool office and training organisations to more directly link welfare programmes with employment. The "Rotterdam Works" programme was designed to move long term unemployed persons into paid employment. The programme had many related activities. "Investment, Rotterdam Works" secured vacancies and apprenticeship positions in companies while, "Training, Rotterdam Works" provided training and nominated candidates to the positions available. Fourth, within each urban district, a great variety of housing should be provided to eliminate concentrations of poverty. Urban renewal which improved housing and neighbourhoods also considered social management. "City Home" dwellings were suitable for a variety of residents -- large migrant households or young people living together. Fifth, greater coherence and co-ordination of care and welfare services were required to serve citizens better. In one case, rather than provide funding to organisations, individuals were given their own care budget so that they could buy the best mix for their needs while living at home.

Three "showpiece" projects are described in detail. The first deals with literacy. The city gave itself five years to ensure that all inhabitants between the ages of 14 and 45 could read, write and count to the lowest primary school level. The city and central governments increased spending for adult education. The 21 organisations involved in adult education were amalgamated but made independent for better coverage and efficiency. The services were professionalised and more minority teachers were employed. Though important benefits were gained, a number of problems remained to be solved such as the question of whether Dutch courses should be mandatory for migrants. The three years required for proficiency resulted in a high drop out rate. The links between adult education and job placement are not well established.

The second project was the establishment of a job pool with the intent of employing the long term unemployed in the implementation of socially useful tasks. "New Jobs, Rotterdam Works" Foundation, with an executive consisting of members from the municipality, employers, employees and minority organisations, managed the job pool. The job pool is confined to full time jobs in the public sector designed under strict constraints: the job must be of evident value to society; it pays the minimum wage with no prospect of advancement; it must be impossible to create the job through normal methods; and no jobs outside or inside the organisation should be displaced. Only those unemployed for at least three years were eligible and preference is given to those with the least chance of finding work. The jobs included building supervision, neighbourhood upkeep and cleaning, administration, housekeeping, cleaning, caring and transport. Though all the targets were not achieved, many positive benefits were recognised from this integrated approach. Low drop-out rates, low absenteeism and satisfaction among employees and employers were cited even though only persons who were hard to employ benefited. Problems were identified with recruitment, acquisition of jobs and organisation of the programme.

The third project, District Management, had four objectives: to promote good citizenship, to reduce dirt on the streets, to increase safety and to deal more quickly with complaints. District management boards were set in every city district. The success of the programme was to be assessed by the residents based on the objectives. Thirty five district maintenance teams were at work all over Rotterdam. Attempts were made to respond to complaints in three days. Residents launched neighbourhood initiatives such as the Opzoomerstraat action described earlier in Inset 22. Though this project requires cultural change within the neighbourhood as well as the city administration, some changes have been achieved and the residents of Rotterdam have a more favourable view of the quality of life in the city.

Despite its recent introduction and its experimental nature, some demonstrable results were achieved through social renewal, but improvements are planned. Some key points were made under evaluation:

-- The starting point for social renewal is not the available instruments and services but with the solutions desired. Then the required central and local policies are activated and cultural and administrative changes are implemented. The process was not fully operational yet.
-- Though the results of social renewal are not yet evident in statistics, the reversal of some negative trends are noticeable and they will eventually have a long term impact.
-- The tension between top-down approaches and grass roots approaches were evident when municipalities on the one hand established targets and on the other hand invited public participation. People want to be involved in setting targets and they resist compulsory participation.
-- Decentralisation has its advantages and disadvantages. Local District Councils emphasised integrated, communicating, project approaches that were responsive to local needs. Citizens knew where to go for help. However, organisations found that they were engaged in separate negotiations with each district council.

--   Co-operation between agencies and organisations was increased however, municipal departments had difficulty adopting the new ways of working. Municipal departments had the difficult task of being both the target and agent of change.

--   Because social renewal was initiated by government, people, particularly the disadvantaged, who have limited faith in the political process, have little confidence in the programme.

Spain

Huelva is one of the eight capitals of the province of Andalusia, located at the junction of the rivers, Tinto and Odiel. On the west bank of the Odiel, is a natural reserve, protected for ecological reasons. The peripheral settlement of Marismas del Odiel is also located here.

By the late 1980s the economy of the province of Huelva was stagnant, and the impact on this community was disproportionate. The average income of residents lay far below the average for the European Union and there was high unemployment.

The project of Marismas del Odiel, Huelva, aimed at the improvement of the housing, urban, social, cultural and economic conditions of about 4 500 residents in six neighbourhoods. The project was linked with an experimental programme of the European Commission, called "Poverty III". The project was implemented by the Autonomous Community of Andalusia in co-operation with the Municipality of Huelva, with the assistance of the national Ministry of Social Affairs. The programme was part of the Districts for Preferential Action of the junta de Andalusia, which focused on health, education, training, labour, social security and urbanism.

The multi-sectoral plan of Andalusia for Districts for Preferential Action had the following major objectives:

--   Youth: full integration of the young into society and the work place through a global policy, developed with their participation.

--   Equality rights of women: improvement of access to the labour force and promotion of positive societal action by women. Development of laws and strategies to protect women in special circumstances and for the improvement of female health.

234

-- Assistance to the gypsy community: integration into the labour force and into the social fabric of the community.
-- Migrants: to assist Andalusian emigrants to return and to improve the conditions of immigrants.
-- Drugs: to prevent exposure to drugs and to rehabilitate addicts.
-- Neighbourhood renewal: to improve marginal settlements by physical improvements and social resources and to introduce integrated programmes against poverty.
-- Solidarity: to improve labour force participation through education, apprenticeships and income support.

Seven principles of action were established. These were a) to develop innovative approaches to combat socio-economic exclusion; b) to promote institutional co-ordination; c) to invite community participation; d) to rely on holistic multi-sectoral approaches; e) to integrate disadvantaged groups; f) to capture visible and transferable results; and g) to conduct evaluation research.

This case study was characterised by its intense use of self help approaches, mobilised by a variety of partnerships formed between government and local community organisations for each activity. The residents were active partners in determining need and selecting solutions and this assured the success of the initiatives. Some of the key elements of the holistic multi-sectoral approaches are described below.

A major objective was to prevent the displacement of residents by legitimising the settlement and improving the quality of the neighbourhoods. The municipality donated the land and residents could purchase their homes over 20 years by making affordable monthly payments. Collectives of people with construction skills were formed to construct new housing, to rebuild and renovate existing homes and to improve the neighbourhood.

Opportunities for occupational, professional and technical training were made available in the community to facilitate participation in the mainstream labour force and consumer market place. In addition to the various levels of government, the unions, churches, neighbourhood associations and co-operatives worked together to create small task forces to develop local training capabilities, to create job possibilities in neighbourhood enterprises and to promote a sustained attachment to the labour force.

The relationship of health to the environment and to market activity was established by partnerships between public health organisations and neighbourhood associations. Through health education, improvements were attained in the use of primary health care and the reduction of insalubrious environments. Better health paid the dividends of further positive health behaviour and of improved labour force participation.

Education, particularly of the young, was a key element of the multisectoral approach. Community participation in developing relevant education aimed to diminish absenteeism and to increase marketable skills. Parents played a key role in the development of local education.

Community development was fostered through the support and training of community groups and through the participation of residents. The preparation and dissemination of information for local use enabled residents to understand the process of urban renewal and to contribute to it.

These multi-sectoral activities stabilised the community of Marismas des Odiel and improved living conditions. The latent skills and motivation that drove residents to work hard to establish squatter settlements were now channelled in legitimate economic activity. Excluded groups were integrated into the social and economic urban community. Empowerment of the residents unleashed latent strengths of self help. The residents had worked with public and non-public agencies to make critical choices and to improve their expectations for the future (see also Inset 21).

Sweden

The Swedish case study summarised evaluation studies of the urban renewal process undertaken during the past decade. Many large scale housing projects built during the "Million homes programme" suffered from functional, physical, visual and technical problems. These problems were exacerbated by a lack of regular maintenance. Social problems such as crime, vandalism and anti-social activities affected the quality of life for residents. The estates had a high turnover and high vacancy rates. As the neighbourhood was considered unattractive and unsafe, those who had the social and economic means moved away, leaving the estate to residents with less resources and greater problems. Public and private services decline in quality or were shut down altogether. Large scale urban renewal processes were launched to redress these problems. In fact, it was noted that the amount of resources (in fixed prices) allocated to renewal in 1990 was twice as large as that in 1980 and seven times the expenditure in 1970.

Municipalities undertook urban renewal by accessing national programmes. Four such programmes were used in combination though the level of subsidies varied among the programmes for each project:

-- The Housing Improvement programme (1983-86) was implemented to repair, modernise and build additions to the housing stock by offering low interest loans and subsidies. Municipalities developed renewal plans for neighbourhoods whereby over 200 000 units were improved.

-- The Social Renewal programme (1986-89) was designed to meet current neighbourhood problems, by reducing vacancies and improving the social environment in multi-problem estates. Grants of Skr 155 million were given to 36 estates to cover half the improvement costs while the remaining costs were shared equally by the housing corporation and the municipality. Resident participation was required and the improvement of the outdoor environment and neighbourhood facilities was emphasised.

-- The co-ordinated Services Programme (1985-90) was initially targeted to provide services for elderly and disabled residents to enable them to remain in their homes rather than moving to institutions. The programme was extended to multi-problem estates to increase neighbourhood amenities by finding new ways to co-ordinate services from different sectors. Grants of Skr 100 million were distributed among 103 projects.

-- Housing Rehabilitation Loans were available for significant improvements to the technical or functional quality of buildings. This programme was dominant, with the flow of subsidies accounting for 60 per cent of the total discounted capital costs.

Though urban renewal activities were integrated, up to 90 per cent of the total renewal investment was dedicated to physical improvements. In fact, in the late 1980s, the average investment for building rehabilitation was close to the cost of new construction. Expenditures for improvement of the exterior environment, for better management practices and for increased public services were low.

The Swedish experience highlights three major difficulties:

-- First, renewal efforts often failed to meet the needs of the residents. Dissatisfaction among the vast majority of residents was due to social problems and they gave high priority to reducing theft, vandalism and disturbances by disruptive neighbours. They also stressed the need for improved commercial and public services, particularly schools and day care. The residents were sceptical about the extensive rehabilitation of buildings. The huge investments in physical improvements to buildings were therefore, misplaced and did not correspond to the priorities of residents.

--   Second, while positive changes were accomplished within the renewal estates, many problems were displaced to adjacent estates or to other problem neighbourhoods. Comprehensive renewal caused unintended migration flows. Tenants moved out during renovation and failed to return after the project was completed. When the attractiveness of the renewed estate increased, hard-to-house tenants and tenants with low resources moved to other problem estates where flats were easier to obtain. Despite efforts to attract residents from a range of socio-economic levels, those with poor social and economic resources were over-represented in public non-profit housing.

--   Third, the overall results of renewal programmes have not been effective given the high economic investments. The measure was considered effective if an equivalent or better result could not be achieved by another measure or a combination of measures at the same or lower cost. From the national perspective, the focus on physical improvements was too expensive and other measures would have met the needs of the residents better at lower cost. The other programmes were more effective, meeting the resident priorities of increasing services and improving social relations among residents at reasonable cost. Municipalities tended to design their renewal programmes according to the availability of programme financing, rather than the priorities of residents. Concentration of effort in one estate shifted problems to other estates, causing greater problems and costs to the municipality. Municipal housing corporations gained because renewal programmes enabled them to correct physical deterioration of buildings due poor maintenance and neglect. Residents often had to pay higher rents after renewal, though their urgent needs were not addressed.

Steps have been taken to amend the renewal process in Sweden. Due to general fiscal constraints, interest subsidies have been greatly reduced and the number of loans have been decreased. Funding will in future be directed more directly to priorities from the point of view of residents. Municipalities were urged to play a co-ordinating role in the design of urban renewal and to strengthen tenant participation in the process. Though discrepancies with public priorities have to be avoided by working with tenants, physical improvements must be guided by professional planners and builders to protect building assets.

Upgrading of services were vital to reduce dissatisfaction and to attract a range of potential tenants. One shot measures must be abandoned in favour of sustained multi-pronged efforts. An ongoing process required the co-operation and co-ordination of many public and private agencies to improve not only housing, but also schools, transportation, employment opportunities and health facilities within the urban mosaic of neighbourhoods.

The United Kingdom

In England, a number of programmes concerned with the economic and social regeneration of cities have, over the last few years, been grouped under the title "Action for Cities". The programmes include, for example, "Estate Action" which is concerned with regenerating social housing developments, and "City Challenge". The latter, particularly, is a strong multi-sectoral partnership model targeted at run-down areas of cities; resources over five years are made available through an initial competitive process. Other major programmes aimed at urban regeneration include Urban Development Corporations and Housing Action Trusts.

The initiative, "Action for Cities", exemplifies a programme of thinking nationally but acting locally. The objectives of the initiative are multi-sectoral and housing-led. They are: a) to enhance job opportunities and to improve the ability of residents to compete for them; b) reclaiming derelict land and buildings for new uses; c) to encourage private investment; d) to improve housing conditions, widen choice and reduce housing stress; and e) to encourage self help and improve the social fabric in inner cities.

The national government has grouped a number of city oriented initiatives from several departments along with its ongoing national policies under this umbrella. Programme expenditure for 1990-91 was £4 billion. Eight City Action Teams, consisting of regional officials of different departments, co-ordinate the range of government programmes for effective implementation. They are the contact point for local community organisations and business. At the community level, there are 16 Task Forces, whose role is to organise the joint effort of government departments, local government, the private sector and the community at large to rejuvenate their inner city neighbourhood. Local organisations take over this task in time. Each City Action Team and Task Force has its own government minister and the committee of ministers with these responsibilities is headed by the Inner Cities Minister.

Two major programmes under the "Action for Cities" initiative are Estate Action and City Challenge. The partnership approach has been developed in England through the City Challenge programme. Selected local authorities with areas of deprivation were invited to bid competitively for inclusion in the programme. The 31 winners from two competitions each receive an additional 7.5 million pounds per annum over five years for the comprehensive regeneration of a targeted inner urban area. The City Challenge areas often include large tracts of social and private sector housing. The government looked for a working partnership to include the community and the private sector, as well as local government and other statutory agencies. The City Challenge partnership takes effect through a board which is responsible for the development and delivery of an action plan. The plan states the vision for the area, and relates the contribution of each partner to the achievement of agreed strategic objectives, targets and outputs. Some losers in the competition have found the partnerships forged to develop their bids helpful in the process regeneration using their existing resources.

A tenant's "right to buy" programme for Council dwellings has been an important programme to increase the diversity of tenure in neighbourhoods. In addition to prices set by discounts proportional to the years of tenant's occupation, shared ownership (part rent, part buy) has also promoted ownership. These measures have increased the number of home owners by some 1.3 million households and reduced the stock of Council housing. The quality of the stock has also been improved by grants for repair and improvement.

All of these programmes are supported by a series of well prepared documents for communities and businesses that guide them through the various programmes and sources of funding that are available. There are also a series of Inner City Research Programme Reports and Case studies of Good Practice.

From 1994/95, the national government is combining the resources of 20 English programmes concerned with economic and social regeneration, including those listed above, into a new "Single Regeneration Budget" (SRB). At the same time in each of the ten English regions, four government departments (trade and industry, employment, environment, and transport) concerned with economic and social regeneration will form new integrated offices. Local authorities and other bodies will be able to formulate bids against the new SRB. Priorities will be set locally, and local innovation and imagination is encouraged. The SRB's objectives include enhancing job prospects, education and skills; levering-in private sector and other resources; encouraging economic development and local competitiveness; improved housing; reduced crime; improved environment and infrastructure; a better quality of life; and community participation. In the first year, the SRB will be £1.4 billion, but initially the money available will be mostly taken up by existing individual programme commitments. The new integrated regional offices will assess bids and allocate SRB resources, while seeking better co-ordination of the constituent department's main resources. The SRB will be overseen by a Ministerial committee. Key cities have sponsor Ministers.

In Scotland, the initiatives are driven by local priorities and implemented under local management by partners, and therefore, each area based programme is unique. However, they channel public funds and rely on government programmes.

The experience of Glasgow provides a good example. The Glasgow City Council, has a corporate strategy, with six objectives for the city. These are to sustain a balanced local economy, tackle deprivation, improve the environment, secure quality of life and equality of opportunity for residents, promote health and effectively manage the city.

One of the key components of the Corporate strategy is the Housing Plan for the 1990s. The Housing Plan describes broad multi-agency strategy to achieve effective renewal of Glasgow's peripheral housing estates and other deprived areas and to develop further a high quality social rented sector. These activities are linked to the inner city renewal programmes for improving commercial districts and increasing home ownership within the city. Council activities revolve around four major policies, which are used to revive city neighbourhoods. The first of these are based on needs, consist of strategies for the homeless, youth and others with special needs. Estate based policies, the second in the list, include clusters of programmes under the Estate Action Programme and the Area Renewal programme. The increased use of concierges and housing alarms are included here. The third, property related policies involves activities such as programmes for repair, thermal efficiency, improvement and property management. Finally, new customer policies, complement the others with programmes such as Action Plan for Racial Equality. Under the Citizens Charter, customer contracts have been drawn up, setting out standards of services and the tenants charter, was developed in consultation with tenants.

Area based policies and estate improvement are well established strategies in Scotland. The rationale for multi-sectoral "area based" initiatives are stated thus: "There has been a long recognition in Scotland that good housing conditions do not, alone, provide an acceptable urban environment and an awareness that poverty and other indicators of social and economic deprivation are not randomly distributed throughout urban Scotland". Therefore, concentrated action in well circumscribed areas are justified.

The area based programmes are based on the following principles:

--   An integrated approach to economic, social and physical regeneration firmly grounded in an initial analysis and long term strategic plan. This requires partnership and concerted action among a wide range of public sector bodies.
--   The inclusion of the private sector in the partnership, both to secure the benefit of advice, expertise and resources and to help break down the economic isolation of the areas.
--   The full involvement of the local community in the decision making processes, partly to ensure that decisions taken reflect the needs of the community, but also to encourage local people to take responsibility for their areas and to generate the commitment required to ensure that regeneration will be sustained in the long term.

In Glasgow, comprehensive area based renewal of public housing estates aims to provide high quality mixed tenure housing and a good residential environment. The city removes surplus social rented stock through well planned demolition to decrease residential densities. Renovation of existing stock is an opportunity for the creation of more popular housing types. To bring private resources into these areas and to diversify tenure, joint ventures are encouraged and new housing for sale is constructed. Discussions on mix of landlords and tenant management continue. Available resources will be used to improve the quality of the existing housing stock.

In addition, to these housing-led policies, there are a number of programmes directed to social renewal. Health Boards are building health centres in areas of multiple deprivation increasing the access to primary health care. Social work resources in these areas are improved in partnership with local voluntary agencies. The links between education and employment have also been strengthened. Public funding was increased to augment the number of teachers in troubled urban neighbourhoods. The Technical and Vocational initiative encourages a school curriculum with work related training and enterprise skills. With support from the Department of Employment and Manpower Services Commission, compacts are signed between schools and employers, where the schools agree to train to agreed standards and the employers guarantee jobs for graduates who meet those standards. Under the Training for Employment programme those unemployed for six months or more will be eligible for a year's training. The Safer Cities programme relies on co-operation not only between levels of government, but also the policy, commerce, industry and community and voluntary organisations. Activities range from increasing the security measures in homes to running "neighbourhood watch". The lack of cheap but reliable transportation links has been a major problem in peripheral estates. Innovative programmes include the running of mini-buses that are economically viable and the introduction of competition to lower prices.

The United States

Cities in the United States have launched experimental programmes to link social welfare policies more closely to the labour market. Private welfare offices like Maximus Inc., in Los Angeles and America Works, in New York, have moved welfare clients into training and jobs, cutting welfare expenses in these cities.

The case study from the City of Minneapolis developed a long term integrated community based strategy that recognised that the causes of joblessness were often inter-related personal, social, economic and environmental conditions which formed barriers to productive employment. The objective of The Minneapolis Neighbourhood Employment Network (NET) was to help residents find and keep jobs close to home.

In 1981, a task force of business and community leaders was established by the Mayor to develop a strategy that would enable "hard to employ" residents to share in the planned economic development of the city. Public sector resources were expected to decrease and efficiencies were to be gained by co-ordinating access to social services. In 1986, NET was incorporated as a non-profit organisation, with excellent access to city government and the private sector. The NET co-ordinator, housed in City Hall, directed programme planning by meeting regularly with facilitators, solicited funding and private sector involvement, and provided direction to the overall network by monitoring and evaluation. A decade later, NET became an integral part of the programmes of the city, dedicated to employment services. NET assisted city residents who had difficulty getting or keeping jobs, generally those with little or now work experience, limited skills, low self esteem, behavioural problems, history of alcohol or drug abuse, inadequate child care options, family instability, lack of shelter and poor access to transportation. Consuming an annual budget of

US$69 000 provided by business and foundations, it has placed approximately 900 people a year in jobs and helped many more with training programmes, job preparedness and daily living skills.

The whole city was divided into geographical units to more effectively utilise existing employment and support services for the benefit of the unemployed in the neighbourhood while drawing on the full range of fiscal and non-fiscal resources available in the public, private and non-profit organisations located there. Each area had a "community facilitator" (a neighbourhood group or community social service agency) and a "lead business" to work in collaboration to match the unemployed with employers and providers of social services. The community-based approach was designed to encourage closer contact between the unemployed and the small neighbourhood employers who generally create new jobs as well as to focus the employment programmes of the larger companies on a single section of the city. Direct corporate involvement was essential, providing jobs, equipment, volunteers, advice and programme support. Under NET, each area had a "job bank" which listed community based employment opportunities while linked to complementary government and social programmes. Each job bank, had a NET facilitator who was knowledgeable about area employers and support services. They met with clients to assess their skills and experience and in some cases supplied training for job preparation skills (résumés, interviewing techniques) or work place behaviour (punctuality). Each client was matched with appropriate services, such as education and literacy programmes, child care, chemical dependency programmes, or with a job opening. They followed up with the client and the employer after placement.

Some innovative special services were added to meet specific client needs. The Emergency Grant Programme, funded through grants from foundations, business and the city, was used for small one-time grants (up to US$200) to clients who were unable to hold a job because they could not afford job related expenses such as tools, work shoes, uniforms, union dues or transportation. An Auto Purchase Programme was tried but cancelled due to difficulties. The Family Self Sufficiency Programme provided rental subsidies in conjunction with supportive services to families on public assistance, participating in self-sufficiency, education or job training programmes. Rents were set at one third of the client's income. The Minneapolis Public Housing Authority (MPHA) selected the families and MPHA case manager developed a self sufficiency plan for the family ranging from six months to five years. The required community resources, such as child care, job training, education, transportation, family services, financial management counselling and pre-employment and post-employment support were tapped. The employment services were provided by

NET. The NET facilitator reviewed the job and income status every three months for a maximum of five years or until the income of the client increased enough to forfeit the rental subsidy. If the job was lost, a new plan was developed and NET assisted clients with their employment search. Additional services such as job-seeking workshops, emergency grants, job referrals, personal support services and job training were provided by NET.

Business/neighbourhood co-operation was fostered to improve employment opportunities for city residents while providing employers with appropriately trained employees. Small community based businesses were formed to provide transitional employment experiences to the hard-to-employ and to prepare them for regular private industry jobs. NET-tie, was an example. This non-profit business was created to convert railroad ties discarded by the Soo Line Railroad to wood fuel useable by the Northern States Power Company. Unfortunately, after a year of operation, the business was sold and moved. NET and Seward Redesign, Inc., collaborated on a customised training programme, where unemployed or underemployed workers were placed in a combined classroom /internship experience for six months to learn to operate computer numeric control machines. Entry level jobs with flexible hours were open to participants during their training period so they had some income while gaining job experience. This customised job training offered part-time training and flexible jobs to participants unable to attend full time day training because they would lose income from their day time jobs. The Job Linkage Programme combined the resources of NET, the Minneapolis Education and Training Programme and the Minneapolis Community Development Agency to more directly link economic development to job opportunities for local residents. NET gained better access to better jobs while business were encouraged to hire locally within the neighbourhood. Any business receiving public funding is required to participate by signing an agreement specifying jobs which will be filled by low income clients. Residents had more direct access to new jobs while businesses had the pick of a pool of applicants screened and tested to match their needs. Customised training and supportive employment services were available under some agreements.

NET was accountable to the city of Minneapolis through a system of performance based payments to the Job Banks for work accomplished and goals met. For example, individual Job Banks received US$25 for each Job Linkage agreement signed with a business. An annual report recorded accomplishments of NET. Data was maintained on intake, placements, retention rates and wages as well as on client characteristics.

The success of NET was, in large measure, due to its ability to grasp new opportunities, experiment with new programmes and to abandon problematic ones. It has managed over the last decade to offer its employment services city-wide, without losing its community based focus.

Key features, identified during discussion by members, were a lean organisation, recognition of neighbourhood-specific needs in different city neighbourhoods, reliance on neighbourhood facilitators within a co-ordinated city-wide programme, multiple ways for social investments by private sector companies, the concept of one window for services, where a client need can be assessed in the round, follow-through of cases over time and the search for linkages and supportive programmes to open blockages.

The characteristics of multi-sectoral initiatives

The characteristics of public intervention to improve cities were examined for patterns that would facilitate the sharing of policy experiences among Member countries. The case studies describing the application of multi-sectoral policies among the OECD countries show similarities and differences. These are shown in Table 7.1. The case studies were examined for patterns in the design of multi-sectoral initiatives, by comparing four factors: role of housing, source of financing, actors involved and agency playing the lead role.

The mix of objectives for the case study project determined whether the approach was housing led or if housing was a major component. Where the area was identified because of deteriorated housing, such as in Sweden, there was a tendency to use housing led policies. In the majority of cases, however, major investments were made in improving the physical structure of housing. There were problems associated with high costs as well as low satisfaction of resident needs when housing improvement was the primary activity.

There is clear recognition in all the Member countries that presented case studies, that the problems of cities cannot be redressed by cities alone. Financing for the projects were consolidated by accessing national funding programmes, supplementing them with municipal programmes, leveraging private sector investments and encouraging individual contributions. Where individuals were unable to contribute financially, other self help instruments were used to involve local residents. This was particularly the case in Spain. This approach seems to be widely used among Member countries.

246

Table 7.1 Characteristics of case studies from OECD Member countries

Characterisitcs	Can	Fra	Jap	Net	Spa	Swe	United Kingdom		USA
							Eng	Scot	
Role of housing									
Housing led			*			*			
Housing component	*	*		*	*		*	*	*
Financing									
Public, national	*	*	*	*	*	*	*	*	*
Public, local	*	*	*	*	*	*	*	*	*
Private	*	*	*	*	*	*	*	*	*
Individual	*	*	*	*		*	*	*	*
Actors									
Public	*	*	*	*	*	*	*	*	*
Private	*	*	*	*	*	*	*	*	*
Non-profit	*	*		*	*	*	*	*	*
Individual	*	*		*	*	*	*	*	*
Lead role									
Centre	*	*	*	*			*	*	*
Municipal			*			*	*	*	
Community					*				

247

The case studies also show that a coalition was built with a variety of actors who played various roles in the renewal process. This characteristic is also common among all the case studies and appears to be a successful approach. Partnerships were built between public and private agencies for specific functions, such as the improvement of commercial zones as in the case study from Canada and for job creation as described in case studies from Scotland and the United States. The non-profit agencies played the lead role in alliances that were built for components of social renewal. Voluntary agencies and tenant organisations were active in several cases, often funded through public subsidies.

The widest variation among the case studies appears to be in the organisation playing the lead role and the type of structures established for implementing the changes. France has a well-developed national structure, proving the national priority placed on urban renewal. They have a structure which cascades to other levels, with strong support flowing to the neighbourhood where local action is taken. On the other hand, many case studies show the key role played by municipal governments in identifying, designing and delivering a programme of positive urban change. The case studies from Sweden, Holland and Japan show city governments playing such roles. The model from the United Kingdom relies on a local committee with representatives of all parties concerned. Each approach has its advantages, and perhaps, evolved to meet the specific needs of the local community within the larger framework of the national culture with respect to economic, social and environmental aspects.

Policy guidelines

From this review of urban regeneration initiatives in a variety of OECD Member countries, it is clear that partnerships have a critical role to play in the development of the multi-sectoral approach. From this part of the project, it is therefore possible to suggest some critical guidelines for policy in relation to the establishment of successful partnerships, as follows:

- **Partnerships are critical to the implementation of multi-sectoral policies. They facilitate the rationalisation of resources, the concentration of effort, the integration of expertise and the assurance of commitment on the part of stake holders.**

- Partnerships should be developed to suit the specific local conditions. The characteristics of the urban problem, the stake holders and vested interests should determine the structure, composition, duration, scope and mode of operation of the partnership.
- Partnerships should be built on shared interest, complementary and joint action. A vision of the future, providing a clear picture of the desired outcomes, encourages partners to align their goals and objectives while making appropriate contributions.
- Partnerships should involve local residents and community organisations as the nucleus. The involvement of local residents and community organisations is necessary in order to ensure their full commitment to achieving the jointly established goals and to ensure that they are the principal beneficiaries of whatever action is taken.
- Partnerships should combine both "bottom-up" and "top-down" initiatives. Capacity building and mutual understanding are essential both at the top and the bottom to ensure that the partnership can work effectively.
- Partnerships that involve the local (neighbourhood) level are essential if communities are to be engaged effectively and social cohesion is to be engendered. However, partnerships working to improve neighbourhoods cannot work in isolation; they require the support of agencies at the level of the city, region and state or nation, if their actions are to be successful and durable.

References

CITY OF MONTREAL (1989), *Habiter Montréal -- A Policy Statement on Housing*, Montreal.

DELEGATION INTERMINISTERIELLE A LA VILLE ET AU DEVELOPPEMENT SOCIAL URBAIN, Information pamphlet, Paris.

DEPARTMENT OF THE ENVIRONMENT (1990), *Renewing the Cities*. Central Office of Information, United Kingdom.

GLASGOW CITY COUNCIL (1992), *Housing Plan for the 1990s*, Glasgow.

JACQUIER, C. (1991), *Voyage dans dix quartiers européens en crise*. L'Harmattan, Paris.

SCOTTISH OFFICE (1988), *New Life for Urban Scotland*, HMSO, Edinburgh.

Chapter 8

The Challenge of the Multi-sectoral Approach

There appears to be widespread acceptance of the need for holistic approaches to deal with the complex problems of contemporary urban systems and to advance strategic objectives for cities as a whole. There has been considerable experimentation with multi-sectoral policies over the last few decades. Even though the experience with multi-sectoral approaches has been piecemeal, the results appear promising. However, several challenges must be met before multi-sectoral approaches can be implemented in a systematic way.

The multi-sectoral approach

Urban problems have been growing in number and complexity and are increasingly attracting the attention of national governments. Traditional policy instruments and local level financing are insufficient to address these problems. For example, it is insufficient merely to renovate housing in declining areas, when more radical action is required to revitalise whole neighbourhoods and change their role in the urban tissue. The need for a new approach is evident.

Throughout OECD Member countries, cities are grappling with the need to understand urban change. New sources of data and the means to inter-relate them have become necessary. The neighbourhoods selected for renewal are typically identified largely on the basis of the severity and complexity of problems within their boundaries. Explicit goals are developed for such areas and timetables for change are established. As such programmes evolve, linkages are set up between sectoral policies and alliances developed between the various actors involved and other stake-holders. Mechanisms for monitoring changes are set up. The need for new integrated powers to manage this process has emerged clearly. In order to widen political support for change, cities need to identify wider benefits than those that flow specifically to dysfunctional neighbourhoods. The linkages between economic, social and environmental benefits require a more holistic perspective.

There is widespread agreement also on the objectives of multi-sectoral interventions. There are five points on which views converge.

-- **The multi-sectoral approach is not an end in itself but it is necessary if the challenge raised by the growing complexity of urban management is to be met.** Sectoral policies are incongruent with urban concerns and, more than ever before, multi-sectoral policies are required to grasp the multi-dimensional links, interactions and implications of current issues. They are essential to build real life solidarities while resolving conflicts. Exclusion has many causes which affect individuals in a variety of ways according to their immediate environment. Therefore, actions covering a whole geographical area are more likely to remedy shortcomings than targeting of special population groups in difficulty.

-- **The multi-sectoral approach is only rarely incorporated into the rationale of prevailing government structures.** It calls, on the contrary, for an overall view transcending administrative power sharing and going beyond the necessarily piecemeal reasoning that governs the choices of decision makers at the various administrative levels. Neither can it always be reconciled with hard-and-fast application of market principles. It calls for the will to act, a federative spirit, an overall reference framework, a strategic "vision" of the problems and how they are to be resolved, and a consensus on what is at stake for the city's future. This goes much further than the purely physical planning of the past decades; the aim now must be to work out a truly community-based plan.

-- **It is a strategy that also involves knowledge and know-how, a better understanding of facts and trends.** Two major areas for improved and reliable data and efficient information systems were identified to support multi-sectoral actions. The first is a body of urban data, where information may be examined at the micro level, whether it be the neighbourhood or groups of households with similar characteristics. The second is information related to policies and their impacts. At present, data is lacking on many key items within the urban context. Redistribution systems must be made more transparent through consolidated accounts covering all the many instruments of official assistance. Though information on single programmes and even sectoral investments are often available, policies for deprived neighbourhoods are multi-layered and incoherent, so that it is difficult to estimate the full benefit flowing to residents.

-- **The multi-sectoral approach calls for long term partnerships among the different actors on whom life in the city depends, central, regional and local government; private sector leaders and organisations and neighbourhood residents.** To mobilise support from all the actors, it is necessary to conclude a pact binding as many as possible of the partners involved. This may be achieved through a charter, a formal agreement or even a contract covering the development of the city as a whole.

Support for city scale activities can be rallied only by combining two approaches, one from the top down, with a plan emanating from the national or provincial governments, the other from the bottom up, drawing on the commitment of local groups and neighbourhood residents. While each of the approaches have been tried, combining the two is relatively untried and requires refinement through trial and error.

-- **Only a multi-sectoral approach can match resources to needs to ensure effectiveness.** There are costs associated with leadership and co-ordination at the decision making level as well as with efficient administration and implementation of the policies and programmes. However, overall savings are also possible due to more rational choices, consistent decisions, elimination of duplication and internalisation of external costs. Efforts to combat exclusion may not require more intensive effort, rather better targeted effort to achieve change within local realities.

Challenges for implementation

Despite extensive agreement on the need for more multi-sectoral actions and on the objectives of such actions, there remain several general concerns regarding how to implement them. Much of the experience with this approach (especially in Europe) is relatively recent and still evolving. As a consequence, many significant questions remain unanswered. These challenges involve all aspects of implementation -- design, organisation, targeting and evaluation. Inevitably they are more controversial and more idealistic.

-- **The multi-sectoral approach potentially has significant implications for the organisation of government.** A complete revamping of government, its roles and its relationships is called for. This should entail a thorough modernisation of the public service, moving away from the administration of individual programmes and subsidies to holistic strategies pursued by government departments at all levels designed to implement coherent and integrated policies. Government relations with other sectors will have to become more flexible and co-operative in order to achieve wholehearted collaboration on complex projects for mutual benefits.

-- **The strategic plan that underpins the multi-sectoral approach is likely to have to confront strong internal contradictions.** The structures and mechanisms that are currently in place in most countries and cities do not support multi-sectoral approaches well. Strategic plans must be developed through public consultations, even though this process is fraught with inherent difficulties. Open, inclusive public discussions do not always result in consensus. Some groups -- the young, for example -- often want no truck with formal societal structures. Nonetheless, consultation is essential to generate enthusiasm among the local actors and to stimulate wider public support.

Furthermore, the rehabilitation of declining neighbourhoods, though beneficial in the long term, has little immediate voter appeal. Many local office holders prefer to keep a low profile and are disinclined to avow such policies in public. The electoral cycle promotes the espousal of popular short term issues rather than long term integrated strategic plans. Initiatives that redefine the responsibilities of citizenship, the elements of social solidarity and the obligations of representative government are needed to build support for multi-sectoral approaches.

-- **The content of a strategic plan for regeneration is bound to depend very directly on the project's perimeter.** The geographical boundaries for a strategic plan, to a large extent, determine the priorities, options, actors and structures. The project's perimeter has to be taken into account in reconciling the demands of the two way approach -- that is the "top-down" and "bottom-up" approaches. But changes in the perimeter may mean that the externalities are not the same and, as a result, the strategic plan will need revision. Any plan for rehabilitating a run-down area must therefore be consistent with the plans for the city as a whole. It should include considerations of the impacts on population, commerce and economic activity of the city as well as specific strategies for the neighbourhood in question.

--   **Planners have to be wary of the specious consensus and allegedly strategic aims that some decision makers may use as an alibi to achieve private objectives.** While trust is an essential element of successful partnerships, care must be taken to put the needs of the project above private objectives that do not benefit a neighbourhood in need of renewal. The design of the multi-sectoral strategy must maintain its integrity if it is to be successful. Implementation procedures may be adjusted according to need without damage to the inter-related goals of the project.

--   **The integrated multi-sectoral approach requires careful monitoring.** The discipline of evaluation is not yet up to the task of measuring the outcomes of multi-sectoral action, at either the neighbourhood or the city level. It is difficult to generalise elements of good practice when customised approaches are taken to meet the mix of local needs.

Specific issues

Apart from these general issues a number of unresolved issues continue to stimulate debate and discussion. These issues are not sufficient in the view of most practitioners to cast doubt on the advantages of the multi-sectoral approach; but they are relevant both to gaining public support and social acceptance and to improving the efficiency of the process. For pragmatic reasons, Member countries tend to have proceeded with multi-sectoral strategies, whilst assuming a definitive position on unresolved issues. In many cases, a better solution requires striking a sensitive balance between two opposing approaches.

How should multi-sectoral policies be targeted?

Because the benefits of city growth are unevenly distributed, there is considerable justification for selecting areas in decline for attention. Such area based renewal strategies have been used in many countries to improve large social housing projects or peripheral estates. The poorest communities need the widest multi-sectoral actions. Nonetheless, if the objective of public investment is overall positive urban change, is the worst neighbourhood first scenario the most productive one for the city to pursue? Will massive investment turn around the neighbourhood sufficiently to diminish a continued drain on public funds while increasing its contribution to city growth? Are there sufficient spill over effects to widen the base of beneficiaries to gain greater public support?

Can multi-sectoral policies eliminate the association between the underclass and declining neighbourhoods to justify area based strategies?

The supporters argue that positive discrimination through concentrated investment is required because of the intensity and density of the problems clustered in declining neighbourhoods. When changes are being forged on many fronts, there are additional benefits to be gained from policy synergy and momentum. Detractors claim that severely disadvantaged neighbourhoods require continued public investment and they revert to decline when government aid is withdrawn. Others claim that problems, such as crime and drugs, are merely displaced to other city locations. This approach is also considered inequitable by some because one area of the city is favoured while others that are equally or slightly less needy do not receive attention. Another reason why this approach is regarded as inequitable is the belief that only a small fraction of individuals that require help are assisted because many live outside the renewal neighbourhood.

Transferability of benefits may depend on recognising the validity of an area-based approach across cities, not just for a few problem neighbourhoods. Some services are best provided on city-wide scale. However, the critical factor is the co-ordination of related policies to meet agreed common objectives.

What should the role of housing be in urban renewal?

Initially, many of the multi-sectoral programmes were housing-led. Because housing is a major asset of cities, deteriorating housing stock received policy attention. Declining neighbourhoods were simple to identify by the condition of their housing. Member countries are now questioning this approach. In considering the needs of the people and of community development, the need to consider urban systems and not simply housing is recognised. Housing access by itself does not address the complex range of needs of people within cities nor the interaction of housing with other aspects of our cities. In recognising this, there is a need to ensure responses are balanced and to be aware of the externalities which may result.

Since many social policies are linked to individuals by their home address, the poor housing of recipients also received attention. Housing-led policies were utilised to deal with the problem of declining neighbourhoods as well as to identify individual households in difficulty.

Some of the assumptions on which housing led strategies were based have not been proven. It was expected that removing the stigma of declining neighbourhoods would result in positive development through normal urban processes. In spite of expensive improvements to housing, it has proved difficult to attract private sector investment, commercial and social services, transportation or affluent households, often for other reasons such as location.

There are other actions that in many cases should precede massive renovation of housing. Though the neighbourhood may be improved, residents may continue to be disadvantaged by virtue of location in relation to job markets and urban services. Scrutiny of the quality and mix of public and private facilities and services may show the inadequacies in the system. Swedish experience has highlighted the fact that massive investments in housing are not necessarily coincident with the priorities of residents. In fact, housing satisfaction is closely related to the quality of non-housing amenities and urban services.

What are the roles of the market in multi-sectoral approaches and how can they be assured?

It is generally accepted that there are clear relationships between macro-economic policy and market forces and that these affect housing affordability and exclusion.

The housing industry is a key economic indicator. Boom and bust cycles are an important factor affecting housing affordability by creating inefficiencies in construction. In addition, unstable land or property markets related to such cycles can cause specific affordability problems such as negative equity and excessive levels of debt, ultimately affecting home purchase. Government intervention, on the other hand, while endeavouring to maintain stability by protecting property values, often results in unintended social and economic effects.

Cities are the primary locus of economic activity. The quality of the urban environment is an important factor for the location of new enterprises which, in turn, has consequences on the creation of jobs. Therefore, the quality and availability of housing, urban form, public and community services and transport in the longer term all support the participation of urban residents in employment.

The challenge is to create greater efficiency in housing stock utilisation and access to urban services and facilities in such a way as to increase individuals' capacity to participate more fully in society.

There is growing evidence that repeated labour market exclusions have a ratchet effect on the economic stability and unemployment of disadvantaged groups. In modern economies, restructuring has resulted in the disappearance of many opportunities for unskilled labour. Where groups and communities are left without marketable skills or motivation for employment, they are marginalised from the labour market. This leads to a potential long term social financing burden and overall lower levels of economic activity.

The dichotomy between "planning" and "market" approaches is called into question by the need for multi-sectoral intervention. Both are integral elements to the operation of cities and the real issue is the interplay between them. It is increasingly recognised that markets need guidance and support to respond to changing circumstances. Planning should be used as a strategy for the pursuit of a vision for the city, providing a framework within which the market can confidently operate. Market activity alone will not solve the problems.

How to manage the interface between planning and markets, and to what ends, remains an unsolved question. In examining the links between planning and the market under present conditions, the need to recognise planning as a system rather than simply as a process has become apparent. Reforms in planning and regulation must ensure balance in the system to prevent social exclusion, as well as higher production costs, while achieving stated goals.

What structures are required for the implementation of multi-sectoral approaches?

The limitations of single policy solutions to narrowly defined problems are generally acknowledged. In particular, the limitations of single tenure strategies as a means of responding to urban needs were evident in the policy experience of several Member countries, especially those European countries which are attempting to diversify and revitalise concentrations of social housing. The need for the development of cross tenure approaches and a richer tenure mix to respond to the full gamut of household circumstances is now accepted. There exist parallels in other policy fields. However, abandoning traditional single policy approaches for multi-sectoral ones raises other problems associated with implementation.

Existing structures and administrative processes were generally designed for traditional single sector approaches. These traditional structures and processes are under stress because of the demands placed upon them. Problems that were analysed within sectors resulted in single sector responses. These are inadequate to redress current complex problems within the urban system. Retaining the existing structures and administrative processes has required the blending of programmes from various departments and levels of government on the ground, where each of funding stakeholders pursued their own specific goals. The difficulties and inefficiencies of this solution have emerged clearly in the experience of many Member countries.

The need for multi-sectoral analysis of problems is also clear, because of the multiple and reiterative causes of urban problems. However, the lack of adequate and appropriate data for such analysis is a frequent matter of complaint. The inter-relationship between economic, social and environmental factors needs to be acknowledged in data collection and analysis. To identify unbalanced development and concentration of social problems in geographic terms, it is necessary to collect fine grained data which may be aggregated and disaggregated in various ways while linked to spatial locations within the city.

While the need to transform existing structures and administrative processes is widely accepted, the forms of specific potential models are yet to be delineated. The difficulties presently being experienced provide some indications of the direction of the reforms required. For example, individual programmes and associated budgets often targeted an individual with multiple problems. However, each has to be accessed separately by meeting separately developed criteria. Not only is this administratively inefficient, but the duplication and overlapping are costly. Some single window type operations can ease the administrative difficulties but budgets tend to continue to be separate. Reforms will therefore be driven to some extent by the need for coherence of programmes and the streamlining of expenditures.

In many cases legal and other restrictions, designed to maintain privacy and confidentiality, prevent the sharing of information about individual circumstances or commercial enterprises, which could simplify the design of multi-pronged initiatives. A sensible balance needs to be struck between the competing objectives.

How should effective partnerships be built for multi-sectoral actions?

The importance of partnerships emerges clearly from the experience of Member countries. However, the mix and roles of the partners have varied widely. Most partnerships were formed after specific areas of the city were identified for action, rather than for city wide strategic action. France was the exception, where municipal participation in the programme for the social renewal of cities was facilitated through the establishment of partners for action.

The advantages of stable partnerships are evident. Where good working relationships are established, it is possible to break down inter-disciplinary barriers and to develop holistic perspectives. Commitment and local buy-in can ensure the success of local ventures. The weaknesses of local individual partners can be overcome by joint action and synergy, while their strengths are consolidated by the partnership (*Cf.* European Foundation for the Improvement of Living and Working Conditions, 1992). Corporate partners provide business acumen and are likely to be more socially responsible, so long as they can continue to make effective business decisions. Tenant associations and voluntary organisations are flexible, close to informal networks and support the long term interests of the community; but they have few financial resources. Governments, local, provincial and national, have key roles to play, in inviting co-operation, supporting local initiatives and decision making, leveraging resources and providing administrative support.

Nonetheless there are likely to be some difficulties. Some partners are difficult to engage. Where partnerships are unstable or where goals are not shared, stakeholders are motivated mainly by the need to protect their vested interests. Variations in power and political clout, in annual budgeting, in planning cycles and work styles put different pressures on partners and can create tensions within the partnerships. Much time and effort therefore needs to be spent in building partnerships with an atmosphere of trust and sharing. Participation and partnerships in fact require a new culture of joint action within the city.

How should the interface between the community and government be designed?

Policies need to reflect both national objectives and local needs. "Top-down" approaches ensure that national priorities and interests are met, while "bottom-up" approaches secure actions that are effective, appropriate and timely for local problems. While most countries have built up considerable experience with the use of one approach at a time, the use of both is an evolving idea. To have both approaches simultaneously requires a sensitive balance and a new code of practice. Strategic directions developed in the broader context must not become a impediment to local initiative.

The issue of power appears in many guises in defining the interface between governments and the community. While the importance of consulting with local residents is widely accepted to be pre-eminent, a balance has to be struck between the power of representative government and the power of citizens to make decisions. Frictions are possible between locally based "consultative democracy" and wider city based "representative democracy". The uneven distribution of power among interest groups and variations in the participation of groups is also a matter of concern. Though the disadvantaged are in greatest need of assistance, they are often excluded from consultation or public participation processes. They lack the time, resources or motivation for civic activities. The empowerment of disadvantaged persons, areas and groups is essential to enable all urban residents to participate economically, socially and politically in the urban setting.

The concept of empowerment is widely accepted in principle as a necessary condition for creating durable change among the disadvantaged. However, different perspectives have been applied to the concept. In some countries, institutional dysfunction is cited as the reason for adopting an empowerment approach, whereas in others the prime concern is with political disenfranchisement. In the former, empowerment is interpreted in terms of ensuring ready access to opportunity, thus relying somewhat more on individual initiative and opportunities; in the latter, empowerment suggests actually placing the resources and tools for the delivery of improved services and conditions in the hands of the disadvantaged. Clearly significant difficulties and differences of opinion remain, when it comes to operationalising the concept of empowerment.

How should national objectives for urban development be achieved?

Global and national factors inevitably affect urban development. Many of the key areas of development are areas of national responsibility, including economic policy and social security. What steps therefore should be taken by national governments to foster positive urban development?

The need for a coherent national urban policy is a central issue. Such an urban policy would establish a consistent framework within which all levels of government could develop specific plans and strategies for development. Markets would be assured of the strategic direction of change as well as clear signals with regard to opportunities for private sector action.

Such an urban policy must be multi-sectoral, based on the concept of the urban system. It must express national aspirations while at the same time offering latitude and flexibility for the achievement of local community goals.

While such a policy would link urban development to overall national growth, practical problems remain. Urban settlements and their hinterlands continue to compete for central government resources and commercial investments. Regional disparities may draw policy attention away from the cities. Regionally differentiated policies and subsidies for development can have a massive impact on the rates of population growth, location of public infrastructure and the industrial diversity.

Moreover, the recognition of the need for a national focus sits more easily with the traditions of those Member countries that have strongly centralised or unitary governmental structures. By contrast, in countries in which government is more decentralised, particularly those with a federal structure, urban policy is more appropriately left to the provincial or regional tier of government, national government intervention being limited to the more general issues of resource allocation and economic management. The tendency towards increased decentralisation in most Member countries (with the notable exception of the United Kingdom) suggests that the definition of the national role in urban policy formulation will become increasingly difficult, though nonetheless important, in the coming decade.

What steps can be taken to direct the future growth of networks of cities?

With present rates of urbanisation and development, cities are displaying new characteristics. Agglomerations are growing, often coalescing two or three cities, sometimes with little regard to political boundaries. The Osaka-Kobe-Kyoto corridor is an example; Detroit and Windsor spill over an international boundary, as do San Diego and Tijuana. This process at the urban level mirrors the larger-scale pattern of regional agglomeration that is affecting areas such as the North-West United States and British Columbia (Canada).

Trade and commercial exchanges increasingly link cities. The European Union has resulted in especially close ties between cities. The shared labour pool results in large movements of people. The liberalisation of trade and the removal of barriers have increased the location options for large business and manufacturing enterprises. Similar developments are under way, or anticipated, between the United States, Canada and Mexico.

Technology and communication "highways" connect cities in different regions or countries. Financial capitals in various countries are increasingly linked through electronic means. Rapid ground transport and air links have reduced travel time and increased exchange of people and goods between cities.

Such cross national and global developments defy direction by cities or even national governments. But they provide the context for the strategic multi-sectoral steps that need to be taken to promote positive changes while protecting urban residents from negative ones. How far cities and governments can be successful remains an open question.

Policy guidelines

- **A clear vision for the future of our cities must guide development: this vision must be based on cities as urban systems. Such a vision would focus strategic planning and provide a framework for decision making.**
- **Multi-sectoral approaches must be designed for the urban system with strategic objectives for growth as well as for the redress of existing problems. Related issues must be tackled holistically. The urban mosaic with its spatial, functional and communication links must be considered.**
- **Multi-sectoral strategies must take a dynamic long term perspective as well as meet immediate needs. Policies must ensure flexibility, keeping options open for multi-dimensional growth. Sustainability is a key objective, with positive impacts for the environment, housing and the quality of life for residents.**

Next steps

Consensus among Member countries regarding the validity of the multi-sectoral approach provides direction for the next steps. Experiments in Member countries must be closely monitored to identify success factors and pitfalls. Results must be examined in a systematic way to enable sharing of policy experiences among Member countries. Transferable ideas must be documented and disseminated to shorten experimentation time and to save expenditures.

Summary and Conclusions

Unbalanced growth and socio-economic separation have, throughout history, been constant realities of urban economic development. The emergence of new forms of exclusion and disadvantage in the course of the 1980s has led to a growing recognition that urban regeneration policy is essentially about reconnecting the links between severely disadvantaged or alienated areas or groups and the rising economic mainstream. Urban policy for the 1990s is increasingly concerned with central societal objectives about growth, equality, and the environment.

The context for housing and urban policy in OECD countries

There is a strong connecting thread among the problems faced by mature OECD cities and metropolitan regions.

Firstly, severely disadvantaged neighbourhoods co-exist with areas of affluence and economic success. These are often in the inner city, but are also to be found on the periphery, especially where large areas of low-cost or social housing have been built at the outer edge of the metropolitan area. Typically these areas lack access to basic amenities and community facilities; employment opportunities are limited; and housing tenure and social mix are uniform. Social deprivation tends to be concentrated in these areas.

Secondly, there are also clear and sometimes related problems of housing affordability. A shortage of cheap rental housing or difficulties of access to finance for first time buyers, combined with high land and housing prices, have made it increasingly difficult for low-to-middle income families to find affordable housing in suitable locations.

Thirdly, there are problems relating to social and demographic change. The growing number of elderly households in the OECD countries, the numbers of young households moving into property for the first time, and, arguably most

267

pressing in much of Europe at least, the upsurge in immigration into the cities of Member nations are each having a major impact on the volume and structure of urban housing demand.

Finally, despite major improvements in recent decades, there remains a problem of overall physical housing quality in many of these neighbourhoods.

Apart from the socio-demographic changes just noted, three main processes account for the emergence of low quality neighbourhoods and persistently disadvantaged groups in contemporary cities: labour market changes; the globalisation of economic processes; and fiscal restraint.

In most OECD Member countries the last thirty years have witnessed a substantial increase in the number of jobs. This has been accompanied in many countries by a significant increase in labour force participation. Women have accounted for a major share of the increase in labour force participation and employment, but many jobs for women, as also increasingly for men, have been part-time or temporary. In almost all countries there has been a widening of wage differentials. Significant differences also show up when these labour market experiences are converted into patterns of household formation. A "new poor" has come to be defined as much by their household status as by their degree of success, or lack of, in finding a secure and stable source of income from employment or from their provision for old age: the single elderly and those of an advanced age, single parent families, families with large numbers of children and, to some extent, older people of working age, living alone, without secure employment.

Associated with these broad changes in the labour market has been a significant change in the economic structure of cities and in the composition of the labour force. This reflects the progressive globalisation of national and local economies, which has had two main effects: to require continuous attention to the need to improve productivity; and to increase uncertainty about the future. This has encouraged upward pressure on the skill mix of those in employment, a new emphasis on training, the loss of many unskilled job opportunities and the increasing reliance of firms on part-time or casual employment. The employment situation of many marginal groups is as a consequence increasingly precarious.

The much greater attention paid by governments to the control of inflation, the imposition of limits on public spending and borrowing and the efficiency of the public sector has had two direct consequences for cities. Firstly, it has seen the loss of large numbers of often unskilled but secure jobs in public sector agencies. And secondly, it has set new limits to the volume of resources available to assist disadvantaged areas and groups and to create programmes for urban regeneration. This has encouraged policy makers to look elsewhere, to the private sector and to local communities, for additional resources to fund their efforts.

Towards Strategic, Multi-sectoral Approaches to Urban Regeneration

The design of appropriate responses to these changes should be based on a recognition of the fundamental characteristics of urban change: cities are open economic systems; cities can choose to change; cities essentially comprise a set of neighbourhoods; and there are basic areal and functional interactions between those neighbourhoods. It follows that, wherever possible, urban policies should be targeted at neighbourhoods, as the essential building block of urban change, and that they should be linked and multi-sectoral, both at the level of the city and at the level of the neighbourhood.

The first pre-requisite for successful regeneration policy is that there should be a clearly articulated "city-wide vision", based on a broad strategic understanding of how housing and other programmes can serve the economic, social and environmental objectives which are components of this "vision". For the areas or neighbourhoods selected for policy action, there needs to be a clear statement of the aims of each proposal and a more detailed scrutiny of these inter-sectoral connections. This should include: definition of the actions which should precede housing change; integration of the tenure and management aspects of housing policies and land market issues; scrutiny of the links between the neighbourhood and the wider urban system; analysis of the appropriate quantity and mix of public and private facilities and services; detailed investigation of environmental effects.

Social integration and livable environments

Programmes for social renewal and environmental improvement need to address a broad range of initiatives.

Social integration, employment and training: Programmes of reintegration usually follow the order: *i)* physical regeneration; *ii)* training programmes; *iii)* education policy. Yet this is often the reverse of the necessary order of

269

priority in terms of timing. The appropriate scale for intervention is small: highly localised populations of 1 000-2 000 are often the most effective grouping for the delivery of the required labour market and training packages.

The re-establishment of pathways between excluded neighbourhoods and the wider urban economy requires local control by organisations working for the area within the area. These should focus expenditure on long-term benefits: basic education, training and vocational-skills building, as well as labour market counselling. Multi-lateral action and collaboration with local or regional governments and with private sector employers are also essential. It is only through "local sensitivity" that job training policies, linked to the community and to housing, can accommodate the special needs of specific groups in terms of job placement such as: women with children, ethnic minorities, the young and the disabled.

Homelessness: There is a need for an internationally defined and agreed measurable concept of homelessness. The legal rights of the homeless also need to be clarified.

Homelessness usually has complex causes. A well co-ordinated strategy involving housing, health, employment, training and social services is needed to combat the problem. Co-operation and co-ordination between service providers is essential. Housing-led policies to address the problem of homelessness are appropriate, since the primary, immediate need is for sufficient housing. But in the longer term assistance needs to be multi-sectoral. Partnerships and joint ventures with the voluntary and non-profit sectors should also be encouraged, including the use of innovative administrative arrangements, since voluntary organisations are more successful than large public organisations in gaining the confidence of homeless people.

A healthy residential environment: The quality of the urban environment depends in large measure on the manner in which the individual experiences both the natural and the man-made environment. The factors responsible for economic, social and environmental stress must be identified. The impacts of dysfunction are experienced in the short term by the residents of blighted neighbourhoods but there may be grave long term consequences as well, due to the inter-generational transmission of poverty, unemployment and disadvantage. Such intractable poverty and exclusion is a drag on economic functionality and city competitiveness. Some of the impacts of rapid urban change on human health and the environment may be long term or even irreversible.

Cross sectoral planning for the environmental improvement of neighbourhoods and areas is essential. Organised implementation and cost effective use of resources is possible only through multi-sectoral policies.

Integration through empowerment: In many countries strategies for empowering local neighbourhood communities are relatively recent. It is already clear that involving residents that are alienated is not easy: it is likely that there will always be a residual group that does not have the ability to become self sufficient due to negative pressures, such as discrimination, which are beyond their control.

Nonetheless local action and community involvement are indispensable for social cohesion. Non-controlling, arm's-length arrangements provide flexibility and room for independent action, in which key partners, such as national voluntary organisations and local groups, should be encouraged to play appropriate roles. A combination of the "bottom-up" and "top-down" approaches is likely to be most successful. Programmes for empowering local communities should be based on a long term perspective and commitment and should be well resourced, with a training component for staff as well as local groups. In this a balance must be struck between representative democracy and local control in order to ensure that local action takes place within a strategic view of the broad urban context.

Social cohesion: Social cohesion contributes to political stability and social collaboration, which in turn create positive conditions for economic investment and urban growth. The success of community relations and social cohesion tends to be measured by community harmony and lack of strife rather than formal indicators.

Social cohesion should be built on the existing strengths of the residential community, by reinforcing networks and "capacity building". A sense of community takes time to develop. It should be nurtured by the residents because they see its value rather than promoted as a necessity for public programmes or funding. External supports to social cohesion moreover should be sensitive and co-operative rather than directive and prescriptive.

Integrating the young: Co-operation between governments, non-government associations and community groups should be encouraged with the aim of formulating and applying co-ordinated policies and programmes for children, adolescents and young adults, especially those living in deprived urban neighbourhoods. A range of remedial and preventive policies should be implemented to reduce illiteracy and innumeracy, improve vocational training, provide for cultural and recreational activities outside of formal school hours, support personal and household coping mechanisms, nurture interpersonal bonds during adolescence, and provide counselling about education, health, legal, nutritional and vocational matters. These programmes should recognise the diversity of requirements of children, adolescents and young adults.

A multi-purpose services unit in one location (preferably at the neighbourhood level) can best provide for both traditional sectoral welfare and non-traditional services. The aim should be to involve children, adolescents and young adults directly in policy formulation and implementation using peer group dialogue, vocational training and job placement. The organisation and co-operation of programmes for youth require long-term commitment and labour-intensive resources from both the public and private sectors. Investments in programmes for children and youth often need to be complemented by policies for family support and investments in urban infrastructure and housing.

Safety in cities: Successful initiatives to improve safety and reduce crime in cities recognise that known and agreed causes can be identified in order to formulate and implement preventive and remedial policies. Multiple counter-measures and strategies are required: building design proposals and technical solutions alone are ineffective.

Preventive and remedial measures should be combined and national and municipal authorities should collaborate with non-government organisations to reallocate funds and invest resources in order to reduce crimes and improve safety in cities. Partnerships between national and municipal authorities, the residents, local businesses, police and service agencies result in the most effective programmes. The emphasis should be on preventive strategies, based on comprehensive risk assessment and priority setting.

Housing affordability

Most OECD governments have encouraged the deregulation of their housing finance systems. As a result, there are more funds available for mortgages through the growth of wholesale and secondary markets. There is a greater variety of mortgage products, including index-linked loans which directly aid affordability by reducing problems of front-end loading. Down-payment conditions have eased in many countries. And consumers are able increasingly to shop at one-stop financial centres when buying a house, thereby greatly reducing transactions costs. However, following the recent downturn in economic activity and the housing market, innovations in the housing finance sector over the next few years are likely to be consumer-oriented, reflecting greater competition between financial institutions, greater flexibility among mortgage products and lower profit margins than in the 1980s. This may lead to problems in later years.

Policies aimed at easing access to owner occupation are common throughout OECD Member countries, relatively successful and increasingly targeted to moderate and lower income households, although recent experience in some countries highlights the dangers involved in attempting to extend home ownership to vulnerable groups, so long as interest rates and house prices remain volatile and the employment situation for many remains uncertain.

Moreover it has to be recognised that easier access to finance for the majority of house purchasers may create additional problems for the more disadvantaged if the supply of new or existing housing is not sufficiently responsive.

To assist low-income renters, policies based on supply subsidies and tax incentives both have a role to play, though the direct provision of housing by the public sector is rarely as cost effective as other forms of "enabling". In the longer run market renting (and social renting) should be allowed to operate in an environment which allows suppliers to make an adequate return for providing housing of an acceptable quality. Demand-side and supply-side initiatives should work in tandem.

Policies to stabilise the housing market need to recognise that market volatility tends to reflect deeper market failures, notably rigidities in the supply system in the face of unstable housing demand. Microeconomic reform, particularly in the fields of taxation, land supply and land use planning, remains the instrument most likely to improve market stability.

The supply of adequate affordable housing in urban areas can be encouraged by reducing regulatory barriers, by creating incentives for simpler and more sensible planning and building controls, through inclusionary zoning and through the more sensitive use of impact fees and other forms of planning impost. The responsiveness of supply to demand pressure is weak in many countries because the conflicts and regulations within the planning system can be exploited by speculators, existing residents and landowners to prevent more affordable forms of housing development. There is therefore a need for serious and continuing consensus-building about the future patterns of land use, about the need for affordable housing, and about its place within the wider questions of the environment, sustainable development, rising property values and mixed land uses.

Data collection and use

The role of data remains critical to the definition, evaluation and monitoring of area-based programmes and policies for urban regeneration. But although there have been encouraging and significant advances in the collection and uses of data in many Member countries of the OECD, in too many cases the overall situation remains unco-ordinated and piecemeal. Relatively few governments, authorities and institutions have collaborated to develop a dynamic, multi-dimensional data base for use as an archive of information for the analysis of living environments in cities. There is a pressing need for the development of Co-ordinated Information Systems.

The collection and updating of data is an important resource for urban policy administration, especially decision making and monitoring. No single-focus information system can equal the potential of a Co-ordinated Information System to support an inter-sectoral and an inter-organisational approach. Much collected data are not only delimited according to traditional administrative and sectoral approaches, but may be even further defined to meet precise project-oriented objectives. In contrast, the aim of an information management policy based on the Co-ordinated Information Systems (CIS) approach should be to enable diverse groups of users to co-ordinate and integrate different types of data and information for multi-sectoral uses.

There is therefore a pressing need to examine: how to formulate and apply a holistic conceptual framework for networking diverse types of data and information within and across sectors; how to elaborate and apply appropriate tools to deal with information flows between the public and private sectors as well as among authorities, institutions and firms in the same sector; and how to promote and co-ordinate the interest and input of authorities, institutions and firms to rationalise the basic units of recorded data and information.

The multi-sectoral approach and the role of partnerships

A wide variety of experience in different Member countries was reviewed in the course of the project. The conclusions of this review highlight the very general acceptance of the need for a multi-sectoral approach to the problems of combating exclusion, encouraging social integration and regenerating outworn urban residential environments. The mix of objectives for each case study project determined whether the approach was housing-led or if housing was a major component. Where the area was identified because of deteriorated housing, there was a greater tendency to use housing-led policies. It is notable, however, that there were often problems associated with high costs, as well as low resident satisfaction, when housing improvement was the primary activity.

There is a clear recognition in many Member countries that the problems of cities cannot be redressed by cities alone: finance for projects needs to be consolidated by accessing national funding programmes, supplementing them with municipal programmes, leveraging private sector investments and encouraging individual contributions. But there remains wide variation between countries in the determination of which organisation plays the lead role and in the administrative structures established for implementing the changes. Some countries, like France, have developed a national structure, reflecting the national priority placed on urban renewal. In many other countries the key role in identifying, designing and delivering a programme of positive urban change is played by municipal governments.

The importance attached to partnerships is notable. Partnerships are critical to the implementation of multi-sectoral policies. They facilitate the rationalisation of resources, the concentration of effort, the integration of expertise and the assurance of commitment on the part of stake holders. They should be developed to suit the specific local conditions. The characteristics of the urban problem, the stake holders and vested interests should determine the structure, composition, duration, scope and mode of their operation. Partnerships need to be built on shared interests and a joint commitment to action. A vision of the future, providing a clear picture of the desired outcomes, encourages partners to align their goals and objectives while making appropriate contributions. They need to involve local residents and community organisations as the nucleus, in order to ensure their full commitment to achieving jointly established goals and to ensure that they are the principal beneficiaries of whatever action is taken. They should combine both "bottom-up" and "top-down" initiatives. Capacity building and mutual understanding are essential both at the top and the bottom to ensure that the partnership can work effectively.

Partnerships that involve the neighbourhood level are essential if communities are to be engaged effectively and social cohesion is to be engendered; but they cannot work in isolation. They require the support of agencies at the level of the city, region and state or nation, if their actions are to be successful and durable.

The multi-sectoral approach is not an end in itself; but it is necessary if the challenge raised by the growing complexity of urban management is to be met. Sectoral policies are increasingly incongruent with urban concerns and, more than ever before, multi-sectoral policies are required to grasp the multi-dimensional links, interactions and implications of current issues. Yet a multi-sectoral approach is only rarely incorporated into the rationale of prevailing government structures. It calls, on the contrary, for an overview that transcends administrative power sharing and goes beyond piecemeal reasoning.

However, the multi-sectoral approach also requires better understanding of the dynamics of urban change. Two major areas where there is a need for improved information systems are *i)* a body of urban data, that can be readily examined at the level of the neighbourhood or of groups of households with similar characteristics; and *ii)* information relating to the impacts of policies. Only a multi-sectoral approach can match resources to needs in a way that ensures cost effectiveness. There may be additional costs associated with leadership and co-ordination at the decision making level as well as with efficient administration and implementation of the policies and programmes. But overall savings are also possible, due to more sensible choices, more consistent decisions, the elimination of duplication and the internalisation of external costs. Efforts to combat exclusion, encourage social and economic integration and improve living environments may not require more intensive effort, rather better targeted effort to achieve change within local realities.

The Project Group's conclusions can be summarised as follows:

-- First, it reasserted the primacy and relevance in contemporary conditions of an area-based approach to the social and economic regeneration of cities. This was not intended to deny the importance of universal or "people-oriented" programmes for education, welfare, employment, housing and other sectoral needs. But it was intended to highlight the need for carefully targeted, area-based initiatives to supplement or replace universal programmes where these were clearly needed to avoid the cumulative social and economic costs of neglect or where the efficacy of initiatives depended on the adoption of a localised, multi-sectoral approach.

-- Second, it singled out the neighbourhood as the most appropriate unit for the design and delivery of area-based programmes. This too was not intended to deny the importance of other scales of action. In particular stress was laid on the importance of linking action at the neighbourhood level to the development of broader city-wide or metropolitan strategies. Nonetheless the neighbourhood appears the most efficient unit in terms of which to develop and deliver multi-sectoral initiatives for urban regeneration and social integration, not least because it is also the scale at which local communities can be involved to the greatest effect.

-- Third, the Project Group stressed the essential need for a multi-sectoral approach. This is based on the evidence that, while in particular circumstances there may be good grounds for giving one sector "lead" status -- for example, in the case of many European concentrations of social and economic disadvantage, housing-related programmes remain the most important requirement -- in the great majority of cases resources will be put at risk, and the objectives of the initiatives will not be achieved, unless a co-ordinated set of programmes, covering such things as community facilities, public transport, training and personal development, is initiated at the same time. This requires the development of a shared vision of the desired future as well as a high level of co-ordination between government agencies and the involvement of all interested parties. These are not easy goals to achieve. But the evidence clearly suggests that the integration of policies and programmes into a uniform framework is most likely to be successful at the local level.

-- Fourth, it reasserted the value of partnership between government, private and voluntary organisations and the community. This is essential both to guarantee the commitment of those affected to successful outcomes and to assemble adequate resources at minimum cost to public expenditure.

Policy Guidelines

The following policy guidelines have been established for each of the main topics covered in the report, after considering the evidence derived from the material supplied by the participating Member countries in the course of the project.

Social integration, employment and training

- The aim of programmes for social renewal and integration should be to re-establish the pathways between excluded neighbourhoods and the wider urban economy.
- Education and training should be an integral part of any programme designed to re-integrate disadvantaged areas or groups into the urban mainstream.
- Employment-oriented programmes for social renewal should usually be directed to highly localised areas of no more than 2 000-3 000 persons.
- Job-training policies, linked to community action and housing renewal, need to display "local sensitivity" to accommodate the special needs of specific groups: such as women with children, ethnic minorities, the young and the disabled.
- Multi-lateral action through local partnerships is essential to make the required changes materialise.
- The methods by which resources for increasing employment are organised, accessed and evaluated are as important as the funds allocated. Recommended approaches include:

    i) the promotion of a "lean" organisation;
    ii) the reliance on neighbourhood-based facilitators within a co-ordinated city-wide programme;
    iii) the recognition of multiple ways in which private sector companies might relate to a social need in a city;
    iv) the recognition of the different needs of different city neighbourhoods;

v) the concept of a one-stop shop where a needy individual can have his or her problems assessed in the round;

vi) the follow-through of cases over a certain period;

vii) the search for linkages and sub-programmes which will open blockages in the path of reaching objectives.

- Innovative approaches to employment creation need to be developed, based on new concepts of employment which replace the traditional jobs lost in industry.
- Specific measures need to be introduced:

  i) to ensure adequate public transportation for disadvantaged groups and areas to encourage labour market participation and widen the range of opportunity;

  ii) to provide adequate child-care; and

  iii) to eliminate high marginal tax rates within the social security system which might act as a disincentive to labour market participation.

Homelessness

- Governments should establish a clear definition of homelessness which is easy to apply and to use as a basis for measuring the extent of the need for shelter.
- The legal rights of the homeless should be clearly codified and applied on a uniform national basis.
- A variety of programmes should be developed to take account of the wide range of circumstances that can result in homelessness.
- Similarly a variety of types of shelter, ranging from crisis accommodation to long term affordable housing, should be made available to meet housing needs.
- Homelessness programmes should be integrated with other initiatives, such as employment and training programmes, to encourage the progressive rehabilitation of the homeless and their re-integration into the mainstream.
- Voluntary organisations should be encouraged to play a central role in the process in partnership with local and national governmental agencies.

Residential environments

- The links between the economic, social and environmental dimensions of living in disadvantaged neighbourhoods need to be recognised: the need for employment, income security and improvements to community facilities goes hand in hand with the need for improvements to the physical quality of the local environment.
- The short-term and long-term costs of deteriorated residential environments in terms of health, social dysfunction and criminality and environmental degradation need to be assessed and made clear to the wider community.
- The potential consequences of actions taken elsewhere in the urban context -- for example, in relation to highway construction or industrial restructuring -- for the quality of the environment and the health of residents in disadvantaged neighbourhoods need to be kept under continuous review.
- Multi-sectoral partnerships between agencies and organisations, such as area health authorities, private sector employers and community groups, need to be established to devise co-ordinated measures to improve the quality of local residential environments and local public health.

The empowerment of local communities

- A local focus should be established for dealing with problems to draw on local knowledge and to establish better co-ordination of services, direct communication and consultation with residents and a focal point for generating solutions.
- Multi-sectoral action, concentrated locally, is essential but the aim should also be to influence the wider community. Failure to approach problems as multi-faceted and to build bridges to wider community needs and perspectives may generate despair and a greater sense of alienation and powerlessness.
- Resources should be allocated directly to local programmes and initiatives. To redirect wasted resources and maximise local impacts, this may be assisted by localising both decision-making and service delivery.
- The latent potential of residents and local resources of the neighbourhood should be harnessed, based on the involvement of neighbourhood agencies and spontaneous networks and partnerships

between public, private and non-profit agencies in the neighbourhood.

- Links to the mainstream community should be fostered. Concentrated neighbourhoods of disempowered persons should not be permitted to become isolated or stigmatised through outside pressures.
- The responsible authorities should enter into long term policy commitments and be patient about resource investments. Fragmented policy approaches, under-resourcing and *ad hoc* funding have been major problems in developing empowered neighbourhoods and residents.

Social cohesion

- Social cohesion should be built on the existing strengths of the residential community resources. It is important to validate the existing sense of community, however fragile, while reinforcing networks and "capacity building". Such a sense of community takes time to develop. Social cohesion should be nurtured by the residents because they see its value rather than promoted as a necessity for public programmes or funding.
- External supports to social cohesion should be sensitive and co-operative rather than directive and prescriptive. Initiatives such as community education, which enables residents to build their community according to their own vision, should be supported.
- The root causes of disadvantage should be recognised as impeding social cohesion. Initiatives that promote social cohesion can lead to the solution of other problems through the participation of residents. It is a means to urban regeneration as well as a positive end in itself.

Integrating the young

- Policies should aim to be both remedial and preventive, covering a wide range of activities, including: illiteracy and innumeracy programmes, vocational training, cultural and recreational activities (including sport) and personal counselling.
- Young people should be involved directly in the formulation of policies and the design and management of programmes both to draw on their knowledge and experience and to maximise their involvement and commitment.

- Multi-purpose centres should be established in deprived neighbourhoods as a focus for a range of services, including: support and guidance in relation to housing problems, job placement and training, health clinics, counselling and after-school care.
- Voluntary and community resources should be encouraged to work in partnership with governmental agencies to provide personalised attention and co-ordinated programmes to meet the diverse needs of the young.

Safer cities

- Governments should encourage the establishment of partnerships between community organisations, private business, government agencies and the criminal justice authorities to formulate local strategies for crime prevention and safety.
- Measures to increase the safety of all members of the community should be an integral part of all strategies of urban regeneration and social renewal.
- Comprehensive risk assessments should be used to target preventive measures and to identify potentially deviant groups or individuals for whom appropriate integrative programmes can be devised.
- The environmental characteristics of neighbourhoods and the ways in which they are used, especially by vulnerable groups such as children, the elderly, women and racial minorities, need to be reviewed to identify measures that could reduce the opportunity for criminal action and assault.

Housing affordability

- The issue of housing affordability needs to be set in a multi-sectoral context. Affordability is not simply about housing finance, housing subsidies or construction costs. It relates also to employment security, macroeconomic policy, land use planning, ecological sustainability, financial competition and a range of other factors.

- Measures to improve housing affordability must be based on a sound understanding of the workings of the local housing market and of the relationship between national, macroeconomic influences -- such as taxation and interest rate policy -- and local market factors -- such as the structure of neighbourhoods, accessibility patterns, the changing location of employment and the responsiveness of local housing supply.
- Policies designed to improve affordability should take into account possible "second round" effects and should assess carefully the risks involved, especially where vulnerable groups -- such as those with unstable incomes or single parent families -- are the targeted clients for affordability initiatives.
- Governments at all levels should recognise the need to involve private sector housing agencies -- landlords, developers, house builders as well as private employers -- in partnership to address the problems of affordability in the local context. There is a clear need to build a political consensus around viable long-term strategies for affordable housing.
- Broadly-based subsidies, and implicit subsidies from below-cost public infrastructure provision, should be replaced by more selective and carefully targeted programmes to assist those groups most vulnerable to problems of housing affordability. Tax subsidies to owner-occupiers should be reviewed.
- Rental housing provision, both private and public, should be based on market prices and a realistic return on capital, to ensure a buoyant long-term supply of accommodation at minimum public expenditure cost. Barriers to efficient, low-cost private supply should be eliminated.
- However, in the desire to make housing more "affordable", governments should not lose sight of the long run environmental costs of different forms of housing provision and should aim to establish a broadly-based consensus concerning the need to make housing, in the future, compatible with the requirements of an ecologically sustainable urban form.

Data collection and use

- The need for adequate and up-to-date area-based data to form a basis for the formulation of policies to address the social, environmental and economic problems of disadvantaged neighbourhoods should be clearly acknowledged.
- Governments should review the data needs for urban regeneration to identify priority categories, with particular reference to:

  i) appropriate geographical scales;
  ii) availability of time series;
  iii) co-ordination between economic, social and environmental data.

- Traditional "hard" data on urban conditions -- such as data relating to housing, employment and transportation -- should be supplemented both by periodic qualitative assessments of local social, environmental and housing conditions in disadvantaged neighbourhoods and by continuous monitoring of community attitudes and aspirations.
- A Co-ordinated Information Management system for urban and housing policy should be instituted, based on the integration of previously distinct data collection exercises.
- Data needs and data collection responsibilities should be assessed in the context of a partnership between public and private agencies, with a view to meeting the diverse needs of groups of users.
- A set of basic indicators should be constructed, in association with community groups, private business interests and voluntary organisations, both to provide a continuing source of information about urban and housing conditions as a basis for building a wider political consensus about the need for action and as a basis for the allocation of scarce resources.
- Standard procedures and protocols should be established to enable all agencies and groups of data users to relate new and existing data sources to the issues under consideration.

The role of partnerships

- Partnerships are critical to the implementation of multi-sectoral policies. They facilitate the rationalisation of resources, the concentration of effort, the integration of expertise and the assurance of commitment on the part of stake holders.

- Partnerships should be developed to suit the specific local conditions. The characteristics of the urban problem, the stake holders and vested interests should determine the structure, composition, duration, scope and mode of operation of the partnership.
- Partnerships should be built on shared interest, complementary and joint action. A vision of the future, providing a clear picture of the desired outcomes, encourages partners to align their goals and objectives while making appropriate contributions.
- Partnerships should involve local residents and community organisations as the nucleus. The involvement of local residents and community organisations is necessary in order to ensure their full commitment to achieving the jointly established goals and to ensure that they are the principal beneficiaries of whatever action is taken.
- Partnerships should combine both "bottom-up" and "top-down" initiatives. Capacity building and mutual understanding are essential both at the top and the bottom to ensure that the partnership can work effectively.
- Partnerships that involve the local (neighbourhood) level are essential if communities are to be engaged effectively and social cohesion is to be engendered. However, partnerships working to improve neighbourhoods cannot work in isolation; they require the support of agencies at the level of the city, region and state or nation, if their actions are to be successful and durable.

Annex 1

OECD Housing Affordability Survey

Introduction

As part of this project, Member countries participated in a small survey on housing affordability. This survey was in two parts, the first asked a series of contextual questions relating to housing costs, quality and other dimensions of affordability, broadly defined. Data was received for nations, and for up to three cities within each Member nation (ideally these would represent restructuring, typical and growth cities, as defined by delegates for their own country. In practice, the cities were not so clearly defined). The second part of the survey requested brief comments on key affordability policies, focusing on description, objectives, instruments, budgeting, outcomes and the overall integration and evolution of the policy. Overall, ten countries (Belgium, Canada, Finland, France, Germany, Japan, Sweden, Switzerland, Turkey and the United Kingdom) responded specifically to Part A and a variety of case studies and general information was sent by all countries in response to Part B.

What follows is a commentary on Part A, the survey data, followed by summary tables for nine questions asked. The shorter, more discursive commentary on Part B concludes the annex.

Part A: Survey Data

Housing expenditure ratios

Apart from the outliers Germany and Belgium (and to a lesser extent, Japan and Turkey), there is a tendency towards a ratio of average house price to household income, at national level, of between 4 and 5. However, at urban levels, there is considerably more volatility, with much lower rates in Leeds and Montreal but much higher ratios in Turkish and German towns, Stockholm,

Gothenberg and Helsinki. The average rent to household income ratios are broadly uniform at between 15 and 25 per cent of income in every case except Bordeaux and Toulouse (at around 28 per cent) and at the other extreme Japan (11 per cent). This constancy may reflect the long term effects of rent controls and other regulations -- even after their removal (Tables 1 and 2). Finally, in terms of tenure distribution, all OECD countries surveyed have a majority of home owners (apart from Germany and Switzerland) (Table 3). However, in almost every case, urban rates of home ownership are lower than national rates. This would appear to identify the existence of affordability constraints in cities.

Price change

Across and within nations, house price inflation (averaged to an annual rate for the five years 1986-90) grew at different, positive rates. West Germany enjoyed low rates of price change; whereas considerably higher rates were experienced in the United Kingdom, Sweden and Belgium. Within Canada, price change varied from 0.28 per cent in Montreal to more than 20 per cent in Vancouver. United Kingdom and Swedish house prices rose more uniformly (Table 4).

Land price inflation (measured for the same period) (Table 5) is a more sensitive and volatile indicator of housing market pressure, recording negative rates in Bremen and Montreal and annual rates in excess of 20 per cent in Stockholm and in excess of 30 per cent in Vancouver and Nottingham. While very sensitive to local planning regimes, there is evidence that this variable is more locally-specific than any other of those surveyed. But this does not mean that a combination of high price to income ratios, high land and house price inflation, coupled with a low rent to income ratio, is not evidence of a poorly-functioning housing system. The five year annual average construction index (Table 6) appears to follow land price change (and supply activity more generally) but with a smaller amplitude, varying from -0.5 per cent in Hanover to 15 per cent in Vancouver and 14 per cent in Stockholm. Finally, annual housing construction output per 1 000 (Table 7) is a standardised measure of supply activity. This is fairly uniform at national level (between 4 and 5.8) apart from the much lower level of activity in the United Kingdom and very high activity in Japan. Interestingly, there is a clear separation between growth cities and other cities, with the former enjoying higher levels of construction. Nonetheless, there is considerable variety within city types. The volatility of these indicators has been reinforced with the recent downturn in international housing and land markets, not fully captured in this data.

Housing quality

Average household size (Table 8) is not surprisingly uniform, apart from the very much larger households in Turkey (national average 5.2), falling between 2 and 2.8. France, the United Kingdom and Canada tend towards 2.8 and Sweden and Finland toward the lower extreme. The average number of rooms (Table 9) is clearly determined by property type and the variety of this variable across the OECD reflects the variety of property size. While the average is only 3.5 rooms in Switzerland, it rises to nearly 6 in Canada. Helsinki records an average of 3 rooms, whereas Antwerp, Milton Keynes and Toronto all exceed 5 rooms.

It does appear that qualitatively, OECD countries enjoy quite high standards of housing. The problem, as borne out in this indicative survey refers to high housing costs, volatility in the land market and relatively low rates of supply responsiveness. Not all of these issues are within the control of policy makers, but some, such as planning and rent regulations, clearly are.

Part B: Policy Responses

Delegates were asked to group this part of the survey into six basic sections that looked at current housing policies designed to increase affordability: a brief description of the relevant policy; its basic objectives; the policy instruments adopted; the budgeting or finance made available; the outcomes associated with the policy; and, the likely evolution of the area considered. A number of countries produced useful and interesting examination of their affordability policies.

Policy objectives

There is a trend throughout the survey for policies to become more targeted and more budget-conscious. Affordability policies, in other words, policies aimed at reducing the cost of housing and for providing more rented and owned housing at affordable prices, have shifted, in large part, toward those most in need and tend to be more orientated towards allowances and financing devices that have lesser impacts on markets than, say, "bricks and mortar" subsidies. The Belgian documentation is explicit in pointing to the necessary budgetary expenditure imposed by social housing and therefore has redirected its affordability policies towards encouraging private sector investment in social housing, targeting the renovating of inner cities, and moving away from the indiscriminate subsidy of home ownership.

In Switzerland, the market is dominated by private, mainly rented housing, market forces. Affordability policy is therefore about improving the performance of the market as far as disadvantaged groups in society require additional assistance. In Finland, the use of allowances and state loans are designed so that households of different means and sizes will not have to face unreasonably high housing expenditure to income ratios. In France, the standard objectives of providing everyone with a decent home is supplemented with a concern for the needy or disadvantaged by focusing on low income households, preventing debt and helping to restructure existing mortgage or rental debt, and, preventing the emergence of ghettos for high-risk populations.

The Australian documentation makes it clear that affordable housing is intimately linked to social security policy. Their concern is with a housing allowance which attempts to protect the needy from allowing their after-housing income to fall below a minimum level (the same principle applies in the United Kingdom). In Canada, the principle of targeting is taken one stage further by defining the key client group as those in "core housing need".

Policy instruments

Across the responding countries, two main policy instruments come across as important: housing allowances and mechanisms for reducing housing finance costs (on the demand and the supply side). With the exception of some innovative support for first time buyers in Finland, there is less evidence of fiscal inducements and large-scale grant assistance.

In France, *l'aide personnalisée au logement* (APL) has recently replaced the older forms of housing allowances (which were family or social category-orientated) and tries to increase household solvency. In Australia, rent assistance is a non-taxable cash payment to social security and war service pensioner claimants who live in the private rented sector. It works by providing maximum rates of assistance to recipients who pay rents above a minimum threshold level and is provided at the rate of 50 per cent of the rent paid (up to the maximum).

In Canada, Rent Supplement reduces eligible tenants' housing costs to 25 per cent of income, provided they are in core housing need and already paid more than 30 per cent of their income and/or had a suitability (overcrowding) or adequacy (condition) problem associated with their accommodation. Finland has a well-developed allowance scheme (aimed at families, students and pensioners). With the general housing allowance, households have a level of "own payment" that they must meet and the allowance covers 80 per cent of the excess.

The Swiss use of financial assistance is of interest and deserves extended comment. *The Federal Law for the Support of Housing Production and the Promotion of Home Ownership (WEG)* is so interesting because there is no practical difference in the support it gives to rental or owned housing, or the renovation of older dwellings. A package of guarantees and interest rate subsidies improve housing construction; non-profit housing is supported by preferential loans and guarantees, plus low interest loans; new rental construction is aided by guarantees on mortgage loans, loans are made repayable in such a way as to reduce the initial level of rents and owner occupier costs (called the basic reduction) and non-repayable grants can further reduce rents or costs.

Policy budgeting

The most important simple finding from the surveys is that, despite the financial pressures on budgets, housing policy continues to attract a considerable volume of public resources. In this respect the link to expanding social security budgets is very important. At the same time fiscal restraint and the growth in cash budgeting will put pressure on social budgets, as is clearly recognised by Canada among others (Belgium). In this light, innovative polices that are low in public costs, earn a large "social" return or promote a large private to public gearing ratio -- all are to be welcomed in the new climate. In this regard, self-financing mortgage insurance which allow higher levels of debt-gearing for first time buyers are useful examples of such policy (Canada).

Policy outcomes and future integration

While it is often true that it can be difficult to quantify the effects of these policies (often there is no counter-factual), several respondents indicate that efforts have been made, for example, in calculating the change in the proportion of "poor" households facing "unaffordably high" expenditure to income ratios (Finland, Australia). The Canadian response also identifies that, by definition, newer policies are harder to measure, evaluate and integrate into complementary policy areas -- simply because they may still be finding their feet. In Finland, changes in tax policy have increased expenditure to income ratios and allowance policy is explicitly directed to compensate poorer households for these changes.

Conclusion

The data presented in Tables 1 to 9 indicate the diversity of experience in OECD countries and also some important common patterns within and between cities and countries. In all tables City 1 refers to cities undergoing restructuring, City 2 refers to cities that are "typical" or stable and City 3 refers to cities undergoing growth. The information found in Part B complements the data and relates closely to the synthesis of country programmes and profiles. It is important to stress, finally, that there is no consensus about what affordability means, and the degree to which unaffordability becomes unacceptable. What is more common is the budgetary constraint found across the OECD and the desire to increasingly use market-facilitating devices as opposed to policies which override market outcomes.

Questionnaire Responses

In all tables:

-- City 1 refers to cities undergoing restructuring.
-- City 2 refers to cities that are "typical" or stable.
-- City 3 refers to cities undergoing growth.

Table 1. **Average house price to household income ratios**

National level	Ratio	City 1	Ratio	City 2	Ratio	City 3	Ratio
Belgium	8.3	Antwerp	6.3	-------	--	-------	--
Canada	4.1	Montreal	2.1	-------	--	Vancouver	3.1
						Toronto	4.1
Finland	3.5	Tampere	3.5	Lappeeranta	3.2	Vantaa	3.8
						Helsinki	4.6
France	4.0	-------	--	-------	--	-------	--
Germany	9.0	Bremen[1]	8.0	Hanover[1]	10.0	Stuttgart	16.0
Japan	6.8	Gifu	4.9	Hiroshima	6.4	Yokohama	8.3
Sweden	3.5	Stockholm	6.1	Gothenberg	5.0	Malmo	3.8
Turkey	7.2	Erzurum	7.6	Denzuzli	7.5	Antalya	10.2
United Kingdom	3.1	Leeds[2]	2.9	Nottingham[2]	3.0	Milton Keynes	3.4

1. Income figures for Germany may be up to 30 per cent too low *i.e.* ratios may be too high.
2. Regional averages.

293

Table 2. **Average rent to household income ratios, percentage of income**

National level	%	City 1	%	City 2	%	City 3	%
Canada	18.0	Montreal	21.0	-------	---	Toronto	18.0
						Vancouver	24.0
Finland	19.0	Tampere	18.0	Lappeeranta	20.0	Vantaa	18.0
						Helsinki	18.0
France	15.1	Lille[2]	24.5	Bordeaux[2]	28.2	Toulouse[2]	27.6
Germany	19.7	Bremen	23.4	Hanover	21.0	Stuttgart	19.5
Japan	10.9	-------	---	-------	---	-------	---
Sweden	17.0	Stockholm	15.0	Gothenberg	18.0	Malmo	18.0
Switzerland	24.6	-------	---	-------	---	-------	---
Turkey	20.0	-------	---	-------	---	-------	---
United Kingdom[1]	23.0	-------	---	Nottingham[1]	16.0	Milton Keynes[1]	21.0

1. Private renters only taken from regional averages.
2. 1989, rent per m[2].

294

Table 3. Percentage owner occupied

National level	%	City 1	%	City 2	%	City 3	%
Belgium	65.0	Antwerp[2]	41.0	-------	--	-------	--
Canada[3]	62.9	Montreal	46.7	-------	--	Toronto	57.9
						Vancouver	57.5
Finland[1]	66.7	Tampere[1]	63.4	Lappeeranta[1]	65.6	Vantaa[1]	66.3
						Helsinki[1]	54.6
France	54.4	Lille	44.7	Bordeaux	48.3	Toulouse	47.0
Germany	39.3	Bremen	31.8	Hanover	16.4	Stuttgart	23.4
Japan	61.3	Gifu	61.9	Hiroshima	46.3	Yokohama	53.9
Sweden	53.0	Stockholm	39.0	Gothenberg	46.0	Malmo	53.0
Switzerland[4]	29.9	-------	--	-------	--	-------	--
Turkey	71.2	-------	--	-------	--	-------	--
United Kingdom	67.1	Leeds	61.4	Nottingham	51.9	Milton Keynes[2]	69.2

1. 1989.
2. 1981.
3. 1991.
4. 1980.

Table 4. **Annual average house price appreciation, 1986-90, percentage increase**

National level	%	City 1	%	City 2	%	City 3	%
Belgium[1]	15.8	Antwerp	23.6	-------	---	-------	---
Canada	9.5	Montreal	0.3	Toronto	12.0	Vancouver	20.6
Finland	11.7	Tampere	12.5	Lappeeranta	10.3	Vantaa	12.0
						Helsinki[3]	11.2
France	11.3	Lille	1.4	Bordeaux	22.7	Toulouse	4.7
Germany[5]	4.0	Bremen	3.0	Hanover	6.0	Stuttgart	6.0
Japan	11.4	Gifu	10.4	Hiroshima	9.3	Yokohama	12.6
Sweden[6]	13.0	Stockholm	17.0	Gothenberg[2]	16.0	Malmo[2]	16.0
United Kingdom	15.0	Leeds[4]	17.0	Nottingham[4]	16.0	Milton Keynes[4]	16.0

1. 1985-89.
2. There is no differentiation of the Swedish cities.
3. Finland provides additional data for Helsinki.
4. Regional averages.
5. All data for Western Germany.
6. Sweden has only three cities of sufficient size.

Table 5. Average annual land price appreciation, 1986-90, percentage

National level	%	City 1	%	City 2	%	City 3	%
Belgium[2]	5.8	Antwerp	13.8	-------	---	-------	---
Canada	18.6	Montreal	-3.4	Toronto	27.3	Vancouver	31.6
France	4.6	Lille[2]	22.0	Bordeaux[2]	14.9	Toulouse[2]	14.9
Germany	0.6	Bremen	-4.8	Hanover	3.1	Stuttgart	6.1
Japan	13.5	Gifu	9.2	Hiroshima	10.4	Yokohama	15.7
Sweden	18.0	Stockholm	23.0	Gothenberg	19.0	Malmo	24.0
United Kingdom[1]	15.0	Leeds	27.0	Nottingham	35.0	Milton Keynes	12.0

1. England and Wales only.
2. 1985-89.

297

Table 6. **Construction cost index annual appreciation, 1986-90, percentage**

National level	%	City 1	%	City 2	%	City 3	%
Belgium[1]	4.5	------	---	------	---	------	---
Canada	8.1	Montreal	0.4	------	---	Vancouver	15.3
						Toronto	6.0
Finland	5.2	------	---	-------	---	-------	---
France	2.1	------	---	-------	---	-------	---
Germany	0.7	Bremen	2.1	Hanover	-0.5	Stuttgart	2.1
Japan	3.0			-------		-------	---
Sweden[2]	12.0	Stockholm[2]	14.0	Gothenberg[2]	9.0	Malmo[2]	13.0
United Kingdom[3]	9.2	------	---	-------	---	-------	---

1. 1985-89.
2. 1987-90.
3. 1985-90.

Table 7. Annual housing construction output per 1 000 people

National level	N	City 1	N	City 2	N	City 3	N
Belgium	5.8	Antwerp	2.3	-------	---	-------	---
Canada	---	Montreal[2]	5.7	-------	---	Vancouver[3]	9.2
						Toronto[3]	4.8
France	5.5	Lille	2.4	Bordeaux	9.7	Toulouse	13.6
Germany	4.0	Bremen	1.5	Hanover	3.7	Stuttgart	3.6
Japan	13.5	Gifu	10.7	Hiroshima	14.7	Yokohama	16.8
Sweden	4.9	Stockholm	4.9	Gothenberg	4.6	Malmo	4.9
Switzerland[2]	5.5	-------	---	-------	---	-------	---
Turkey	---	Erzurum	1.4	Denzuzli	4.2	Antayla	9.4
United Kingdom	2.9	Leeds[1]	1.9	Nottingham[1]	1.9	Milton Keynes[1]	10.7

1. Regional averages.
2. 1991.
3. Extremely high number relative to city figures, to be treated with caution.

Table 8. **Average household size**

National level	N	City 1	N	City 2	N	City 3	N
Belgium	2.6	Antwerp	2.1	-------	---	-------	---
Canada[3]	2.8	Montreal[3]	2.5	-------	---	Vancouver[2]	2.6
						Toronto	2.8
Finland[1]	2.4	Tampere[1]	2.1	Lappeeranta[1]	2.4	Vantaa[1]	2.5
						Helsinki[1]	2.0
France	2.6	Lille	2.7	Bordeaux	2.5	Toulouse	2.5
Germany	2.4	Bremen	2.1	Hanover	1.9	Stuttgart	2.0
Japan	3.2	Gifu	3.2	Hiroshima	2.9	Yokohama	3.0
Sweden	2.1	Stockholm	2.0	Gothenberg	2.1	Malmo	2.0
Switzerland	2.4	-------	---	-------	---	-------	---
Turkey	5.2	Erzurum	6.5	Denzuzli	4.5	Antayla	4.8
United Kingdom	2.5	Leeds[2]	2.4	Nottingham[2]	2.4	Milton Keynes[2]	2.6

1.   1989.
2.   Regional averages.
3.   1991.

Table 9. **Average number of rooms**

National level	N	City 1	N	City 2	N	City 3	N
Belgium	5.0	Antwerp	5.2	-------	---	-------	---
Canada[4]	5.8	Montreal[4]	5.1	-------	---	Toronto[4]	5.9
						Vancouver[4]	5.7
Finland[1]	3.6	Tampere[1]	3.3	Lappeeranta[1]	3.5	Helsinki[1]	3.0
						Vantaa[1]	3.6
France	3.8	Lille	4.0	Bordeaux	3.6	Toulouse	3.6
Germany	4.4	Bremen	4.1	Hanover	3.9	Stuttgart	4.0
Japan	4.9	Gifu	5.5	Hiroshima	4.4	Yokohama	4.0
Sweden	4.3	Stockholm	3.9	Gothenberg	3.9	Malmo	4.2
Switzerland[5]	3.5	--------	---	--------	---	--------	---
Turkey	3.0	--------	---	--------	---	--------	---
United Kingdom[2]	5.2	--------	---	--------	---	Milton Keynes[3]	5.1

1. 1989.
2. England only.
3. 1991.
4. 1986.
5. 1990.

301

Contacts for Case Studies

Project: Job Placement and Employment Training Program

Address: Commonwealth Department of Health, Housing,
Local Government and Community Services
PO Box 9848
Canberra City
ACT 2601
Australia

Project: Association for Street Kids (ASK), Victoria

Address: 658 View
Victoria, BC
Canada

Project: The Montreal Strategic Approach

Address: Ville de Montreal
303 Notre Dame est
Montreal, QC, H2Y 3Y8
Canada

Project: Safe Neighbourhoods Initiative

Address: Metro Toronto Housing Authority
Suite 7000, 365 Bloor Street east
Toronto, ON, M4W 3LH
Canada

Project: Self-help Housing
(Rural and Native Housing Demonstration Program)

Address: Canada Mortgage and Housing Corporation
700 Montreal Road
Ottawa K1A 0P7
Canada

Project: European Organisation for the Integration
and Housing of Young People

Address: European Organisation for the Integration
and Housing of Young People
12, avenue du Général de Gaulle
94307 Vincennes
France

Project: Protection Under Rental Laws for Persons
70 Years and Over

Address: Chargée du logement des personnes âgées
et des personnes handicapées
Ministère de l'urbanisme et du logement
L'Arche de la Défense
92055 La Défense
France

or

Address: Secrétariat d'Etat chargé des personnes âgées
61, rue Dutot
75732 Paris
France

Project: Social Renewal of Cities

Address: Délégation interministerielle à la ville
10-12, rue du Capitaine-Menard
75015 Paris
France

Project: Union nationale des foyers et services
pour jeunes travailleurs

Address: Union des foyers de jeunes travailleurs (UFJT)
12, avenue du Général de Gaulle
94307 Vincennes
France

Project: The Solar Village

Address: Stavros Tsetsis and Associates
Stratiotikou Syndesmou 4
106 73 Athens
Greece

Project: ERGO

Address: European Foundation for the Improvement of
Living and Working Conditions
Loughlinstown House
Shankhill
Co. Dublin
Ireland

Project: Finglas Enlivenment Project

Address: Planning Development, Block 2
Irish Life Centre
Dublin Corporation
Lower Abbey Street
Dublin 1
Ireland

Project: Focus Point, Dublin

Address: Focus Point
15 Eustace Street
Dublin 2
Ireland

Project: Limerick Youth Service

Address: Limerick Youth Service
5 Lower Glentworth Street
Limerick
Ireland

Project: RESPOND

Address: Voluntary Housing Organisation
Luke House
Alexander Street
Waterford City
Ireland

Project: River City 21

Address: Housing and Urban Development Corporation (HUDC)
1-14-16 Kudan-kita, Chiyoda-ku
Tokyo
Japan

Project: Delft Anti-crime Project

Address: Department of Crime Prevention
Ministry of Justice
PO Box 20301
2500 The Hague
The Netherlands

Project: HALT, Dutch Programme to Reduce Vandalism

Address: Department of Crime Prevention
Ministry of Justice
PO Box 20301
2500 The Hague
The Netherlands

Project: Havezicht Hight Lodging

Address: Centrum voor Dienstverlening
Willem Ruyslaan 10
3061 TV Rotterdam
The Netherlands

Project: Social Renewal in Rotterdam

Address: The Social Renewal Project Office
Rotterdam Municipality
Rotterdam
The Netherlands

or

Address: Erasmus Universiteit Rotterdam
Room L 04.21
PO Box 1738
3000 DR Rotterdam
The Netherlands

Project: Van Speyk Day Centre

Address: Centrum voor Dienstverlening
Hr Vrankenstraat 29
3036 LE Rotterdam
The Netherlands

Project: City of Barcelona Youth Project

Address: Barcelona City Council
Social Welfare Department
C/- Ciutat 4, 5a planta
08002 Barcelona
Spain

Project: Marismas del Odiel, Huelva

Address: Avenida Miramar
s/n. 21002 Huelva
Spain

Project: Renovation of the Historical Centre of Zaragoza

Address: Gerencia de Urbanismo
Edificio "el Cubo"
c/Eduardo Ibarra
s/n.50009 Zaragoza
Spain

Project: Decentralisation to Sub-municipal Levels, Örebro

Address: Örebro University
PO Box 923
701 30 Örebro
Sweden

Project: Renewal of Housing Estates

Address: The Royal Institute of Technology
Department of Regional Planning
100 44 Stockholm
Sweden

Project: Action for Cities

Address: Housing Management and Estate Action
Department of the Environment
2 Marsham Street
London, SW1P 3EB
United Kingdom

or

Address: Inner Cities Directorate
Department of the Environment
2 Marsham Street
London, SW1P 3EB
United Kingdom

Project: Foyer Federation for Youth

Address: Foyer Federation for Youth
91 Brick Lane
London E1 6QN
United Kingdom

Project: Interact Initiatives for North and West Belfast

Address: Community Care Belfast
Glendinning House
6 Murray Street
Belfast
Northern Ireland

Project: The Learning Shop, Whitfield

Address: The Dundee Compact Administration Unit
Craigie High School
Garnet Terrace
Dundee, DD4 7QD
United Kingdom

or

Address: Partnership Office
Lothian Crescent
Whitfield
United Kingdom

Project: New Life for Urban Scotland

Address: Scottish Development Department
New St. Andrew's House
Edinburgh, EH1 3TA
United Kingdom

Project: New Life for Urban Scotland, Example of Glasgow

Address: Glasgow City Housing
City of Glasgow
United Kingdom

or

Address: Glasgow Action
Franborough House
123 Bothwell Street
Glasgow G2 7JP
United Kingdom

Project: Los Angeles Skidrow Corporation and Single Room Occupancy

Address: City Hall of Los Angeles
Los Angeles
California
United States

Project: The Minneapolis Neighbourhood Employment Network (NET)

Address: Minneapolis City Hall
Minneapolis
MN 55415
United States

Project: Omaha Public Housing Education Support

Address: Omaha Public Housing Authority
Omaha, Nabraska
United States

Project: Public-private Partnership for Crime Prevention

Address: The Milton Eisenhower Foundation
Suite 504, 1725 I Street N.W.
Washington D.C. 20006
United States

Project: Renovation of Tampa Heights

Address: City Hall of Tampa
Tampa
Florida
United States

Project: Resident Management Corporations, Public Housing

Address: US Department of Housing and Urban Development
Washington D.C. 20410-6000
United States

MAIN SALES OUTLETS OF OECD PUBLICATIONS
PRINCIPAUX POINTS DE VENTE DES PUBLICATIONS DE L'OCDE

ARGENTINA – ARGENTINE
Carlos Hirsch S.R.L.
Galería Güemes, Florida 165, 4° Piso
1333 Buenos Aires   Tel. (1) 331.1787 y 331.2391
Telefax: (1) 331.1787

AUSTRALIA – AUSTRALIE
D.A. Information Services
648 Whitehorse Road, P.O.B 163
Mitcham, Victoria 3132   Tel. (03) 9210.7777
Telefax: (03) 9210.7788

AUSTRIA – AUTRICHE
Gerold & Co.
Graben 31
Wien I   Tel. (0222) 533.50.14
Telefax: (0222) 512.47.31.29

BELGIUM – BELGIQUE
Jean De Lannoy
Avenue du Roi 202 Koningslaan
B-1060 Bruxelles   Tel. (02) 538.51.69/538.08.41
Telefax: (02) 538.08.41

CANADA
Renouf Publishing Company Ltd.
1294 Algoma Road
Ottawa, ON K1B 3W8   Tel. (613) 741.4333
Telefax: (613) 741.5439
Stores:
61 Sparks Street
Ottawa, ON K1P 5R1   Tel. (613) 238.8985
12 Adelaide Street West
Toronto, ON M5H 1L6   Tel. (416) 363.3171
Telefax: (416)363.59.63

Les Éditions La Liberté Inc.
3020 Chemin Sainte-Foy
Sainte-Foy, PQ G1X 3V6   Tel. (418) 658.3763
Telefax: (418) 658.3763

Federal Publications Inc.
165 University Avenue, Suite 701
Toronto, ON M5H 3B8   Tel. (416) 860.1611
Telefax: (416) 860.1608

Les Publications Fédérales
1185 Université
Montréal, QC H3B 3A7   Tel. (514) 954.1633
Telefax: (514) 954.1635

CHINA – CHINE
China National Publications Import
Export Corporation (CNPIEC)
16 Gongti E. Road, Chaoyang District
P.O. Box 88 or 50
Beijing 100704 PR   Tel. (01) 506.6688
Telefax: (01) 506.3101

CHINESE TAIPEI – TAIPEI CHINOIS
Good Faith Worldwide Int'l. Co. Ltd.
9th Floor, No. 118, Sec. 2
Chung Hsiao E. Road
Taipei   Tel. (02) 391.7396/391.7397
Telefax: (02) 394.9176

**CZECH REPUBLIC –
RÉPUBLIQUE TCHÈQUE**
Artia Pegas Press Ltd.
Narodni Trida 25
POB 825
111 21 Praha 1   Tel. (2) 242 246 04
Telefax: (2) 242 278 72

DENMARK – DANEMARK
Munksgaard Book and Subscription Service
35, Nørre Søgade, P.O. Box 2148
DK-1016 København K   Tel. (33) 12.85.70
Telefax: (33) 12.93.87

EGYPT – ÉGYPTE
Middle East Observer
41 Sherif Street
Cairo   Tel. 392.6919
Telefax: 360-6804

FINLAND – FINLANDE
Akateeminen Kirjakauppa
Keskuskatu 1, P.O. Box 128
00100 Helsinki
Subscription Services/Agence d'abonnements :
P.O. Box 23
00371 Helsinki   Tel. (358 0) 121 4416
Telefax: (358 0) 121.4450

FRANCE
OECD/OCDE
Mail Orders/Commandes par correspondance :
2, rue André-Pascal
75775 Paris Cedex 16   Tel. (33-1) 45.24.82.00
Telefax: (33-1) 49.10.42.76
Telex: 640048 OCDE
Internet: Compte.PUBSINQ @ oecd.org
Orders via Minitel, France only/
Commandes par Minitel, France exclusivement :
36 15 OCDE
OECD Bookshop/Librairie de l'OCDE :
33, rue Octave-Feuillet
75016 Paris   Tel. (33-1) 45.24.81.81
(33-1) 45.24.81.67
Dawson
B.P. 40
91121 Palaiseau Cedex   Tel. 69.10.47.00
Telefax : 64.54.83.26

Documentation Française
29, quai Voltaire
75007 Paris   Tel. 40.15.70.00

Economica
49, rue Héricart
75015 Paris   Tel. 45.78.12.92
Telefax : 40.58.15.70

Gibert Jeune (Droit-Économie)
6, place Saint-Michel
75006 Paris   Tel. 43.25.91.19

Librairie du Commerce International
10, avenue d'Iéna
75016 Paris   Tel. 40.73.34.60

Librairie Dunod
Université Paris-Dauphine
Place du Maréchal-de-Lattre-de-Tassigny
75016 Paris   Tel. 44.05.40.13

Librairie Lavoisier
11, rue Lavoisier
75008 Paris   Tel. 42.65.39.95

Librairie des Sciences Politiques
30, rue Saint-Guillaume
75007 Paris   Tel. 45.48.36.02

P.U.F.
49, boulevard Saint-Michel
75005 Paris   Tel. 43.25.83.40

Librairie de l'Université
12a, rue Nazareth
13100 Aix-en-Provence   Tel. (16) 42.26.18.08

Documentation Française
165, rue Garibaldi
69003 Lyon   Tel. (16) 78.63.32.23

Librairie Decitre
29, place Bellecour
69002 Lyon   Tel. (16) 72.40.54.54

Librairie Sauramps
Le Triangle
34967 Montpellier Cedex 2   Tel. (16) 67.58.85.15
Tekefax: (16) 67.58.27.36

A la Sorbonne Actual
23, rue de l'Hôtel-des-Postes
06000 Nice   Tel. (16) 93.13.77.75
Telefax: (16) 93.80.75.69

GERMANY – ALLEMAGNE
OECD Publications and Information Centre
August-Bebel-Allee 6
D-53175 Bonn   Tel. (0228) 959.120
Telefax: (0228) 959.12.17

GREECE – GRÈCE
Librairie Kauffmann
Mavrokordatou 9
106 78 Athens   Tel. (01) 32.55.321
Telefax: (01) 32.30.320

HONG-KONG
Swindon Book Co. Ltd.
Astoria Bldg. 3F
34 Ashley Road, Tsimshatsui
Kowloon, Hong Kong   Tel. 2376.2062
Telefax: 2376.0685

HUNGARY – HONGRIE
Euro Info Service
Margitsziget, Európa Ház
1138 Budapest   Tel. (1) 111.62.16
Telefax: (1) 111.60.61

ICELAND – ISLANDE
Mál Mog Menning
Laugavegi 18, Pósthólf 392
121 Reykjavik   Tel. (1) 552.4240
Telefax: (1) 562.3523

INDIA – INDE
Oxford Book and Stationery Co.
Scindia House
New Delhi 110001   Tel. (11) 331.5896/5308
Telefax: (11) 332.5993
17 Park Street
Calcutta 700016   Tel. 240832

INDONESIA – INDONÉSIE
Pdii-Lipi
P.O. Box 4298
Jakarta 12042   Tel. (21) 573.34.67
Telefax: (21) 573.34.67

IRELAND – IRLANDE
Government Supplies Agency
Publications Section
4/5 Harcourt Road
Dublin 2   Tel. 661.31.11
Telefax: 475.27.60

ISRAEL – ISRAËL
Praedicta
5 Shatner Street
P.O. Box 34030
Jerusalem 91430   Tel. (2) 52.84.90/1/2
Telefax: (2) 52.84.93

R.O.Y. International
P.O. Box 13056
Tel Aviv 61130   Tel. (3) 546 1423
Telefax: (3) 546 1442

Palestinian Authority/Middle East:
INDEX Information Services
P.O.B. 19502
Jerusalem   Tel. (2) 27.12.19
Telefax: (2) 27.16.34

ITALY – ITALIE
Libreria Commissionaria Sansoni
Via Duca di Calabria 1/1
50125 Firenze   Tel. (055) 64.54.15
Telefax: (055) 64.12.57
Via Bartolini 29
20155 Milano   Tel. (02) 36.50.83

Editrice e Libreria Herder
Piazza Montecitorio 120
00186 Roma　　　　　　　　　Tel. 679.46.28
　　　　　　　　　　　　　　Telefax: 678.47.51

Libreria Hoepli
Via Hoepli 5
20121 Milano　　　　　　　　Tel. (02) 86.54.46
　　　　　　　　　　　　Telefax: (02) 805.28.86

Libreria Scientifica
Dott. Lucio de Biasio 'Aeiou'
Via Coronelli, 6
20146 Milano　　　　　　　　Tel. (02) 48.95.45.52
　　　　　　　　　　　　Telefax: (02) 48.95.45.48

JAPAN – JAPON
OECD Publications and Information Centre
Landic Akasaka Building
2-3-4 Akasaka, Minato-ku
Tokyo 107　　　　　　　Tel. (81.3) 3586.2016
　　　　　　　　　　Telefax: (81.3) 3584.7929

KOREA – CORÉE
Kyobo Book Centre Co. Ltd.
P.O. Box 1658, Kwang Hwa Moon
Seoul　　　　　　　　　　Tel. 730.78.91
　　　　　　　　　　　Telefax: 735.00.30

MALAYSIA – MALAISIE
University of Malaya Bookshop
University of Malaya
P.O. Box 1127, Jalan Pantai Baru
59700 Kuala Lumpur
Malaysia　　　　　　Tel. 756.5000/756.5425
　　　　　　　　　　　Telefax: 756.3246

MEXICO – MEXIQUE
OECD Publications and Information Centre
Edificio INFOTEC
Av. San Fernando no. 37
Col. Toriello Guerra
Tlalpan C.P. 14050
Mexico D.F.
　　　　　Tel. (525) 606 00 11 Extension 100
　　　　　　　　　Fax : (525) 606 13 07

Revistas y Periodicos Internacionales S.A. de C.V.
Florencia 57 - 1004
Mexico, D.F. 06600　　　　　Tel. 207.81.00
　　　　　　　　　　　Telefax: 208.39.79

NETHERLANDS – PAYS-BAS
SDU Uitgeverij Plantijnstraat
Externe Fondsen
Postbus 20014
2500 EA's-Gravenhage　　　Tel. (070) 37.89.880
Voor bestellingen:　　Telefax: (070) 34.75.778

NEW ZEALAND – NOUVELLE-ZÉLANDE
GPLegislation Services
P.O. Box 12418
Thorndon, Wellington　　　Tel. (04) 496.5655
　　　　　　　　　　Telefax: (04) 496.5698

NORWAY – NORVÈGE
NIC INFO A/S
Bertrand Narvesens vei 2
P.O. Box 6512 Etterstad
0606 Oslo 6　　　　　　　Tel. (022) 57.33.00
　　　　　　　　　　Telefax: (022) 68.19.01

PAKISTAN
Mirza Book Agency
65 Shahrah Quaid-E-Azam
Lahore 54000　　　　　　Tel. (42) 353.601
　　　　　　　　　　Telefax: (42) 231.730

PHILIPPINE – PHILIPPINES
International Booksource Center Inc.
Rm 179/920 Cityland 10 Condo Tower 2
HV dela Costa Ext cor Valero St.
Makati Metro Manila　　　Tel. (632) 817 9676
　　　　　　　　　Telefax : (632) 817 1741

POLAND – POLOGNE
Ars Polona
00-950 Warszawa
Krakowskie Przedmieście 7　　Tel. (22) 264760
　　　　　　　　　　Telefax : (22) 268673

PORTUGAL
Livraria Portugal
Rua do Carmo 70-74
Apart. 2681
1200 Lisboa　　　　　　Tel. (01) 347.49.82/5
　　　　　　　　　　Telefax: (01) 347.02.64

SINGAPORE – SINGAPOUR
Gower Asia Pacific Pte Ltd.
Golden Wheel Building
41, Kallang Pudding Road, No. 04-03
Singapore 1334　　　　　Tel. 741.5166
　　　　　　　　　　Telefax: 742.9356

SPAIN – ESPAGNE
Mundi-Prensa Libros S.A.
Castelló 37, Apartado 1223
Madrid 28001　　　　　Tel. (91) 431.33.99
　　　　　　　　　Telefax: (91) 575.39.98

Mundi-Prensa Barcelona
Consell de Cent No. 391
08009 – Barcelona　　　　Tel. (93) 488.34.92
　　　　　　　　　Telefax: (93) 487.76.59

Llibreria de la Generalitat
Palau Moja
Rambla dels Estudis, 118
08002 – Barcelona
　　　　　(Subscripcions) Tel. (93) 318.80.12
　　　　　(Publicacions) Tel. (93) 302.67.23
　　　　　　　　　Telefax: (93) 412.18.54

SRI LANKA
Centre for Policy Research
c/o Colombo Agencies Ltd.
No. 300-304, Galle Road
Colombo 3　　　　Tel. (1) 574240, 573551-2
　　　　　　　Telefax: (1) 575394, 510711

SWEDEN – SUÈDE
CE Fritzes AB
S–106 47 Stockholm　　　Tel. (08) 690.90.90
　　　　　　　　　Telefax: (08) 20.50.21

Subscription Agency/Agence d'abonnements :
Wennergren-Williams Info AB
P.O. Box 1305
171 25 Solna　　　　　Tel. (08) 705.97.50
　　　　　　　　　Telefax: (08) 27.00.71

SWITZERLAND – SUISSE
Maditec S.A. (Books and Periodicals - Livres
et périodiques)
Chemin des Palettes 4
Case postale 266
1020 Renens VD 1　　　　Tel. (021) 635.08.65
　　　　　　　　　Telefax: (021) 635.07.80

Librairie Payot S.A.
4, place Pépinet
CP 3212
1002 Lausanne　　　　　Tel. (021) 320.25.11
　　　　　　　　　Telefax: (021) 320.25.14

Librairie Unilivres
6, rue de Candolle
1205 Genève　　　　　Tel. (022) 320.26.23
　　　　　　　　　Telefax: (022) 329.73.18

Subscription Agency/Agence d'abonnements :
Dynapresse Marketing S.A.
38 avenue Vibert
1227 Carouge　　　　　Tel. (022) 308.07.89
　　　　　　　　　Telefax: (022) 308.07.99

See also – Voir aussi :
OECD Publications and Information Centre
August-Bebel-Allee 6
D-53175 Bonn (Germany)　　Tel. (0228) 959.120
　　　　　　　　　Telefax: (0228) 959.12.17

THAILAND – THAÏLANDE
Suksit Siam Co. Ltd.
113, 115 Fuang Nakhon Rd.
Opp. Wat Rajbopith
Bangkok 10200　　　　Tel. (662) 225.9531/2
　　　　　　　　　Telefax: (662) 222.5188

TUNISIA – TUNISIE
Grande Librairie Spécialisée
Fendri Ali
Avenue Haffouz Imm El-Intilaka
Bloc B 1 Sfax 3000　　　Tel. (216-4) 296 855
　　　　　　　　　Telefax: (216-4) 298.270

TURKEY – TURQUIE
Kültür Yayinlari Is-Türk Ltd. Sti.
Atatürk Bulvari No. 191/Kat 13
Kavaklidere/Ankara
　　　　　　Tel. (312) 428.11.40 Ext. 2458
　　　　　　　　Telefax: (312) 417 24 90
Dolmabahce Cad. No. 29
Besiktas/Istanbul　　　　Tel. (212) 260 7188

UNITED KINGDOM – ROYAUME-UNI
HMSO
Gen. enquiries　　　　Tel. (171) 873 8242
Postal orders only:
P.O. Box 276, London SW8 5DT
Personal Callers HMSO Bookshop
49 High Holborn, London WC1V 6HB
　　　　　　　　　Telefax: (171) 873 8416
Branches at: Belfast, Birmingham, Bristol,
Edinburgh, Manchester

UNITED STATES – ÉTATS-UNIS
OECD Publications and Information Center
2001 L Street N.W., Suite 650
Washington, D.C. 20036-4922　　Tel. (202) 785.6323
　　　　　　　　　Telefax: (202) 785.0350

Subscriptions to OECD periodicals may also be placed
through main subscription agencies.

Les abonnements aux publications périodiques de
l'OCDE peuvent être souscrits auprès des principales
agences d'abonnement.

Orders and inquiries from countries where Distributors
have not yet been appointed should be sent to: OECD
Publications Service, 2, rue André-Pascal, 75775 Paris
Cedex 16, France.

Les commandes provenant de pays où l'OCDE n'a pas
encore désigné de distributeur peuvent être adressées à :
OCDE, Service des Publications, 2, rue André-Pascal,
75775 Paris Cedex 16, France.

1-1996

OECD PUBLICATIONS, 2, rue André-Pascal, 75775 PARIS CEDEX 16
PRINTED IN FRANCE
(04 96 02 1) ISBN 92-64-14663-6 – No. 48241 1996